Maintenance Planning and Control

To those students at the Simon Engineering Laboratories, University of Manchester, whose investigations have helped to provide much of the information on which this book is based.

Maintenance Planning and Control

Anthony Kelly
Senior Lecturer in Engineering, University of Manchester

Butterworths
London Boston Singapore Sydney Toronto Wellington

 PART OF REED INTERNATIONAL P.L.C.

First published 1984
    Reprinted 1986, 1987, 1989

© Butterworth & Co (Publishers) Ltd, 1984

British Library Cataloguing in Publication Data

Kelly, Anthony
    Maintenance planning & control.
    1. Plant maintenance
    I. Title
    620'.0046   TS192

    ISBN 0-408-03030-5

Library of Congress Cataloging in Publication Data

Kelly, Anthony
    Maintenance planning & control.

    Includes bibliographical reference and index.
    1. Plant maintenance.   I. Title
    TS192.K428   1983   658.2'02   83–7601

    ISBN 0-408-03030-5

Typeset by Scribe Design, Gillingham, Kent
Printed in Great Britain at the University Press, Cambridge

Preface

In writing this book my main aim has been to expand and revise the discussion and analysis of maintenance organisation and planning that was my principal contribution to *Management of Industrial Maintenance* (published by Butterworths in 1978).

Most publications in this area have concentrated either on operational research aspects or on the minutiae of organisation and documentation. They have therefore lacked that analysis of maintenance management principles and maintenance organisational structure that is essential for the development of the subject as an academic discipline. I hope that in trying to correct this situation I have provided a book that will assist not only students of industrial management, but also practising engineering managers, towards a fundamental understanding of the management of maintenance resources.

Chapter 1 looks at maintenance costs in terms of decisions taken at other phases (e.g. design, commissioning) of the plant-life cycle; a case study illustrates the applications of the principles outlined. Chapter 2 considers the reasons for, and nature of, maintenance work and develops models of maintenance management structure that underlie the analysis in the remainder of the book. Chapters 3 and 4 develop a systematic procedure for establishing a maintenance plan for different industrial plants. The principles of maintenance organisation and control are discussed in Chapter 5, which also introduces the idea of an 'organisation snapshot'. Chapter 6 discusses the documentation systems needed to operate a maintenance organisation and implement a maintenance plan; a model of such a system is developed. Case studies of manual and computerised documentation systems are outlined in Chapters 7 and 8 respectively. An important feature of Chapter 8 is a survey of computerised systems and guidelines for matching such systems to maintenance user requirements. Many of the ideas of the early chapters are reinforced through the case studies (on the planning of major overhauls via network planning and on short-term planning) of Chapters 9 and 10. Chapter 11 examines the use of failure statistics in diagnosing the cause of failure, and in prescribing the appropriate maintenance procedure. One of the most important sections is Chapter 12, which reviews the factors that influence the motivation of the maintenance tradeforce.

A.K.

Acknowledgements

I am deeply indebted to colleagues in the industrial world who have most generously contributed several important sections of my book, viz. *Harry Moody*, Consultant (formerly with Imperial Chemical Industries, Organics Division), who wrote Chapter 9, and *Bernard Wilson*, of Lever Bros, who wrote Chapter 10.

The following have also contributed, through collaboration in various research projects and courses, by providing material for case studies, and through discussion and correspondence arising out of my own industrial consulting work. *Peter Anthill*, COMAC Systems, *David Brooks*, Imperial Chemical Industries (Organics Division), *Joe Balfour*, British Tools, *Bob Christie*, Shell International Petroleum, *Roger de la Mare*, University of Bradford, *Peter Flegg*, British Steel Corporation, *Professor Bill Geraerds*, Eindhoven Technical University, The Netherlands, *Tim Henry*, Wolfson Industrial Maintenance Unit, *Russell Herbert*, North Thames Gas, *Brian Holcroft*, Greater Manchester Transport, *David Mayers*, Central Electricity Generating Board, *Chris Mentham*, Ford Motor Company, *Professor Floyd Miller*, University of Illinois, USA, *Bob Moss*, R.M. Consultants, *S. Nakajima*, Japanese Management Association, *Mohammad Nassief*, Yanbu Refinery, Saudi Arabia, *Harry Riddell*, University of Manchester, *Knut Sward*, Ali Rati, Sweden, *Bill Telford*, Mainwork, *Alan Walton*, Kennings Tyres, *Roy Warburton*, British Insulated Callender's Cables, *Paul Williams*, Design Audit Group, British Steel Corporation, *David Wood*, Van den Bergh, *Richard Wynne*, University of Manchester, *Olav Vikane*, Rogaland Regional College, Norway.

Significant contributions were also made by the following while they were students at the Simon Engineering Laboratories: *Mark Bamford* (Chapter 8), *Chang Ho* (Chapter 4), *Greville Seddon* (Chapter 4).

Finally, I must acknowledge special gratitude to the following: *John Harris*, Senior Lecturer and colleague at the Simon Engineering Laboratories, who has edited the complete text and also contributed valued suggestions and ideas; *Christer Idhammar*, Senior Consultant, Idhammar Konsult, Sweden, work with whom gave rise to many of the industrial examples quoted; and *Jack Diamond*, Emeritus Professor of Engineering at the University of Manchester, who read the complete draft manuscript and suggested numerous improvements.

Contents

Chapter 1

Maintenance in context

Maintenance and profitability

Industrial organisations exist to make a profit—they use equipment and employ labour to convert raw material of relatively low value into finished products of higher value. One way of considering the profitability of a plant is on a life cycle basis (see Figure 1.1). Investment in the plant occurs from its conception to its commissioning. If all goes well the return on this investment begins when the plant comes into use and continues until the plant is disposed of. To maximise profit the lead time from conception to first use, and the total investment, should be as small as possible, while the operating life and the total return should be as large as possible. Such aims

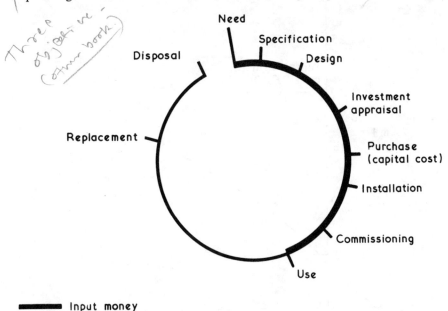

Figure 1.1 Plant life cycle and costs

1

TABLE 1.1. Economic sensitivity of 1000 t/d Ammonia complexes based upon Discounted Cash Flow (DCF) rates of return on investment for a normal two years construction period

Year	Annual availability (%)	DCF return (%)		
		No delay	6 months delay	12 months delay
1	100	26	23	21
1	60			
2	80	16	14	13
3	100			
1	30			
2	80	12	10	9
3	90			
1	30			
2	70	7	6	5
3	90			

may be obvious but their achievement is difficult and the main reason for this is uncertainty—uncertainty about continuing product demand, uncertainty about the eventual onset of obsolescence, uncertainty about reliability and life cycle costs. During the last decade there has been considerable development of techniques for assessing plant reliability[1] and life cycle costs[2], which can influence the choice of plant. There is, however, another factor affecting life cycle profitability which is of growing importance, namely *maintenance*.

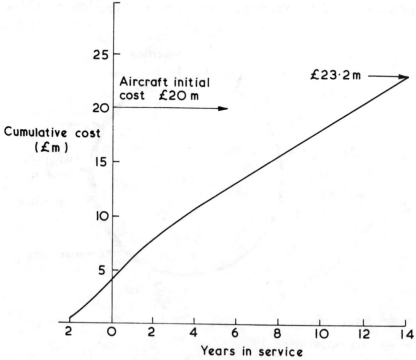

Figure 1.2 Cumulative engineering cost (at 1968 prices) per aircraft

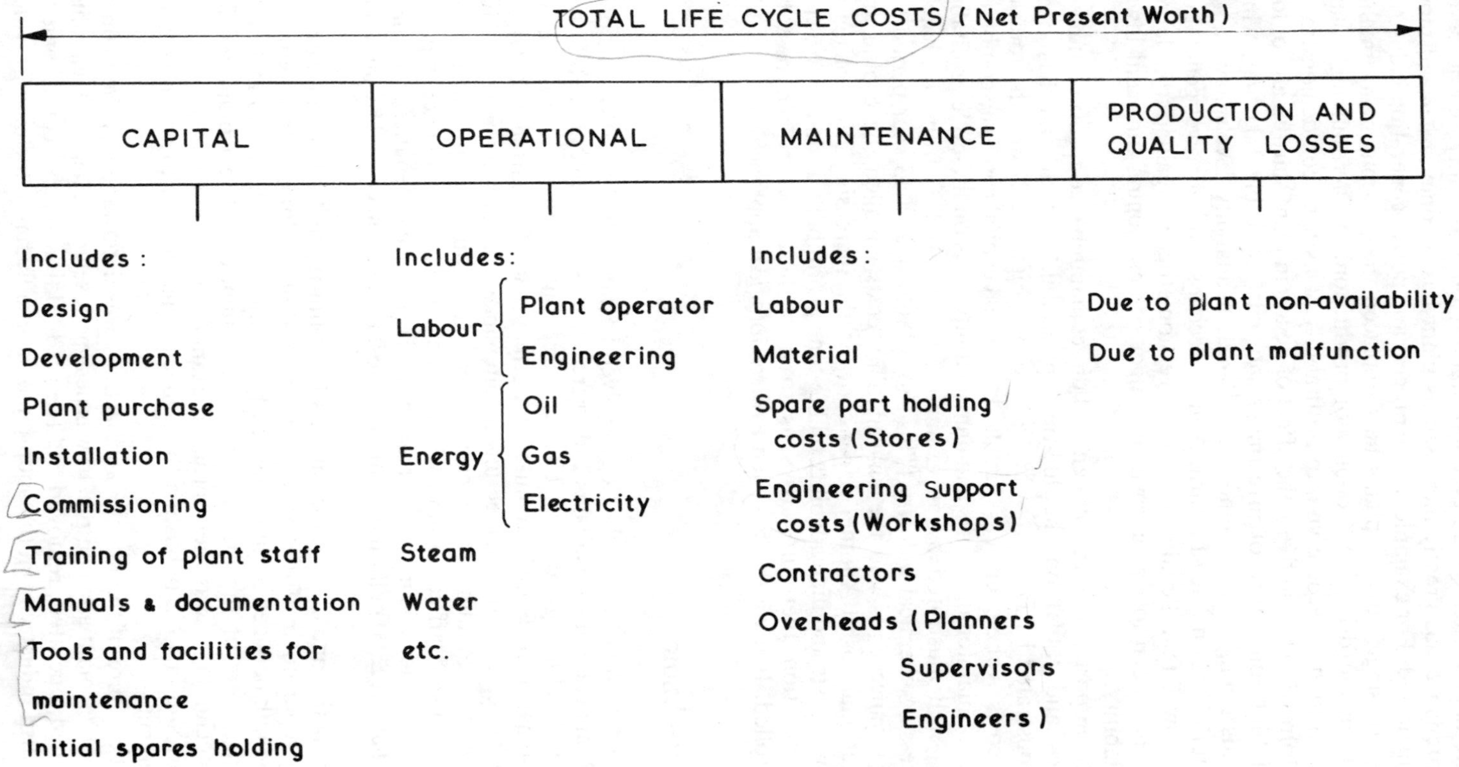

Figure 1.3 Factors and area considered for build-up of total life costs (Plant and Equipment)

The dependence of life cycle profitability on availability and hence on maintenance has greatly increased as plant has become larger and more sophisticated. For example, in the process and power generation industries large, or single-stream, plants have replaced the previous many smaller plants in the drive for economy of production. As a result high plant availability has become vital to profitability. This has been demonstrated by Holroyd[3] who, studying the effect of delays in plant start-up and of low availability on return of investment showed (see Table 1.1) that, while commissioning delays cannot be ignored, availability levels have a far greater effect on rate of return. A more recent study[4] of power generation sets showed that the advantage in conversion efficiency gained from larger units had been lost as a result of longer commissioning time and lower availability.

The importance of the influence of direct maintenance cost (i.e. of men, spares and tools) on the life-time profitability of aircraft has been demonstrated by Doggett[5] who showed (see Figure 1.2) that the total of such costs over eleven years equalled the initial capital cost. The combined effect of maintenance costs and unavailability costs on life-cycle profitability is well illustrated by an example (see Figure 1.3) from the batch-processing chemical industry. This shows[6] that over a 15 year period the maintenance costs and the unavailability costs equalled the capital and operational costs. Another paper showing the increasing effect of maintenance costs and unavailability on life-time profitability is that of Brown[7]. The question therefore arises as to how these factors can best be controlled. Is it via the so called *terotechnological* approach?

Terotechnology

The definition of terotechnology evolved between 1970 and 1975. In 1968 PA Management Consultants Ltd. were commissioned by the then Ministry of Technology of the UK to carry out a study of engineering maintenance in British Manufacturing industry. It reported that (i) the total direct cost of engineering maintenance was approximately £1100 million per annum (value circa 1968), (ii) improved productivity of maintenance staff could have led to a reduction in maintenance expenditure of around £250 million per annum, (iii) better maintenance could have saved about £300 million per annum of lost production caused by unavailability.

Using this and other information a UK Ministry of Technology working party reporting in 1970 emphasised, amongst other things, the importance of the link between maintenance costs and the feedback of information to the designers of the plant. A steering committee (The Committee for Terotechnology) was then set up to examine the broader findings of this report and in 1972 published their conclusions, central to which was the statement—

'The nature of the maintenance activity was determined by the manner in which plant and equipment was designed, selected, installed, commissioned, operated, removed and replaced. Major benefits could come to British Industry from the adoption of a broadly based technology which embraces all these areas, and because no suitable word existed to describe such a multidisciplinary concept, the name 'terotechnology' (based on the Greek work 'terein'—to guard or look after) was adopted'.

In 1975 the Committee for Terotechnology defined terotechnology as follows[8]—

'A combination of management, financial, engineering and other practices applied to physical assets in pursuit of economic life cycle costs'

The following was then added—

'..... its practice is concerned with the specification and design for reliability and maintainability of plant, machinery, equipment, buildings and structures, with their installation and replacement, and with the feedback of information on design, performance and costs'.

It can be seen that the concept of terotechnology had drifted from a point where maintenance and unavailability costs were of central importance to a very general and less tangible subject area, the relevance and applicability of which is, as yet, far from gaining full acceptance by industry.

The author is inclined to the view that the definition attempts to encompass too diverse a range of 'physical assets' (e.g. from school buildings to steel processing plant) across which the main cost factors may differ by many orders of magnitude. This book will therefore be mainly concerned with industrial plant where the main maintenance-related costs are those of resources, unavailability and, in life cycle terms, useful life. The author has arrived at a clear preference[9] for understanding this important subject area in terms of the 'optimisation of total maintenance costs over the equipment's life cycle'. It is implicit in this definition that certain categories of unavailability can be classified as indirect maintenance costs, and the cost of maintenance resources as direct maintenance costs.

The demand on maintenance resources and the achieved plant availability during the operation stage (see Figure 1.4) are affected by factors at the other stages. At the design stage, reliability and maintainability are important and must be considered in relation to equipment performance, capital cost and running cost. In the past far too much emphasis has been put on performance and on capital cost at the expense of reliability and maintainability.

The method of production is particularly important. For example, if a continuous rather than a batch process is adopted careful consideration should be given to the much higher maintenance costs that inevitably occur. In addition, it must be understood that design stage considerations of reliability and maintainability can also affect the duration and cost of commissioning[3].

It is self-evident that quality control during plant manufacture will strongly affect the subsequent level of maintenance. At the installation stage, maintainability continues to be an important consideration because it is only then that the multi-dimensional nature of many of the maintenance problems becomes clear. The commissioning stage is not only a

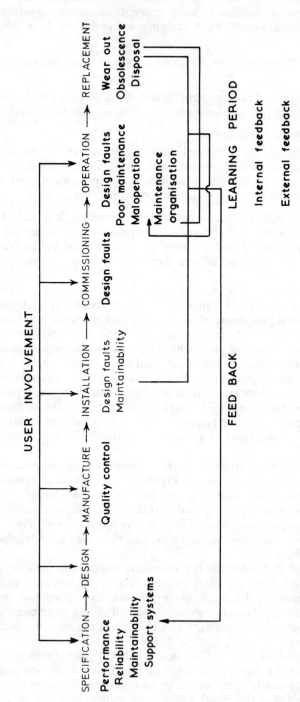

Figure 1.4 Factors influencing maintenance costs over life cycle

period of technical performance testing but also a learning period where primary design faults that might affect equipment availability can be located and designed out. Failure to do this will mean serious maintenance problems and high unavailability early in the operational life[7]. Similar problems will occur if the plant is operated past its useful life period and into the replacement period.

Clearly, the best time to influence maintenance and unavailability costs is before the plant comes into use. It is essential that management appreciates this and provides the necessary resources to create systems e.g. the Design Audit[10], which will ensure that plant, when handed over to production, will not only perform its function but will be fully serviced by an efficient maintenance department. In this respect the following points need emphasising:

(1) The operator of the plant should co-operate with the designer–manufacturer–installer in a full analysis of its reliability, maintainability and safety characteristics. Such a 'plant procurement' exercise should include assessment of spare-part provisioning, of maintenance personnel training and of supplier support systems. The higher the potential costs of maintenance and unavailability the more vital is this exercise.

(2) Decisions to buy new or replacement equipment should be based on a present value life-cycle analysis of costs. Such an analysis must take into consideration both maintenance and unavailability costs, these being estimated, wherever possible, from documented experience (see below).

(3) The plant operator and supplier should co-operate in the collection and analysis of plant failure and maintenance data in order to identify problem areas and to determine the plant's optimum maintenance operation. Since the design of equipment is a continuing process, information thus gathered should, ideally, be fed back to the equipment manufacturer and, in certain circumstances, to a data bank which could be shared on an inter-company, national or international basis[11]. The difficulties of these last operations continue to pose a major obstacle to the successful implementation of a terotechnological approach; communication systems are expensive and different organisations (with different objectives) are involved during the equipment life cycle.

Application of terotechnology

Some of the advantages of the terotechnological approach are illustrated in Harvey and Eastburn's plant procurement case study[12]. The project described was part of a steel bar mill rationalisation. It involved an investment of £34 million in a 400,000 ton/year plant occupying a 265 acre site.

Preliminary work was started in mid-1970 by the development engineering department who set up a Preliminary Project Steering Committee chaired by a Works Manager and having representatives from engineering, quality control, sales, accounts, market research, strategy studies, and

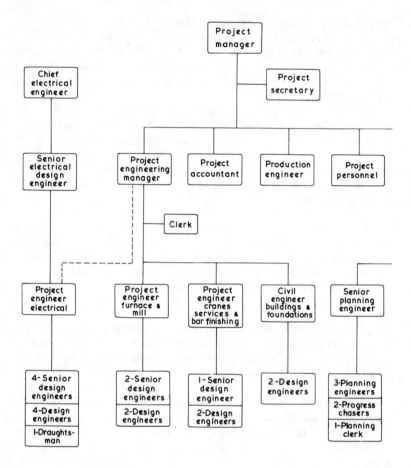

Figure 1.5 Project management structures

research and development. The basic parameters such as product range, size, output rate, packaging and process requirements were established by this committee.

When approval for the project was given, in 1972, a project management organisation (see Figure 1.5) was formed. At an early stage, consideration was given to the problem of organisational communication. To ensure adequate control, several committees covering production control, quality control, production and commissioning, engineering co-ordination, recruitment and training, and project management, were established.

In addition, Joint Consultative Working Groups were established, involving management and labour. These groups discussed plant designs, working procedures, safety, and so on. Regular design, manufacture, installation and other co-ordination meetings were held with contractors. A computerised network analysis of the project was used for planning and control of all phases of work. The Factory Inspectorate were involved from a very early stage to advise on, and approve, safety features and procedures.

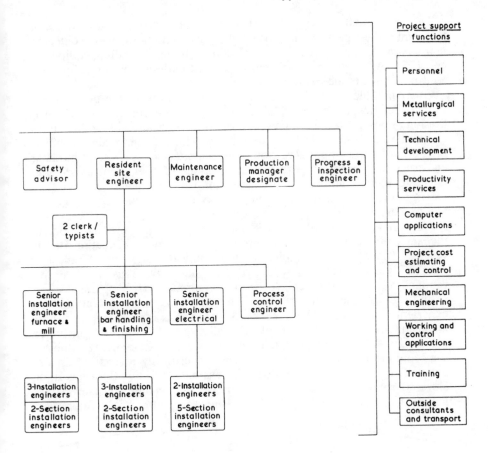

Specifications were drawn up for all items of plant covering performance, reliability and maintainability. This was not easy and plant personnel were closely involved with suppliers in explaining, training and assisting with the preparation of logical fault finding systems. (See section 4.4 and Appendix I of Functional System Documentation FSD). Maintenance manuals, including preventive maintenance schedules, overhaul schedules, lubrication programmes, spares listings, fault diagnosis information and training programmes were also specified and the need for modular construction, ease of access for maintenance and ergonomic considerations were included. A percentage of the purchase cost was withheld until delivery of all maintenance manuals and initial spares was completed.

Initial design work included the collection of historical information on plant performance, listing of maintenance characteristics, layout and flow studies. Maintenance records for previous plant were examined in detail in order to estimate maintenance manpower and frequencies for preventive maintenance schedules. Plant availability estimates were based on recorded mechanical and electrical breakdown.

The productivity services department carried out simulation studies of the plant's likely performance. The 'lowest bid' temptation was avoided on many occasions, notably so when selecting automatic bundling equipment and FSD. An ergonomist was employed in the design of control-panels, control cabins, crane cabs, etc.

Other notable terotechnological design features were the quick stand-change facilities, the stand-by lubrication system, the considerable rationalisation of pumps, drives and motors, rigorous application of modifications to standard equipment in order to improve reliability and maintainability, the design for maximum accessibility for maintenance, the use of modular construction concepts, the functional grouping of equipment in order to facilitate FSD, plant-mounted sensors for vibration detection and fault location, the use of an 'alarms computer' for detecting and reporting faults and process variations.

All equipment drawings were examined for *spares* requirements, one of the aims of the rationalisation programme being the reduction of the variety of spares. For example, all pipework was designed in seven basic sizes and only three types of hydraulic pump were used. Extensive rationalisation was also achieved in the required electrical spares.

In order to carry out much of the above it was essential that an experienced maintenance engineer was recruited as a senior member of the management team. He was involved in all stages of the project, including the design. A notable consequence of this was that the building exhibited some unique features that were designed specifically to facilitate maintenance organisation. The mill bay, for example, had two floor levels, an elevated rolling level and a lower services and maintenance level (see Figure 1.6). The advantages of this underground services floor were

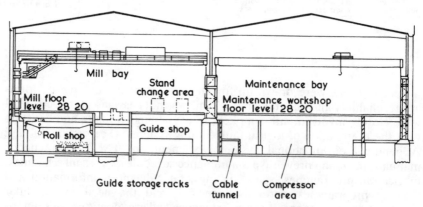

Figure 1.6 Two-floor arrangement of mill bay and maintenance shop

considerable and included routing of distribution and services pipework which was an improvement from the point of view of both installation and maintenance. It gave ease of preventive maintenance (with underground test points), lubrication points and readily accessible drive equipment, without disrupting production flow on the upper level. In addition, scrap collection was facilitated by a 'drive-in; arrangement for road vehicles. Maintenance of rolls was facilitated by passing the roll assemblies through the floor of the production bay directly into the roll and guide shop. After preparation the new roll assemblies were simply craned up to the production floor and refitted.

Installation was supervised by a team of installation engineers who formed part of the project management team and normal recording of plant installation problems was carried out.

Commissioning procedures (plant performance testing, training programmes, a commissioning check-card system) were rigorously formalised for both the static and running phases. The installation engineers compiled lists of checks required for each plant, this work demanding considerable study of drawings and design information prior to installation and ensured that they gained considerable familiarity with the plant design. Control of the issue of the commissioning check cards was related to a computerised installation network programme and cards were issued to appropriate staff when predetermined stages were achieved in the programme. A computer terminal was available for regular updating of the network, and for reviewing checks required, on a day-to-day basis while maintaining an overall picture of the installation and commissioning phase.

The company's own experience, supplemented by visits to similar plants in other countries, suggested that lengthy plant commissioning times had been due to insufficient attention to *training*. It was therefore decided that all management, operatives, craftsmen, engineers and supporting personnel should be adequately trained in the theory and practice needed to meet both the desired reduction in commissioning time and the required operational performance of the new mill. A recruitment and training committee was established, consisting of the project manager, production engineer, personnel officer, production manager, maintenance engineer and training officer. Initial instruction and training was given in two to four weeks of formal lectures and discussion groups. Multi-skill training was given where considered desirable. Simulated control panels and layouts were built and used extensively.

Each craftsman's dossier of experience was matched against a skill and knowledge matrix based on a job description, and was then used to compile a training programme designed to suit the individual's needs. Electricians and fitters were recruited three months before mill start-up and were given formal lectures, site work and project work. Regular tests were given and the training programmes were also reviewed in the light of the participants comments on their effectiveness. Pipefitters were recruited two months before mill start-up and welders, boilersmiths and auxiliaries one month before start-up.

Selection of maintenance engineering staff was given some thought at an early stage. The recruitment of the installation engineers, for example, took account of their potential for subsequent transfer to maintenance when the mill became operational. As a result, nine installation engineers were transferred to permanent maintenance engineering positions. Team training was also applied and the management team were involved in a series of courses designed to improve personal and team effectiveness. Weekend sessions, for fostering teamwork, were undertaken by the management, production operatives, craftsmen and engineers of each shift.

As a result of the considerable prior effort described, the *operational* and *maintenance* practice that will now be outlined was made much easier.

The plant was to be operated on a continuous 15 shift system for 5 days a week. During initial commissioning a one shift system was run, this being subsequently increased to two and eventually three shifts.

Performance standards were derived for output, yield, defectives, accidents, fuel consumption, labour, maintenance, etc., for each product group. These were supported by a formal system of reporting production problems, delays, utilisation, scrap, lost time and many other factors, such reporting being completed on a shift basis. Daily meetings were held between production and maintenance staff at top management level and formal reports issued on a weekly and monthly basis. Preventive maintenance routines and tasks were designed to be carried out, wherever possible, while the plant was running, the remainder being done at week-ends or when the plant was standing for product changes, etc.

As equipment was installed, plant history cards were opened, maintenance routines analysed, frequency of preventive maintenance determined and a computer-controlled preventive maintenance system adopted. A readily assessed and continually up-dated inventory of routines and repetitive jobs was established in the computer data bank, which also contained more detailed information for the execution of specific jobs. Work planning was based on computerised job cards and used 'work measured' job times for repetitive work. Information on cause of failure could also be recorded on the job cards for subsequent analysis alongside the maintenance reports compiled for each shift by the shift engineer. Any delays that could clearly be attributed to design faults were charged to the design department and booked separately on the shift report for further investigation.

Downtime plots were kept up-to-date and displayed in the maintenance engineer's office and the planning office. Availability figures were recorded and graphed for major items of plant and a maintenance engineering report issued monthly. Standards for maintainability and plant availability were established. Network analysis was used on major maintenance jobs.

As a continuing, long-term operation, *feedback* of the experience gained would be directed both to the company's maintenance data bank and to the equipment suppliers.

In achieving its worked-up tonnage level in one year, the plant outstripped the performance of any other recent and major bar mills, world-wide. A planned second commissioning year was not needed.

A 5.4% target for engineering delays was seen as unrealistic and in 1977 management agreed to set the standard at 6.6%. As it turned out the level attained in 78/79 was 5.6% which compared favourably with the 8% figure of the other major mills.

Summary

The application of the approach that has been outlined involves a much higher capital expenditure than the traditional lowest-bid, lowest-cost, shortest-time approach. The difficulties of implementing such an approach are many, e.g. cash constraints, time constraints, the uncertainty of forecasting demand and product life; therefore in some situations it has to be accepted that the additional effort and cost might not be worth the return. However, with the present trend towards automated, large, expensive plant, the adoption of this approach can, in the majority of cases, benefit a company to a considerable extent. It requires the commitment and foresight of the most senior management. It is therefore no accident that the successful industrial examples of the application of terotechnology appear to have at least one common factor—an Engineering Director who is convinced of the long term advantages of keeping maintenance firmly in mind when designing, installing and commissioning.

The chapters that follow will be devoted to maintenance management, i.e. to a function of the *operational* phase. The maintenance manager's basic tasks are two : the determination of strategy, and the organisation and control of the requisite men, spares and equipment. Although these are difficult and important tasks in their own right, what must be emphasised is that failure on the part of the organisation to appreciate the fundamental ideas of terotechnology will probably mean that the maintenance manager will be wasting his time on unnecessary maintenance when the plant comes into operation.

References

1 Moss, T.R. *Plant availability assessment.* Proc.Inst.Mech.Eng., p 91, C 64/79, 1979.
2 Dahlberg, L.E., *Maintenance and Support Analysis Systecon A.B.*, Krunggatan 8 S-11143, Stockholm, Sweden.
3 Holroyd, R. *Chem.Ind. 1310.* 1967.
4 Kelly, A.C. *Conference on Economic Unit Size,* Proc.Inst.Mech.Eng., C65, 1979.
5 Doggett, R.H. *Practical applications in airline maintenance:* National Conference on Terotechnology in Higher Education : Dept. of Industry, 1979, April 1979.
6 Riddell, H.S. *Life Cycle Costing in the Chemical Industry.* Terotechnica 2(1). 1980.
7 Brown, G. *Improvement of reliability in the engineering of process plant and power plant equipment.* Proc.Inst.Mech.Eng., C87, 1973.
8 *Terotechnology—an introduction to the management of physical resources* (HMSO 1975).
9 Kelly, A., and Harris, M.J. *The Management of Industrial Maintenance,* Butterworths, 1978.
10 Jeffries, B., Sadler, J. and Williams, P.R., *The Design Audit.* Terotechnica 1(4). 1980.
11 Ablitt, J.F., Moss, T.R., and Westwell, F. *The role of quantitative assessment and data in predicting system reliability.* Proc.Inst.Mech.Eng., C89. 1973.
12 Harvey, G., and Eastburn, K. *Terotechnology : a case study in the application of the concept.* Terotechnica 1(1). 1979.

Chapter 2

Principles

It has already been pointed out that the maintenance manager's main function is to formulate a maintenance plan, and then to construct an organisation and a control system which will ensure the implementation of that plan. *In carrying out this task he should follow the same guide-lines as for any other industrial management problem.* He needs to understand the nature of maintenance, its relationship with production, and what the *function* of the maintenance department really is. In other words, he needs to be familiar with the situation for which he is responsible, to recognise the dynamic nature of the maintenance-production system, and to understand the mechanics of such a system. From this the *maintenance objective* can be defined and then, and only then, can the *maintenance plan, organisation, schedule* and *control system* be established.

The structure of plant

For the present purpose what is recognised as a *plant* could vary from a chemical plant on the one hand to a fleet of dump trucks in a mining operation on the other. In either case the plant performs the overall function (produces chemicals, transports ore) for some forecasted production life. This function is usually measured by the output of the plant over some production period where

Average Output (tons/h) = Design Performance (tons/h) × Availability (%)

One way of regarding a large and complex industrial plant is as a hierarchy of parts ranked according to their function and replaceability. Figure 2.1 shows a chemical plant divided into its useful functional groupings which, for simplicity, have been called *units*. An example of a unit from this plant is shown in Figure 2.2. The way in which these units are connected together, *the plant structure*, (in series in this case but in parallel in the case of the plastic moulding plant of Figure 2.3), has considerable influence on the reliability and maintenance characteristics of the plant. The series configuration may be particularly difficult to maintain because of long production runs, limited plant redundancy (provision of which can

14

Raw Materials → Charge → React → Filter → Wash → Dry → Product 'X'

Figure 2.1 Process flow chart (Unit level, illustrating plant structure)

be expensive) and the absence of inter-stage storage. This means that the cost of plant unavailability as a result of unit failure can be extremely high. In general, the opposite is the case with a parallel configuration.

A unit of plant can itself be further sub-divided on a hierarchical basis, e.g. the chemical reactor of Figure 2.2 can be classified on a replaceability basis (see Figure 2.4) into *assemblies* (agitation section), *sub-assemblies* (gearbox) and, at the lowest level of replaceability, *components* (gear).

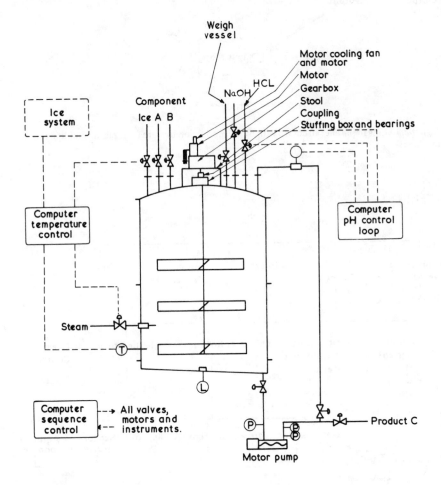

Function : To perform defined stages of an operating process (e.g. coupling under controlled pH and temperature.)

Figure 2.2 A batch chemical reactor

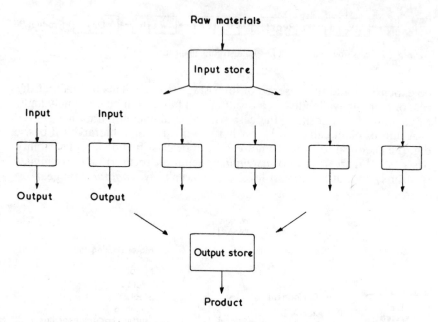

Figure 2.3 Units in parallel structure with batch production to store (e.g. plastic moulding machines)

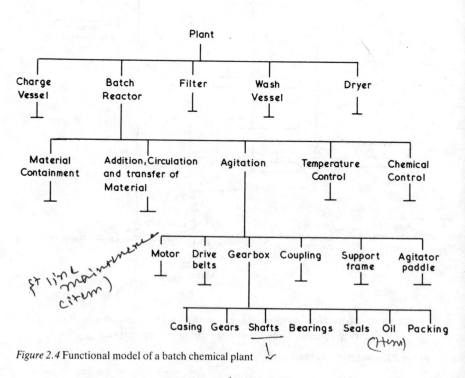

Figure 2.4 Functional model of a batch chemical plant

The reason for, and nature of, maintenance work

Over a century ago Oliver Wendell Holmes wrote the following in one of his poems, 'The Wonderful One-Horse Shay',

'For the wheels were just as strong as the thills
And the floor was just as strong as the sills,
And the panels just as strong as the floor,
And the whipple-tree neither less nor more,
And yet as a whole it is past a doubt,
In another hour it will be worn out!'

The implication was that the vehicle was designed for zero maintenance, since each of the constituent parts had a life of exactly 100 years. When considering the complexity and expense of modern plant, it will be readily realised that designing for zero maintenance, even if possible, would be uneconomic. Many of the constituent components will have been designed, for technological and economic reasons, with a useful life greater than the longest production cycle but less than that of the plant itself. Other components may well have a high possibility of failure during their useful life. Thus, maintenance* is inevitable and generated from failure at component level.

In most cases 'weak' components will have been identified at the design stage and made easily replaceable. Obviously such components are relatively easy to deal with since the need for maintenance can be forecast and planned for; this is the 'expected maintenance load'. In addition, a need for maintenance will also arise due to failures that occur for reasons that are difficult to anticipate, such as *poor design, poor maintenance*, or *maloperation*; this is the 'unexpected maintenance load'. Although such work is difficult to forecast, experience suggests that it is inevitable, especially in the early life of the plant, and therefore needs systems for its detection, recording and analysis. An added complication is that failure to carry out the expected maintenance load generates a larger unexpected load.

Thus, the major problem of the maintenance manager is to decide on the best way of dealing with this complex and uncertain workload, i.e. should he replace or repair the weak component (or some higher level part containing the weak component) before failure (preventive maintenance*) or after failure (corrective maintenance*) or should he design-out the weak component to prevent maintenance? It is to these questions that this book will be addressed.

---

*BS 3811[1]:Maintenance—a combination of actions carried out to return an item to, or restore it to, an acceptable condition.
Preventive Maintenance—maintenance carried out at predetermined intervals, or to other prescribed criteria, and intended to reduce the likelihood of an item not meeting an acceptable condition.
Corrective Maintenance—maintenance carried out to restore an item which has ceased to meet an acceptable condition.

The production-maintenance system—a dynamic model

Consider a large process plant. The objective of the production department is to manufacture a planned output (so many tons of product) over
some given production period. This planned output will depend on the
sales demand (see Figure 2.5) and while its long-term total can be forecast,

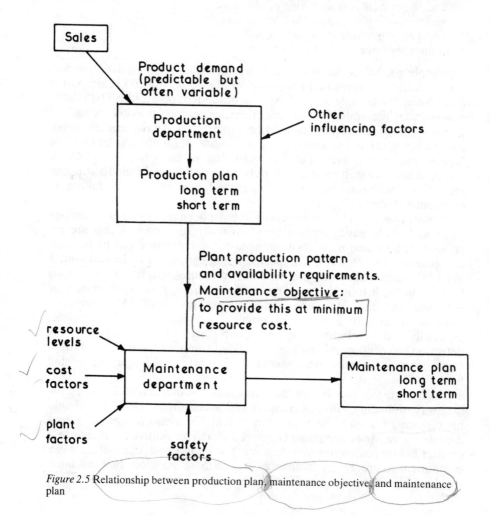

Figure 2.5 Relationship between production plan, maintenance objective and maintenance
plan

there may be short term fluctuations. Thus, the long term production plan
will determine the working pattern and availability requirements of the
plant, e.g. 2 shift/day, 6 days/week, 48 weeks/year at an average availability level of, say, 90%. Obviously, this plan could change in the short term.
The situation can be represented as in Figure 2.6. The plant, or some part
of it, may be in one of the following states—

(a) In production and only running maintenance† can be carried out.
(b) Not wanted for production, e.g. night shift, or feedstock shortage, and available for maintenance without production loss. This is the 'production window' where 'shutdown maintenance'† will not incur production loss. Production windows may be scheduled or may occur with random incidence (as in the case of feedstock shortage).
(c) Taken out of production for scheduled (preventive and corrective) maintenance. Major shutdown work can be carried out but there is production loss.
(d) Failed unexpectedly and corrective maintenance is being carried out under 'emergency'† conditions. Obviously, production is being lost and the maintenance is difficult to plan.
(e) Failed, but due to shortage of maintenance resources is 'waiting for maintenance'. This is the worst state of all.

The plant availability is therefore

$$A = \frac{T_{up}}{T_{up} + T_{down}} = \frac{(a) + (b)}{(a) + (b) + (c) + (d) + (e)}$$

$$= \frac{\text{mean-time-to-failure}}{\text{mean-time-to-failure} + \text{mean time for maintenance}}$$

and is one measure of the effectiveness of the maintenance department. Caution is needed when using this definition of availability since

(i)   it is often difficult to cost unavailability,
(ii) the cause of failure may not be due to maintenance,
(iii) the definition assumes only two levels of performance, namely working and failed, whereas usually there will be a spectrum of intermediate states of partial failure or reduced performance. Amendment of the formula to take account of this is not difficult and does not alter the underlying concept.

In the model of Figure 2.6 maintenance is presented as the operation of a pool of resources (men, spares and tools) directed towards controlling the level of availability and the condition of the plant. Thus it can be considered that the function of maintenance is to use those resources to repair, replace, adjust or modify the parts of plant to enable it to operate at a specified availability and performance over a specified time and for a specified life.

In order to decide on a maintenance plan it is first necessary to establish a maintenance objective. This must be compatible with the company objective—in other words, it must be linked to profitability.

---

†BS 3811 Running maintenance—maintenance which can be carried out whilst the plant or unit is in use (in this book **on-line maintenance** is used for running maintenance)
Shutdown maintenance—maintenance which can only be carried out when the plant or unit is not in use (in this book **off-line maintenance** is used for shutdown maintenance)
Emergency maintenance—corrective maintenance which it is necessary to put in hand immediately to avoid serious consequences.

20

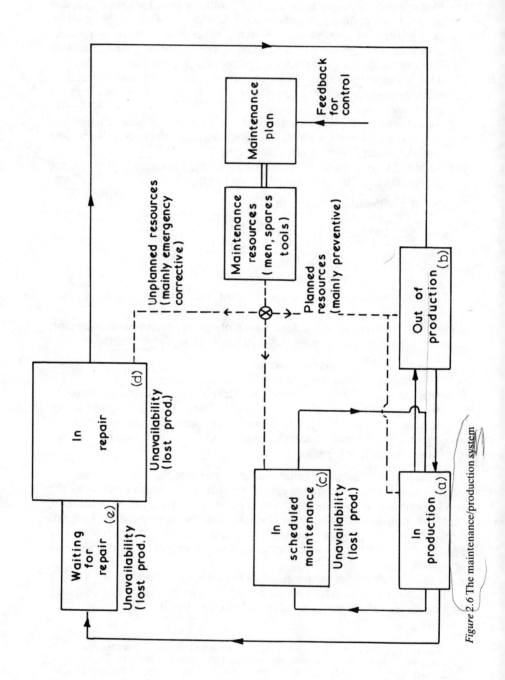

Figure 2.6 The maintenance/production system

Maintenance affects company profitability in a number of ways, the most important of which are:

(i) through its relationship with availability; this is the *indirect cost* of maintenance which might occur when the plant is in states (c), (d) and (e) of Figure 2.6.,

(ii) through the cost of maintenance resources; this can be considered to be the *direct cost* of maintenance,

(iii) through its relationship with the useful life of the plant; the longer the plant life, the greater is the life-cycle profitability.

In general, the greater the level of maintenance resources (higher direct cost) the lower the level of unavailability (lower indirect cost) and the longer the useful life of the plant. Thus, in most industrial situations the proper maintenance objective should be *to minimise the sum of the direct and indirect costs*, always taking into consideration the *long term effect of any maintenance decision*. The problem here, however, is that the cost of unavailability can vary greatly, due to sales and storage factors. Where this is so it is essential to recognise the dynamic nature of maintenance decision making, to clearly understand the maintenance objective and to ensure that systems exist to provide the right information at the right time.

The practical reality of the production-maintenance system is that production dominates, the maintenance objective often being established as shown in Figure 2.5. The maintenance objective can then be restated as 'to provide production with the long- and short-term plant availability requirements (the planned production) at minimum resource cost'. In this form the objective allows for the dynamic nature of the situation.

The *maintenance plan* should consist of a *schedule* of preventive maintenance work and *guidelines* for the implementation of corrective maintenance work. It should ensure that maintenance resources are directed in the best way to achieve the planned output.

Preventive maintenance is one of the two principal means (the other being 'design-out') of controlling the level of corrective maintenance. The difficulty is fixing the level and type of preventive maintenance. Figure 2.7

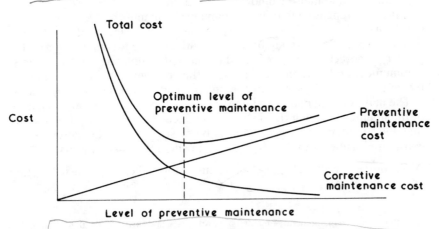

Figure 2.7 Relationship between preventive maintenance and total maintenance cost

shows a model that is often used to illustrate the relationship between level of preventive maintenance and total maintenance cost. In practice it is very much more complex than this because we are not only concerned with the level of preventive maintenance resources, but also the type of preventive maintenance (e.g. should it be time-based or inspection based?) in a situation where unavailability and other influencing factors can change. For example, if the plant in Figure 2.6 has a high unavailability cost, then it would be advantageous to carry out preventive maintenance in states (a) or (b) and, where possible, to use inspection procedures in (a) and/or (b) in order to schedule the resultant maintenance in either (b) and/or (c). This will only be effective if there is close liaison between maintenance and production to establish the scheduling of (b) and the best time for (c). The minor failures not causing plant, or unit, failure (deferred corrective work) can be handled in a similar way.

Carrying out maintenance in this way has a number of advantages[2]: since the maintenance resources can be planned and scheduled, their high utilisation can be achieved; achievement of the required plant availability is easier; the effect of unavailability can often be minimised and premature deterioration of plant can be avoided. Conversely, if the plan is to operate the plant to failure, its condition will rapidly go out of control. This will lead to a difficult planning problem, high unavailability, failures often at the worst time, poor plant condition and a short useful life. Obviously, a plan based on some form of *planned maintenance*‡ would appear to be essential.

This problem is further illuminated by the idea of a maintenance resource curve[3] (see Figure 2.8). This is a plot of the increase with operating time of the level of resources required to bring a plant back to acceptable condition. It is suggested that each plant type will have its characteristic resource curve. If the maintenance plan is to be effective then the preventive maintenance (inspections, adjustments, replacements, etc.) should take care of the expected and unexpected maintenance loads, respectively, before the condition of the plant deteriorates past the 'elbow'. If the elbow is passed then the resource demand may be such that preventive maintenance cannot be carried out.

It is worth repeating that the maintenance plan must be based on the real situation and be designed to respond to the dynamics of production demand. In addition, the importance of adhering to the maintenance plan must be appreciated in both production and maintenance departments, communication between them being sufficiently good to enable an effective and, where necessary, flexible, maintenance schedule to be operated.

The maintenance plan, to a large extent, determines the level and nature of the maintenance workload. It is through consideration of this workload that the maintenance *organisation* is best established. This latter can be considered as being made up of the following inter-related parts :

A Resource Structure : men, spares and tools—their level mix, function and location.

‡BS 3811 : Planned maintenance—maintenance organised and carried out with forethought, control and the use of records to a predetermined plan.

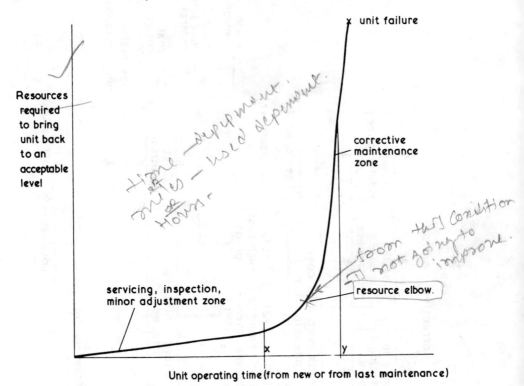

Figure 2.8 Deterioration characteristic of a simple mechanical item

An Administrative Structure : maintenance decision makers, in a hierarchy of authority and responsibility.

A Work Planning System : planning and documentation for matching the resources to a dynamic and complex workload.

Figure 2.6 shows the close link between plan and organisation. If preventive maintenance is omitted due, say, to lack of resources, then more corrective maintenance is generated and still less resources are available for preventive maintenance. This can very quickly result in pure *emergency maintenance* where the whole plant has deteriorated beyond the 'resource elbow'.

The ever-changing nature of the maintenance/production complex makes it necessary not only to establish a plan and organisation but also a *control* system to ensure that the plan and organisation are continually updated. There are three principle mechanisms of maintenance control: work control, plant condition control and availability and cost control. (See Figure 2.9).

At the lowest level, work control complements work planning and is closely linked to the system for spare parts control. Work control is the most important mechanism because it ensures not only that resources are matched to workload but that the failure and cost information, upon which the other control systems depend, is provided.

24

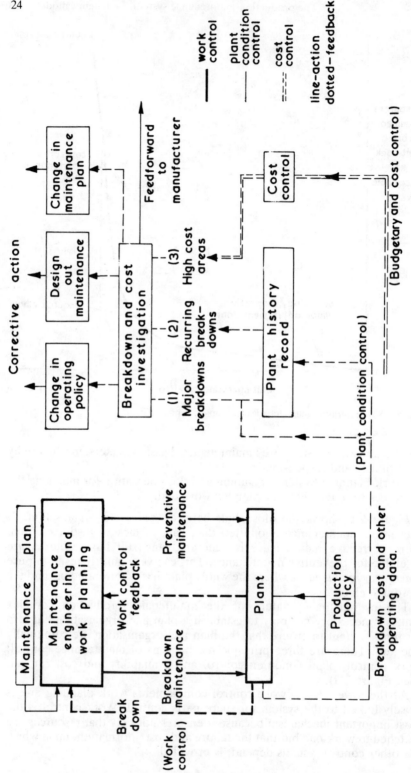

Figure 2.9 A maintenance control model

A plant condition control system is needed to achieve optimum long-term plant performance and its function is to identify the most important problems, diagnose causes, and to prescribe solutions. In this aspect (and bearing in mind the causes of equipment failure—poor design, maloperation, poor maintenance) modification of the maintenance plan is only one of a number of alternative actions which would achieve the maintenance objective. Others are design-out maintenance (aimed at the unexpected load—especially early in the plant life) and changes in the production plan or method of plant operation.

At the highest level (and in the longest term) a maintenance cost and availability control system is needed in order to monitor the effectiveness of the maintenance effort, i.e. are the budgeted resource levels being sustained and unit availability targets met?

It is in the area of control that *maintenance indices* [4,5,6,7] are used to monitor the effectiveness of such variables as labour performance (work control), failure frequency (plant condition control) and availability (cost control). Although indices may be used with advantage in each of these areas, the maintenance activity in total is too complex, too dynamic and too dependent upon the production function for one index or, indeed, set of indices, to properly monitor its overall effectiveness. Indices are likewise not particularly useful for comparing the effectiveness of maintenance at different plants.

Summary

The aim of this chapter has been to introduce the reader to the characteristics of maintenance work and the overall operation of the production/maintenance system. The inter-dependency of maintenance and production has been emphasised. This approach should have provided a basic understanding of the elements of maintenance management (see below).

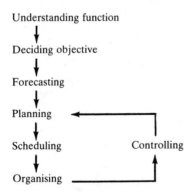

Understanding function

↓

Deciding objective

↓

Forecasting

↓

Planning

↓

Scheduling   Controlling

↓

Organising

With suitable modification the models and concepts discussed can provide a basis for the analysis of most maintenance situations and will therefore provide the presentational framework of the rest of the book. Maintenance plan and schedule will be discussed in detail in Chapters 3 and 4, organisation and control in Chapters 5 and 6.

References

1 BS 3811 British Standard Glossary of *'Maintenance Terms in Terotechnology'* British Standards Institution (1974)
2 Kelly, A., and Harris, M.J., *'The Management of Industrial Maintenance'*, Butterworths (1978)
3 Leadbeater, A.A., *'Station Planning—The Stability Problem'* C.E.G.B. Internal Report (1979)
4 Corder, G.G., *'Modern Maintenance'* Seminar Publication by the British Productivity Council, Sect 2, p.5, 1962.
5 Priel, V.Z., *'Twenty ways to track Maintenance performance'* Factory, pp 81–91, McGraw Hill, (March), 1962.
6 Luck, W.S., *'Now you can really measure maintenance'* Asian Productivity Organisation, 1977.
7 Hibi, S., *'How to measure maintenance performance'* Asian Productivity Organisation, 1977.

Chapter 3

Establishing a maintenance plan—preliminary considerations

Figure 2.4 on page 16 illustrated the division of a complex plant according to function and replaceability into a number of levels from *units* to *components*. The delegation of responsibility for the replacement decisions of a given level differs from plant to plant but higher management usually has responsibility for replacement of units (or, indeed of the manufacturing plant itself) and maintenance management for the replacement and repair of assemblies and components. This division of responsibility is obligatory because replacement policy for units (and plant) is influenced by external factors (mostly long term) such as obsolescence, sales or cost of capital, as well as internal factors (mostly short term) such as the cost of maintenance resources and unavailability costs. Consequently, the *replacement* of units (replacement policy) can be considered as part of the corporate strategy. However, a shorter term plan (schedule of preventive actions and corrective maintenance guidelines) is required for the *maintenance* of units. Replacement policy and maintenance plan are, however, closely interrelated, maintenance cost and actions influencing unit replacement which, in turn, affects the maintenance plan (see Figure 3.1).

In order to establish a maintenance plan it is necessary to identify the parts of the plant which need maintenance, the plant *items*, to determine the most appropriate procedure for each item, and then to list the procedures in the form of a *plan and schedule*.

The item

This can be defined as the lowest grouping of parts of a unit that is likely to require in-situ replacement or repair (1st line maintenance) during the expected life of that unit. In the example of Figure 2.4 the motor, drive belts, gearbox, coupling, agitator paddle and support frame can be considered as items. Since the gearbox oil can be independently replaced, it too can be considered as an item. On the other hand, the gearbox shaft is more likely to be replaced in the maintenance workshop (2nd line maintenance) and is not considered as an item.

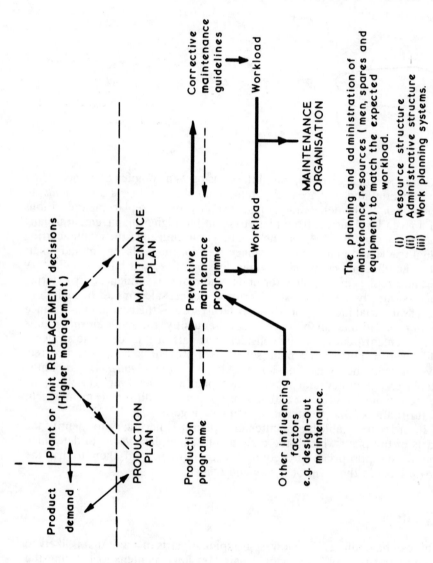

Figure 3.1 Relationship between maintenance plan and plant replacement policy

Maintenance, cost and safety characteristics of an item

The following is a summary of the information essential for the identification of the best way to maintain an item—

Maintenance characteristics:	*Deterioration characteristics* : mean-time-to-failure (MTTF); failure mode; nature of deterioration parameter—if any (detectability of the onset of failure). *Repair characteristics* : mean-time to repair/replace (MTTR); time after failure before unit function is affected.
Economic factors:	Material cost; repair cost; cost of unexpected failure; cost of replacement prior to failure, monitoring cost.
Safety factors:	Internal, environmental, statutory regulations.

Maintenance characteristics

The mean life of an item can be used as an indication of the need for maintenance. Maintenance is likely to be needed where the mean life of the item is less than that of the unit to which it belongs. This being so, the mean life of the item should be greater than the longest expected production run of the unit—if this is not the case the item should be designed-out. The problem is that there is usually considerable statistical uncertainty about the mean life, especially so with expensive long-life items such as gearboxes.

Figures 3.2 and 3.3 illustrate the concepts of detectability and statistical predictability (see Chapter 11 for fuller explanation). Figure 3.2(a) illustrates a failure mechanism (wear, fouling, corrosion etc) where the resistance to failure decreases with use. Thus, if the approach of failure is monitorable successive failures could be represented as in Figure 3.2(b). The life of any one particular item will not be predictable but will fall somewhere in a band centred about the mean value (see Figure 3.2(c)). The more predictable the mean life of such items and/or the more easily the onset of failure can be monitored, the easier it is to decide upon the best maintenance procedure.

Figure 3.3(a) illustrates a time independent failure mechanism. The resistance to failure of the item remains virtually constant. Failure is caused by randomly occurring excessive stress (due to maloperation, faulty feedstock etc) the approach of which will probably not be monitorable. Successive failures of a single item might then be represented as in Figure 3.3(b). Since the cause of failure is external to the item, replacement will not forestall failure; there is no optimum replacement period.

Economic factors

These are a function of the plant to which the item belongs and of the way the plant is operated. Data is obtainable only from the plant user and will be subject to large fluctuations. Estimates of failure cost are, however, relatively straightforward to obtain.

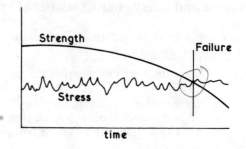

(a) The mechanism

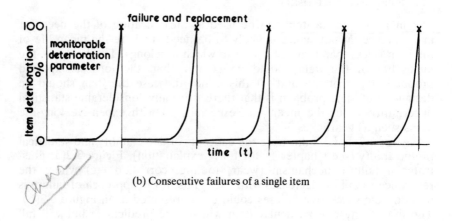

(b) Consecutive failures of a single item

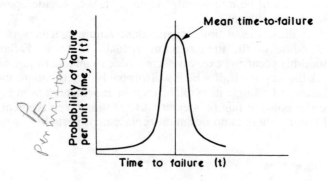

(c) Statistical representation of (b)

Figure 3.2 An age-related failure

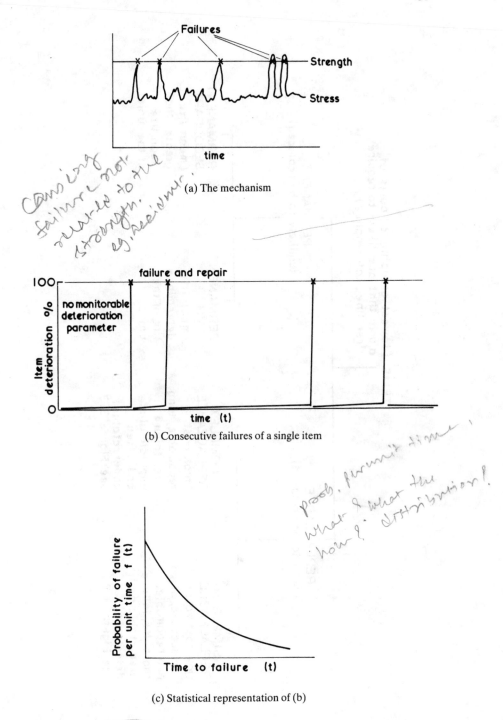

(a) The mechanism

[handwritten margin note:] Causing failure not related to the strength. eg, accidenter.

(b) Consecutive failures of a single item

(c) Statistical representation of (b)

[handwritten margin note:] prob, per unit time ' what & what the how? distribution!*

Figure 3.3 A time-independent failure

32

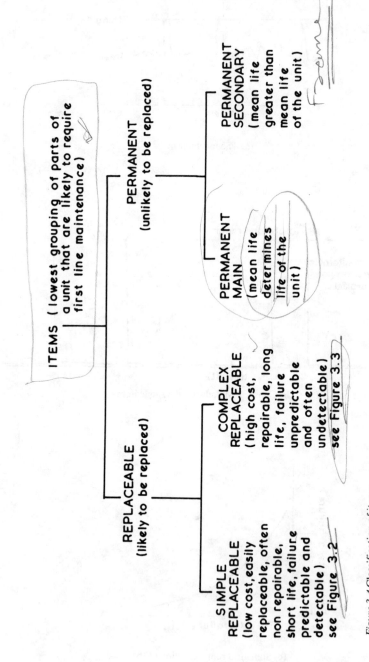

Figure 3.4 Classification of items

Safety factors

These[1] will also depend on the nature of the plant. They are usually well understood and documented.

Classification of items

This can be based on maintenance and cost characteristics (see Figure 3.4).

The first division is into those items that have been designed to be directly replaced—*replaceable items* (e.g. the gearbox of Figure 2.4), and those items that are unlikely to be replaced—*permanent items* (e.g. the support frame of Figure 2.4).

Permanent items can be further divided into those whose life determines the life of the unit (e.g. the reactor shell of Figure 2.4) and those whose life is expected to be longer than that of the unit (e.g. the support frame of

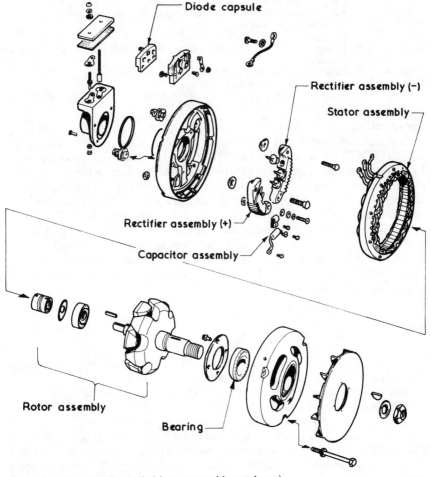

Figure 3.5 Alternator dismantled (cover assembly not shown)

Figure 2.4). In the case of the reactor-shell replacement is possible but uneconomic. The same is true for a badly corroded car body.

The replaceable items can be divided into *simple-replaceable* and *complex-replaceable*. The simple items are made up from a relatively few components, failure of one of which causes the failure of that item. Such items are low cost, easily replaceable, often non-repairable, have a short mean life and the approach of failure is usually detectable (e.g. the drive belts of Figure 2.4). Simple items are particularly significant since they are the main source of the 'expected maintenance load' and can be handled through preventive maintenance procedures.

Complex items are made up from many components into a complete replaceable module (e.g. an alternator, see Figure 3.5). Failure can be caused by failure of any one of the components (see Table 3.1) and the

TABLE 3.1. Causes of alternator failure

Brushes	Wear, faulty slip rings.
Stator	Open circuit on winding; short circuit on winding; high temperature due to high current consumption, i.e. faulty regulator or flat batteries.
Rotor	Open circuit; short circuit.
Heat sink	Overgreased.
Diode	Heavy current. High internal temperature due to external faults e.g. faulty regulator
Bearings	Lack of greasing; worn shafts; end plate wearing.
Fan	Affected by bearing failure.

approach of failure may be difficult to detect by simple monitoring techniques. Probability of failure is often time-independent (see Figure 3.3). The MTTF is usually long and the cost of replacing or repairing high. For these reasons such items present the maintenance manager with his biggest engineering problem, since there is difficulty in determining what, if any, is the best preventive procedure and what is the best corrective procedure in the event of failure. In addition, complex items are the largest sources of unexpected maintenance. It must be emphasised that many items will not fall neatly into one of the divisions of the foregoing, rather simplistic classification. It is offered only as a guide which will help the maintenance manager towards a clearer understanding of the maintenance characteristics of his plant.

The maintenance procedure

This will be taken to be the *maintenance action and its timing* for a particular item (e.g. valve replacement at 3-monthly intervals).

The basic procedures are shown in Table 3.2. The maintenance can be carried out to prevent failure (procedures 1 to 3) or as a result of failure (procedure 4), opportunity maintenance being used in conjunction with the other procedures listed. Design-out is not strictly maintenance but is an option open to the maintenance manager. The main decision is one of timing since, in most cases, the action itself cannot be decided until after the maintenance-demanding event has occurred.

TABLE 3.2. Alternative maintenance procedures

Timing	Action
1. Fixed time maintenance	Adjust or repair or replace at fixed periods
2. Fixed time inspection	Inspect via equal or variable inspection periods then adjust/repair/replace on condition
3. Continuous inspection	Inspect on continuous basis then adjust/repair/replace on condition
4. Operate to failure	Replace or repair after failure
5. Opportunity maintenance	Inspect item at time based on some other item's maintenance/inspection period

Timing

Fixed-time maintenance

Maintenance actions that are carried out at regular intervals, or after a fixed cumulative output, fixed number of cycles of operation etc. This includes item replacement, repair and major strip-down for inspection (the author regards condition-based maintenance as inspection carried out without major strip-down). In most cases, the periodicities, actions and resources for such work can be anticipated and scheduled well beforehand with ample time tolerances. However, *this procedure is only effective where the failure mechanism of the item is clearly time-dependent* (see Figure 3.2), the item being expected to deteriorate over a period much less than the life of the unit to which it belongs.

Obviously, the more predictable the time-to-failure, the more effective is fixed-time-maintenance. Whether this is necessarily the best procedure, even then, will depend upon the cost of the alternative effective procedures. If approach of the failure is detectable, condition-based maintenance is effective and in the majority of cases more economic. Comparing fixed-time-maintenance to operate-to-failure, a rough guide is that fixed-time-maintenance is only effective where the total cost (of resource and unavailability) per maintenance action is substantially less than that of operate-to-failure. The implication is that 'fixed-time-maintenance and adjust or replace' is an effective procedure for simple replaceable items, but is inappropriate for complex replaceable items because of their far less predictable time-to-failure and their high cost. With such items, it is often better to seek a suitable condition-monitoring technique[2, 3, 4, 5].

Condition-based maintenance

An attractive concept is that the proper time for performing maintenance ought to be determinable by monitoring condition and/or performance, provided of course, that a readily monitorable parameter of deterioration can be found. The probabilistic element in failure prediction is therefore reduced or, indeed, almost eliminated, the life of the item maximised and the effect of failure minimised. One of the major benefits of this policy is that the resulting corrective maintenance can, in most cases, be scheduled in the short term without production loss.

The monitored parameter can provide information about a single component (e.g. the wear of a brake pad), or provide information that can indicate a change in any number of different components (e.g. vibration from a turbo-generator). The more specific is the information provided, the better from the point of view of maintenance decision making. Condition-monitoring can be applied in three ways:

Simple inspection—   qualitative checks based on look, listen and feel (e.g. rope worn/rope not worn).

Condition checking—   done routinely and measuring some parameter which is not recorded but is only used for comparison with a control limit. Such checking only has value where there is extensive experience of identical systems.

Trend monitoring—   measurements made *and plotted* in order to detect gradual departure from a norm.

The desirability of the monitoring, the technique used, and its periodicity will depend upon the *deterioration characteristics* of the item and the costs involved.

Simple Inspection Procedures are sufficiently effective to account for 70% of a typical condition-based-programme. Such procedures are usually cheap and carried out as part of a routine. The important points are that the cost should be insignificant, relative to the cost of repair and that the periodicity should be sufficiently short to detect minor, and often unexpected problems before they develop. One form is 'short-period blanket inspections' of on-line plant carried out in order to identify obvious minor defects before serious damage can arise.

Condition checking could be used in such items as brake pads which have well documented linear deterioration characteristics of the type shown in Figure 3.6. Because of the predictability of the time-to-failure the actual inspections need not begin until well into the item's life. The subsequent

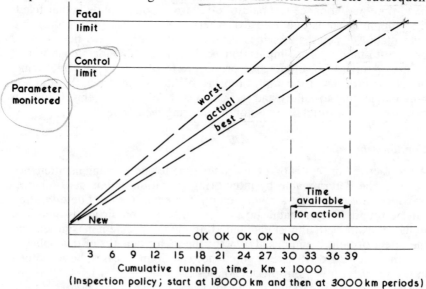

Figure 3.6 Linear deterioration characteristics

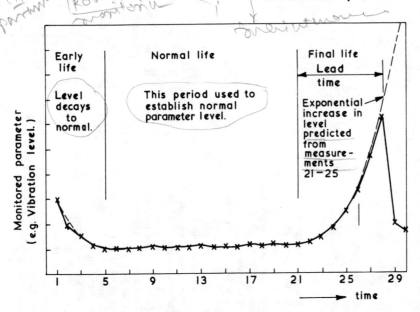

Figure 3.7 Typical vibration characteristics

periodicity can be adjusted to give the desired level of warning using a control limit. Obviously, the deterioration characteristics shown in Figure 3.6 are preferable to the more usual characteristics shown in Figure 3.7 in as much as the failure developing period, or 'lead time', is longer. The shorter the lead time and the higher the cost of failure, the greater the inclination towards shorter inspection period and, in special cases, continuous monitoring (e.g. vibration monitoring of turbo-generators).

Trend monitoring is most effective where little is known about the deterioration characteristics. Since this is mostly the case, it will be appreciated that trend monitoring is of the widest application. Experience is accumulated as monitoring progresses and, when enough knowledge of deterioration characteristics has been acquired, condition checking can be substituted for trend monitoring.

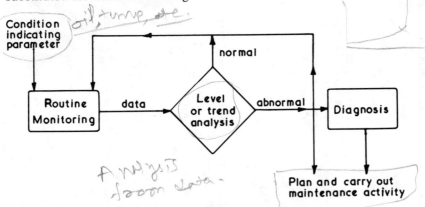

Figure 3.8 Flow diagram of a condition monitoring procedure

TABLE 3.3. Summary of condition monitoring techniques

Type	Method	On-line or off-line	Comments	Skill of operator	Equipment cost
1) Visual	Human eye	on	Covers a wide range of ad hoc methods. Surface inspection only	4	5 (zero)
	Optical probes	off	Can be used for internal inspection of aero engines, steam turbines, chemical vessels, etc.	3	4
	Optical probes with television	off			2
2) Temperature	Temperature crayons and tapes. Thermometers. Thermocouples	on	Mainly surface temperature over a wide range of temperatures	3	5
	Infra-red meter	on	Use of infra-red to monitor surface temperature of equipment surfaces. Covers a wide range of temperatures but limited area	2	3
	Infra-red scanner	on	As above but can cover much wider surface area. Can provide surface temperature picture and can be calibrated to give quantitative measure	2	1
3) Lubricant monitoring	Magnetic plugs, filters	on	Analysis of debris picked up by plugs or filter in an oil washed system. Mainly large debris picked up, 100–1000 microns.	2	5
	Ferrography		Instrument to separate ferrous debris by size to enable microscopic examination. Non-ferrous debris also separated. Direct reading instrument also available. Wide range of debris size analysed. 3–100 microns.	2	1
	Spectroscopy		Spectrographic analysis of oil samples to determine elements present. Analysis for small debris size 0–10 microns. Contract service usually available.	2	2 but contract service available
Vibration	Total signal	on	Monitors vibration signal from rotating or reciprocating machine as an averaged no. Problems on one freq. can be masked by overall signal.	3	4
	Freq. analysis	on	Records vibrations signal over wide freq. range (signature) and monitors. Can establish out of balance or roller element bearing problems.	1	2
	Shock pulse monitoring (SPM) S pulse energy and kurtosis meter	on	All three techniques use high freq. signals for roller element bearing monitoring. Considerable experience built up in the use of SPM methods. SPM can also be used for leak detection	3	3

				Skill	Cost
Crack	Dye penetrant	on and off	Detects cracks bearing surface	3	5
	Magnetic flux	on and off	Detects cracks at/near surface of ferrous materials	3	5
	Elect. resistance	on and off	Detects cracks at surface and can be used to estimate depth of crack	3	4
	Eddy current	on and off	Detects cracks near to surface. Also useful for inclusion and hardness, etc.	1	3 & 4
	Ultrasonic	on and off	Detects cracks anywhere in component. Directional sensitivity, therefore general searches lengthy. Use to back up other techniques	1	3
	Radiography	off	Detects cracks anywhere in component. Section and source (steel). Access to both sides of component necessary. Radiation hazard.	1	2
Corrosion monitoring	Weight loss coupons	off	Coupons weighed when plant off-line	4	5
	Corrosometer	on	Electrical element and potentiometer. Detects less than 1 mm corrosion loss	3	4
	Polarisation resistance	on	Only indicates corrosion. No accuracy with estimate of rate	3	3
	Pulse indicator holes	on	Indicates that present amount of corrosion has occurred—	3	3

Key

Skill
1 Considerable
2 Skill needed
3 Some skill
4 Little skill

Cost
1 £10000
2 £2000–10000
3 £500–2000
4 £50–500
5 £50

In general, monitoring techniques (see Table 3.3) can be used for both condition checking and trend monitoring. It will be appreciated that condition monitoring routines are predetermined and, in most cases, can be carried out with little or no unit/plant unavailability (i.e. they can be categorised as on-line maintenance). If the resulting corrective maintenance requires the plant to be stopped this can be short-term scheduled to minimise inconvenience (see Figure 3.8).

Operate-to-failure

No action is taken to detect the onset of, or to prevent failure. The corrective work that results occurs with random incidence and with little or no warning. Where such maintenance results in plant failure the failure can cause a complete plant outage, the determination of the 'best' action is both difficult and expensive. This will be discussed below under 'corrective maintenance'.

Opportunity maintenance

Timing is determined by the procedure adopted for some other item in the same unit or plant. Consideration of this possibility is a major factor in formulating the maintenance plan for the whole plant (see Chapter 4).

Actions

The main 'first line' actions are replace, repair and adjust (see Table 3.2). Obviously, this is a simplification because, in practice, each of these groups can be further sub-divided (e.g. permanent or temporary repair).

Only in the case of fixed-time-maintenance is action established beforehand (e.g. replace sparking plug at 18000 km, replace engine at 150,000 km, etc). In all other situations the action is established after the maintenance-causing event. This is the area of corrective maintenance decision-making.

Corrective maintenance arises not only when an item fails but also when indicated by condition monitoring. The first task is to establish the most economic method of restoring the failed unit/plant to an acceptable state (see Figure 3.9). Clearly, it is only after the maintenance causing event that the influencing factors (cause of failure, cost of replacement or repair, availability of resources, cost of unavailability, time to next window, etc) can be assessed and the type of repair determined. This is a particularly difficult task when the failure has occurred as a result of an operate-to-failure policy and results in a plant shutdown. Condition monitoring avoids this since it provides time for decision making and scheduling. Some failures do not stop the plant immediately and allow time for decision making. Once such work is identified (sometimes called 'deferred jobs') it can be scheduled for the most suitable time.

Accepting that corrective work occurs, it is essential to plan for it. This means deciding on the type of corrective maintenance actions (and resources) needed, i.e. it calls for the formulation, as part of the maintenance plan, of corrective maintenance guidelines to assist in the determination, at short notice, of the maintenance procedure to be adopted.

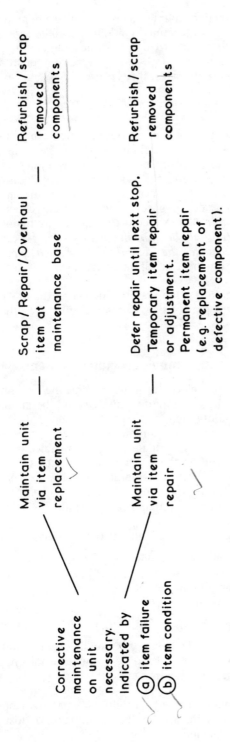

Figure 3.9 Example of alternative corrective maintenance actions for a complex replaceable item

Clearly, corrective maintenance via replacement of complex items, in the light of the predetermined guidelines, will be reserved for critical units since item holding costs are high. A critical item in this context is one which (when adopting an operation-to-failure policy) might fail with little warning and where the unavailability costs are high.

Design-out-maintenance

By contrast with the above procedures, which aim to minimise the effect of failure, design-out aims to eliminate the cause of maintenance. Clearly, this is an engineering design problem but it is often part of the maintenance department's responsibility. It is appropriate for items of high maintenance cost which arises either because of poor maintenance, poor design or operation outside design specification. In many cases design-out is aimed at items that were not expected to require any maintenance. Therefore, *such a policy can only be implemented effectively if an information system exists which facilitates the identification of such items*. The choice to be made is between the cost of re-design and the cost of recurring maintenance.

Where design-out is the maintenance department's responsibility, it can be considered as part of the preventive effort (see the dynamic model of Figure 2.6).

Guidelines for matching procedures to items

The problem is to select, for a given item, the best procedure from those listed in Table 3.2, taking into consideration the maintenance characteristics, cost and safety factors.

The maintenance characteristics of an item can be used to establish the *effective* procedures (see Figure 3.10). The choice of the most *desirable* of these is then based on the safety and cost factors.

Where the mean life is considerably less than expected the problem boils down to establishing the cause of this and, if possible, designing it out. Often a temporary maintenance procedure is adopted until a more permanent solution is found.

Figure 3.10 gives an *initial* ranking of the effective procedures as follows:

1. condition-based-maintenance (on-line)
2. condition-based-maintenance (off-line)
3. fixed-time-maintenance
4. operate-to-failure

Such a ranking is justified on the following grounds:

> *Condition-based-maintenance* is usually cheaper and more positive than fixed-time maintenance because of the uncertainty of the time-to-failure (caused either by inherent variability or by lack of data, especially early in the plant's life).
> *Fixed-time-maintenance* is usually cheaper than operate-to-failure because of the high cost in the latter case of lost production and/or consequent damage.

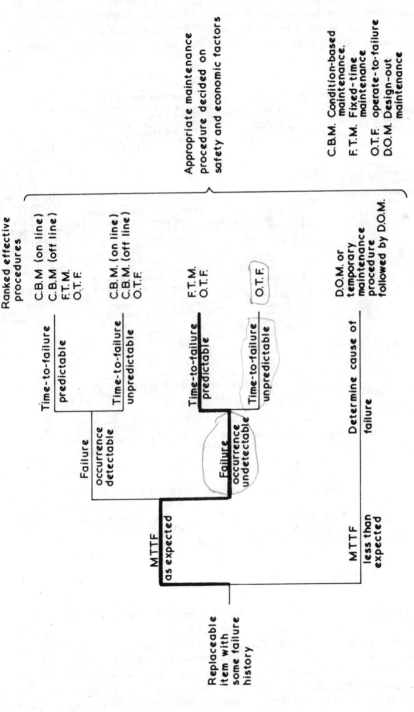

Figure 3.10 Decision diagram for selection of 'best' maintenance procedure

This simple reasoning, and the properties of the items as classified and discussed in the section on classification of items, leads to the guidelines of Table 3.4. These *are* only guidelines. Each item would be considered individually and the best of the effective procedures selected on the basis of

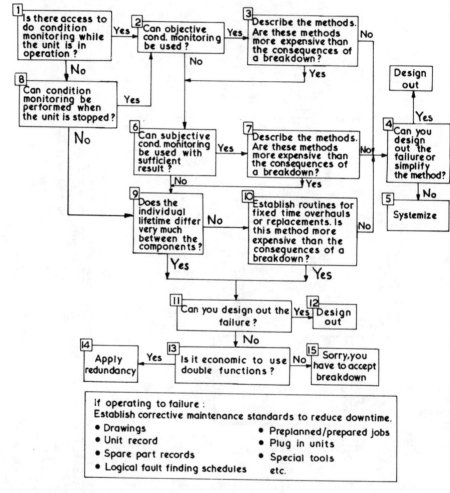

Figure 3.11 Idhammar decision diagram

the known cost and safety factors by applying engineering judgement (Note the relationship between the maintenance plan and the spares inventory policy[7]). Various diagrammatic aids to this decision making process have been published. The Idhammar diagram[8], see Figure 3.11, is based on the idea that, wherever possible, a condition monitoring procedure should be used. The United Airlines method[9], see Figure 3.12, has two parts; a diagram for determining the effective actions and a diagram for establishing the most desirable of these.

TABLE 3.4. Maintenance guidelines for a critical unit

Item category / Plan	Simple replaceable items			Complex replaceable items			Permanent items	
							Main	Secondary
Maintenance procedure	Adjust or replace	via	F.T.M. or C.B.M.	Repair or replace	via	C.B.M. or F.T.M. or O.T.F. or D.O.M.	Repair via C.B.M.	No. action
Preventive policy	Inspection routines Lubrication routines Service periods			Condition based routines Overhaul periods	or D.O.M.		Inspection routines	None
Corrective policy				Decision guidelines Diagnostics Corrective methods				
Spares inventory policy	Carry mostly items— some components Demand predictable			Carry mostly components— some items in special cases. Demand difficult to forecast			None carried unless insurance spares	

Key
C.B.M.   Condition based maintenance
F.T.M.   Fixed time maintenance
O.T.F.   Operate to failure
D.O.M.   Design out maintenance

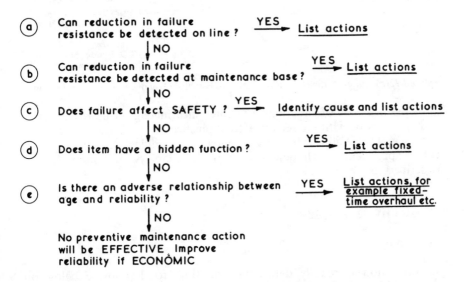

Figure 3.12(a) United Airlines Decision Diagram. Determination of effective maintenance procedures

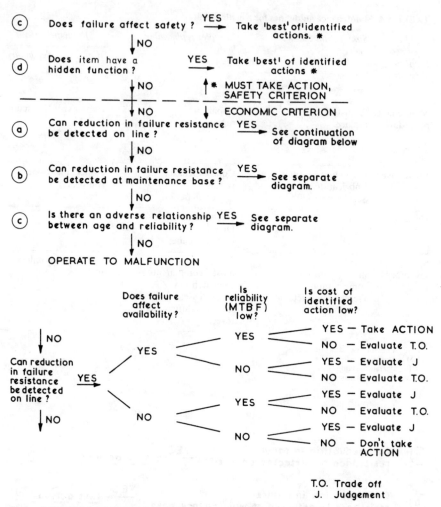

Figure 3.12(b) United Airlines Decision Diagram. Establishment of best effective procedure

In the majority of situations a maintenance manager can arrive at the best procedure without recourse to sophisticated statistical and/or cost analyses. This is illustrated in the following examples. A more sophisticated approach, which depends on the availability of failure data is described in Chapter 11.

Illustrative examples

Spark plug

Deterioration is readily detectable and time to deteriorate below an acceptable level fairly predictable. Consequently, the most likely timing is via visual inspection although fixed-time maintenance is also effective.

However, when costs are considered (low material cost, low labour cost for replacement, which is the same as that for inspection) then the best procedure is fixed-time-replacement, the periodicity being determined from the deterioration rate of the electrodes. The precise periodicity actually adopted will be a convenient compromise with the periodicities identified for other engine-items.

Paper-machine bearing-assembly

The assembly has been in use in-plant for some time and the main cause of failure has been identified as bearing wear. The time-to-failure is not predictable but the approach of failure is detectable by shock pulse monitoring (SPM) of the high speed roller bearings. The consequences of failure are very serious and the cost of replacement, in terms of material and labour, is very high.

The first question is concerned with the mean-time to failure. Is it acceptable or not? If it is too short the cause of MTTF must be established and design-out considered. In our case the MTTF is acceptable and the onset of failure detectable via SPM. Therefore, the effective procedures (see Figure 3.10) are condition-based-maintenance and operate-to-failure.

Operate-to-failure is unacceptable because of the high unavailability and repair costs. The economically appropriate procedure is condition-based-maintenance via shock-pulse monitoring of the bearings[10]. The condition-based policy most appropriate for the type of bearing and the SPM technique is trend monitoring based on monthly inspections.

The most appropriate maintenance action (replace assembly or repair assembly) can be decided (assuming a spare assembly is kept) when the monitored parameter passes a defined limit.

Chipping machine wearplate

The chipping machine (Figure 3.13) is part of a series-structured continuously-operated sawmill. The life of the mill is expected to be nine years. The customary period for maintenance is during the two-week annual shutdown. Outside this 'window' production is lost if the mill is stopped.

The main task associated with the chipping machine is the replacement of the wear plate. Unexpected failure of the plate results in 10 hours lost production while it is replaced. If the production department is given advance notice of plate replacement, only 2 hours of production is lost. Wear on the plate is due to abrasion by the wood chips. This cannot be seen from the mouth of the chipping machine. The costs involved are as follows :

Production loss per hour of downtime	£100
Labour, for replacement after failure	£350
Labour, for planned replacement or for removal for inspection	£100
Plate	£1000

The life of the wear plate is thought to be about 18 months with a range of plus or minus 3 months. The bearings and blades have lives well in excess

TABLE 3.5. Determination of best procedure for wearplate maintenance

Maintenance procedure	Average No. replacements over 9 years	Expected production-loss cost (£)	Labour cost (£)	Materials cost (£)	Total cost (£)	Objective
Operate to failure and replace	6	$6 \times 10 \times 100$ = 6000	6×350 = 2100	6×1000 = 6000	14100	
Fixed time replacement 12 m period	8	0	8×100 = 800	8×1000 = 8000	8800	Minimise total costs
15 m period (Other period)	7	$6 \times 2 \times 100$ = 1200	7×100 = 700	7×1000 = 7000	8900	
Condition-monitor and replace	6	$6 \times 2 \times 100$ = 1200	6×100 = 600	6×1000 = 6000	7800	Select

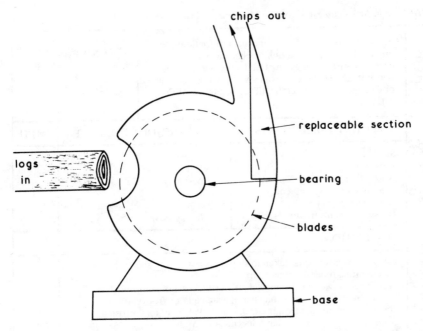

Figure 3.13 Schematic of chipping machine

of 18 months. It is known that wear progresses linearly with time with a worst rate of about 2.5mm per month.

The life is fairly predictable so, fixed-time replacement would be effective. What is not obvious is the method to be used to monitor the wear of the plate should condition-based-maintenance be employed. Ultrasonics could be used, but a far less sophisticated method would be to drill one or more small diameter holes (where the wear is likely to occur) to a depth of say 5 mm and to check monthly with piano wire if the hole has been penetrated. This would give adequate warning of wear plate failure.

Table 3.6 shows that, of the effective procedures, condition-checking is the cheapest. Operate-to-failure is too expensive because of lost production cost. Fixed-time-maintenance is too expensive because of material cost.

Universal maintenance procedures

Ideally, the equipment manufacturer should specify the maintenance procedure necessary for each item. Alternatively, the manufacturer should describe the maintenance characteristics of his products so that the user may establish the best procedure. In practice, manufacturers supply limited information on procedures (mainly for short-life simple-items) and even less on maintenance characteristics. This is especially true with process plant.

A number of consultants can now provide guidelines, or what they call 'universal maintenance procedures' for many of the common items that

TABLE 3.6. An example of Universal Maintenance Procedures

ITEM	CLASSIFICATION: Brake: mechanical friction: operated by mechanical link mechanism: strongly corrosive surroundings; operated more than 5 times per shift; sudden breakdown may cause fatal accident or damage exceeding £1500. (Treat separately: Lifter 3.)		UNIVERSAL MAINTENANCE ITEM GUIDE LIST

STANDARD DEFECTS	DEFECTIVE COMPONENTS	DESCRIPTION OF DEFECT	MTTF
	Steel parts	Corrosion	4y
	Link bearings	Wear	4y
	Nuts, other fastening elements	Loosening	Never
	Operated braking element, friction area	Wear	3m
	Braked element, friction area	Wear, grooved	4y

UNIVERSAL MAINTENANCE OPERATORS	DESCRIPTION	Freq.
	Activate. Measure time taken to stop (max a = _____ secs, 0.5 secs + operating time of mechanism)	8h
	Watch out for wear on braking element (thickness of lining min b = _____ mm, 70% of new thickness); watch out for grooves on braked element (depth max c = 0.5 mm); watch out for corrosion, lubricate d = _____ General Specification M.38)	1m
	Watch out for loose bolts; check play of link bearings (total free movement should not exceed 30% of normal lifter travel, i.e., max e = _____, 30% watch out for wear of braked element (wall thickness min f = _____ mm, minimum 70% of original).	ly

REMARKS	COMPONENT BREAK-DOWN:	
	1. *Mechanism*	2. *Friction elements*
	1.1 Levers	2.1 Braking el. (Shoes, etc)
	1.2 Links and Bearings	2.1 Braking el. (Drum, disk, etc).
	1.3 Bolts	3. *Lifting elements*
		(not included)
		4. *Closing elements*
		4.1 Spring, weight, etc.

make up industrial plant. An example of universal maintenance procedures[11] for a mechanical brake is shown in Table 3.6. It can be seen that much useful information, for determining the best procedure, is provided.

Quite the most valuable aid to maintenance decision making and control is, however, the routine collection, via the normal maintenance function, of failure and repair data and its compilation into a history record which can be easily accessed for subsequent analysis. This continuing exercise should be done at item level where first-line decisions are taken. A full discussion of this area is given in Section 5.

References

1. Lees, F.P., *Loss Prevention in the Process Industries*, Butterworths, London (1980).
2 Henry, T.A. *A simple approach to condition monitoring*, Terotechnica, 1, 131–139, Elsevier, Amsterdam (1979).

3 Neale, M., and Associates, *A guide to the condition monitoring of machinery*, HMSO, 1978.
4 Collacott, R.A., *Mechanical Fault Diagnosis and Condition Monitoring*, Chapman Hall, London (1977).
5 *Industrial Corrosion Monitoring*, HMSO 1978.
6 Kelly, A. and Harris, M.J., *Management of Industrial Maintenance*, Chapter 9, Butterworths, London (1978).
7 Harris, M.J. *An introduction to maintenance stores organisation and spares inventory control.* Terotechnica, 1 47–57 (1979).
8 Idhammar, C. *Maintenance Course Notes for Developing Countries.* Ali Rati, Fack 1213, Lidingo, Sweden.
9 Nowlan, F.S. *Decision Diagrams Approach to On Condition Philosophies.* Aircraft Engineering, March and April (1972).
10 Brown, P.J. *Preventive Maintenance of Machinery Bearings*, Maintenance Engineering, 20 (8) : 54–56.
11 Grothus, H., Plant Engineering Institute, D-427, Dosten 2, Wettring 4, West Germany.

Chapter 4

Establishing a maintenance plan and schedule

The previous chapter considered the best way of maintaining individual items. Consideration of the plant as a whole, seeking opportunities for co-ordinating the aggregate of procedures, will now be examined. This will involve a compromise between the individual optimum periodicities, the most economic use of labour and the maximum plant availability.

A systematic six-step method

We need a method for establishing the most appropriate combination of maintenance procedures for the many plant items. In a sense the following method (which the author calls the *Top-Down Bottom-Up* Approach) encapsulates what has been said in Chapters 2 and 3.

Step 1—Determine critical plant units and production windows

Determine the nature of the plant process (continuous, batch, etc.). Classify the plant into units and construct a process flow diagram (e.g. see Figure 4.1). Carry out a simple consequences of failure analysis and estimate the cost of lost production. Determine the production plan, the pattern of plant operation and the expected plant and unit availabilities. From such information determine (a) the critical plant units, perhaps even ranking them according to the cost and consequences of failure, (b) the schedule of production windows (including consideration of the possibility of random production stops). In addition, and also as part of Step 1, determine the existing maintenance plan—if any.

Step 2—Classify the plant into constituent items

This will be a complete classification in the case of critical units, and a partial classification in the case of non-critical units (see Figure 2.4).

52

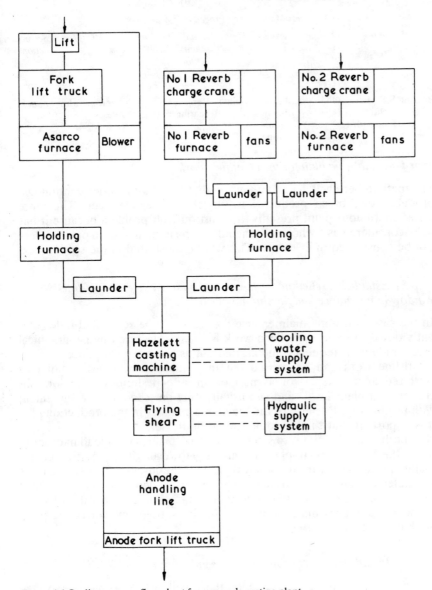

Figure 4.1 Outline process flow chart for an anode casting plant

Step 3—Determine and rank the effective procedures

Determine the effective procedures for each item and the best of these from a cost and safety viewpoint (see Figure 3.10). In general the procedures for the simple items will be reasonably certain and will be mostly on-line maintenance. However, this will not necessarily be so in the case of the complex items and the *best approach is often to try to identify a simple method of condition checking.* Such a procedure should result in a table such as the following for each item.

Best Maintenance Procedure for an Item

Item	Timing	On-line (ON) or Off-line (OFF)	Periodicity	Time	Initial maint. action	On-line (ON) or Off-line (OFF)	Periodicity	Time	Secondary action
Bearing	S.P.M. trend monitoring	ON	M as running maint. routine	(mins)	Replace bearing	OFF during agreed shutdown	Approx. 2 years (Random)	2 hrs.	none

Step 4—Establish a plan for the identified work

The method here will depend upon whether the plant is series-continuous, product flow, batch product flow, batch, or vehicle fleet. The large series-continuous plant presents the most difficult problem because it has to be considered as a whole for scheduling; the item in a batch plant or fleet can be considered individually. This will be illustrated in the sections.

Step 5—Establish a schedule for the on-line maintenance, the off-line window maintenance and the shutdown work

In the case of on-line maintenance the work can be scheduled independently down to item level. Such work is usually classified by geographical area, trade and frequency and carried out as short-term routines.

Off-line work can be carried out in production-windows (small jobs clustered at unit level) or as part of an agreed shutdown (major jobs clustered at plant level) and can usually only be scheduled by agreement with production. Because of the inevitable changes in the production plan it is important that this schedule should be flexible.

In both cases the aim is to smooth the maintenance workload in order to make the best use of in-plant resources. However, if a condition-based-maintenance plan is in operation then only the inspection checks can be scheduled because timing of the subsequent work depends on the results of these checks. However, it is important to take into consideration (where known) the approximate periodicity of the subsequent corrective work load when planning resources.

Step 6—Establish corrective maintenance guidelines

In spite of preventive maintenance there will still be some unexpected failures, e.g. those due to items which fail randomly and without monitorable warning. Such failures have to be planned for in terms of spares and manpower. In the case of critical units, careful consideration must also be given to repair methods, documentation and decision guidelines.

A maintenance plan for a paper machine

The machine (see Figure 4.2) makes paper 4 m wide and runs at speeds varying between 100 and 374 m/min. The output is 75,000 t/y. The machine

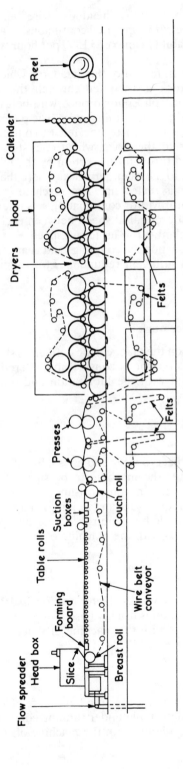

Figure 4.2 The paper machine

can be divided into six sections: headbox, wire belt, conveyor, press, dryers, calender and reel. It is operated continuously 24 hours per day, 365 days per year. Unavailability can cost £1500 per hour when the machine is production limited.

Liquid paper stock is fed into the headbox which has a corrosion resistant lining, the stock is then fed through the slice (a controlled aperture) on to a moving phosphor-bronze wire-belt conveyor on which the paper is formed as the water drains away. The paper then passes to the press section where it is carried by the felt (a continuous belt) into the presses. It then passes to the dryer which consists of 22 steam heated cylinders, being assisted through this section by the felt.

The paper is then fed to the calender stocks where the final finish is given to its surface before it is reeled up. The machine is driven, section by section, by AC-Generator/Motor combination sets interlinked in a control system such that the differential in speed between each section can either be maintained, as the plant is run up to full speed, or varied as necessary. The motors drive each section via couplings and gears. This driving section is very reliable and has sufficient redundancy for running maintenance to be possible.

Definition of maintenance work

The maintenance work on the plant can be defined as shown below. It must be emphasised that this outline is considerably altered and simplified for illustrative purposes and with the lubrication and other on-line maintenance omitted.

Headbox (1)

(a) Rubber seals are subject to wear and have a life of 7 ± 1 months. Wear is detectable but requires the machine to be stopped. Seal replacement takes about 2 hours with the machine off-line.
(b) The headbox lining requires repair (welding) at approximately 6 month intervals. Wear is detectable but requires the machine to be stopped. The repair takes about 2 hours with the machine off-line.

Wire Belt Conveyor (1)

Has a life of about 4 ± 1 weeks. Deterioration is detectable while it is running but failure detection is usually based on product quality. Replacement takes about 8 hours with the machine off-line.

Felts (3)

The felts on both press and dryer section have a life of about 2 months ± 1 week. Deterioration is detectable under running conditions. Replacement of each felt takes about 3 hours with the machine off-line.

Calender (1)

Has a life of about 8 ± 1 weeks. Deterioration is detectable while it is running. Replacement takes about 8 hours with the machine off-line.

Rotary Joints on the Steam-Heated Cylinders (22)

Steam enters each joint (see Figures 4.3 and 4.4) via a flexible hose and passes through the joint on the outside of a syphon pipe. The steam condenses in the cylinder and returns to the joint via the syphon. The condensate leaves the joint through the condensate head, a flexible hose carrying it to sink. The rotating part of the joint is made up of the quick release mechanism, shank, spherical washer and gland assembly. During

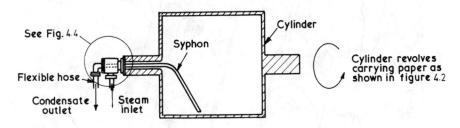

Figure 4.3 Rotary joint of heated cylinder assembly

operation seals A and B (see Figure 4.4) wear, but it has been found that seal A fails first, allowing steam to escape, damaging the paper and therefore precipitating machine shutdown. The spring provides the sealing force between the shank/seal-B and washer/seal-A interfaces and also promotes self-adjustment of the joint as the seals wear. The seals have a life of anything between 6 and 30 months. Steam leaks often require the machine to be taken off-line. Replacement of the joint after failure or for seal inspection takes about 2 hours of off-line work.

Roller Element Bearings (High-Speed) (120)

Time-to-failure varies randomly, with a mean of about 5 years. Unexpected failure involves 2 hours of off-line work.

The existing maintenance plan is to replace the calenders every 8 weeks, taking the opportunity to do other jobs as necessary. The six-step method will be used to see whether there might be an alternative better plan.

Step 1

There is little point in constructing a flow chart. The mill is obviously series, continuous product flow and production limited. Thus, all the units are equally critical and there are no production windows. The cost of unavailability is £1500/hr. The existing maintenance plan is given above.

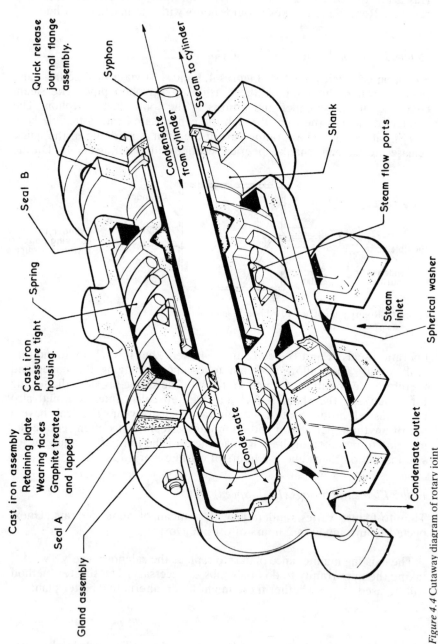

Cast iron assembly
Retaining plate
Wearing faces
Graphite treated
and lapped

Seal A

Seal B

Spring

Cast iron pressure tight housing.

Quick release journal flange assembly.

Syphon

Steam to cylinder

Condensate from cylinder

Shank

Steam flow ports

Steam inlet

Spherical washer

Condensate

Gland assembly

Condensate outlet

Figure 4.4 Cutaway diagram of rotary joint

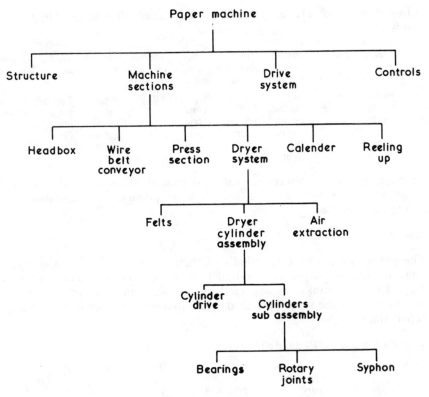

Figure 4.5 Functional analysis of a paper machine

Step 2

See Figure 4.5.

Step 3

A typical complex item is the rotary joint (Figure 4.4). The alternative maintenance procedures worth considering are as follows :

(a) operate to failure,
(b) fixed-time replacement of the seals at say 6 months periodicity,
(c) condition-based-maintenance—based on a simple visual external means of monitoring the wear of the seals.

— Alternative (c) is suggested from careful consideration of Figure 4.4, which reveals that the spring takes up wear by pushing the housing and condensate head away from the rotating part of the joint[1], the flexible hose on the steam inlet and condensate outlet allowing this movement. Therefore the wear on the seals can be monitored by measuring the movement of the housing relative to the rotating part of the joint.

In this case option (c) is by far the most economic. It is outlined in detail below :

Item	Timing	On-line or Off-line	Periodicity	Time and labour	Initial maint. action	On-line or Off-line	Periodicity	Time and labour	Secondary action
Rotary joint (22 off)	Visual condition checking	On	M on-line maint. routine for 22 joints	1 hr for routine 1 fitter	Replace joints (about 1 per month)	Off	About 1 per month on agreed shutdown	2 hrs per joint (1 fitter)	Recondition

Similar reasoning determines the best procedure for the other items (headbox, wire belt, etc.) listed. Where possible condition-based-maintenance is used.

Step 4.

The previous steps have revealed that there are no production windows, unavailability is the predominant cost and off-line maintenance is necessary. Table 4.1 ranks the expected off-line work in order of increasing periodicity; for the same periodicity the ranking is in order of decreasing repair time.

TABLE 4.1. Ranking of identified off-line work

No.	Item	Description of off-line work	Approx. average periodicity wear-out (W) or random (R)	Time	Comments
1	Wire belt (1)	Replace	M (W)	8 hr	on visual check
2	Rotary joints (22)	Replace	M (R)	2 hr per bearing	on visual check (approx. 1 per month) random failure
3	Bearings (120)	Replace	M (R)	2 hr per bearing	on SPM check (approx. 2 per month) random failure
4	Headbox seals (1)	Visual check	M (W)	mins	
5	Headbox lining (1)	Visual check	M (W)	mins	
6	Calender (1)	Replace	2 M (W)	8 hr	on visual check
7	Felts (2)	Replace	2 M (W)	3 hr	on visual check
8	Headbox seals (1)	Replace	6 M (W)	2 hr	on action 4
9	Headbox lining (1)	Repair	6 M (W)	2 hr	on action 5

TABLE 4.2. A maintenance plan for a paper machine

No.	Item	Timing	On-line or off-line	Periodicity	Time and labour	Initial maintenance action	On-line or off-line	Periodicity wear-out (W) or random (R)	Time and labour	Secondary action
1	Wire belt	Visual on output quality (Production check)	ON	D	Mins	Replace belt	OFF	M (W) as an agreed shutdown	8 hrs (1 fitter 2 riggers)	None
2	Rotary joints (22)	Visual condition checking	ON	W as part of an on-line maintenance routine	1 hr for routine (1 fitter)	Replace joints 1 per month	OFF	M (R) at wire belt stop	2 hrs each joint (1 fitter)	Re-condition
3	Bearings (120)	S.P.M. trend monitoring	ON	W as part of an on-line maintenance routine	4 hr for routine (1 fitter)	Replace bearings 2 bearings per month	OFF	6 M (W) at wire belt stop	2 hrs (1 fitter 1 rigger)	None
4	Headbox seals (1)	Visual inspection	OFF	M at wire belt stop	Mins (1 fitter)	Replace seals	OFF	6 M (W) at wire belt stop	2 hrs (1 fitter)	None
5	Headbox lining (1)	Visual inspection	OFF	M at wire belt stop	Mins (1 fitter)	Repair lining	OFF	6 M (W) at wire belt stop	2 hrs (1 welder)	None
6	Calender	Visual inspection	ON	W as part of an on-line maintenance routine	Mins	Replace	OFF	2 M (W) at wire belt stop†	8 hrs (1 fitter 2 riggers)	None
7	Felts	Visual inspection	ON	W as part of an on-line maintenance routine	Mins	Replace	OFF	2 M (W) at wire belt stop†	3 hrs (1 fitter 2 riggers)	None

†Guideline only—left as a dynamic decision

Among several alternatives carrying out all off-line work during replacement of the wire belt conveyor (see Table 4.2) appears the most attractive. Having the shortest periodicity (one month) and the highest expected off-line time (8 hours) this replacement provides an opportunity for maintenance at minimal downtime cost. Since, in this case, downtime is an order of magnitude more expensive than material or labour, the maintenance objective will thus be largely met. The plan amounts to condition checking to determine the replacement time of the wire belt and condition checking of everything else, either before or during the resultant shutdown, to determine the additional work to be undertaken. The plan relies on the inspection giving enough information to determine whether an item will last the maximum life of the wire belt, i.e. 5 weeks.

The plan will be an economic success if the extra income resulting from the higher availability will be greater than the extra resource costs incurred by performing the maintenance during the belt stoppages. Items 2 to 5 of Table 4.2 have mean lives very much greater than the mean life of the wire belt and incur relatively low material and labour cost. The value of any unused life is therefore small and the decision to carry out their maintenance during the belt stoppage is an easy one to make. However, as regards felts and calender the decision is not so straightforward; their material cost is high and their mean lives are only twice that of the wire belt.

Thus, because of statistical variability two replacements of the wire belt could have occurred within, say, six weeks leaving the calender with an estimated two weeks of life remaining. The calender should then only be replaced if its residual value (i.e. one quarter of its initial cost in this case) is considerably less than the cost of an unscheduled stop—in this case £12 000. This example typifies the dynamic nature of maintenance decision making and shows how the maintenance plan is used only as a *guide*.

Step 5

Since it is a daily *production* check that is used to indicate the condition of the wire belt, production must liaise closely with maintenance to ensure maximum notice of replacement. The on-line maintenance can be scheduled as a weekly routine. Off-line work, on the other hand, is based on the belt stoppages and the actions (and resources) are partly dependent upon the on-line checks. The resources for such work can therefore only be scheduled approximately into monthly, two-monthly, six-monthly packages. A job package will include the provision of information on methods, tools, spares and manpower required. Added to these packages will be deferred corrective work that will have accumulated during the production run.

Step 6

Since most items of the plant provide monitorable parameters of their condition, the incidence of unexpected failure, leading to serious disruption should be low.

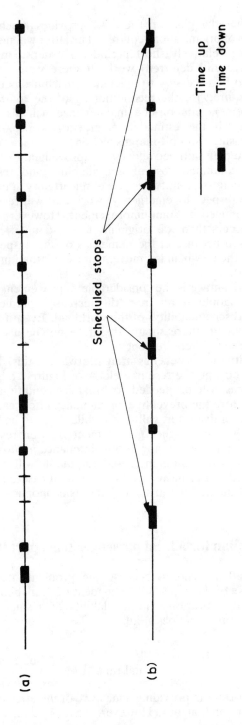

Figure 4.6 Paper machine operating pattern

Summary

It can be seen that the plan of Table 4.2 provides much information indicating the type of organisation required. The latter will need to provide large resources for relatively short periods in order to undertake the planned (preventive and deferred) work. If there were, say, 16 paper machines, it would be necessary to schedule 4 machines per week. Some facility will be required for the reconditioning of the rotary joints (and other complex items). The on-line maintenance will also have to be provided for, as will the estimated emergency work and additional corrective work arising from off-line inspection.

Is the alternative plan outlined above an improvement over the existing plan, i.e. is the combined cost of unavailability and resources less? Although it is difficult to quantify because of uncertainty in forecasting the level of corrective (especially emergency) work that will result, it is clear that there should indeed be some improvement. However, even if more corrective work occurs than was originally forecast, its effect on output should be minimised because of the numerous on-line inspections. What should result from the new plan is a movement from Situation (a) of Figure 4.6 to Situation (b).

An additional advantage is the considerable improvement in utilisation of resources that should result from the increased predictability (and therefore increased schedulability) of the workload. Even if the new plan increases the workload, there should therefore not be a corresponding increase in total resource requirement.

In practice the situation is never as straightforward as this. The plant will have deteriorated beyond the resource elbow of Figure 2.8 and considerable extra resources will be needed to bring its condition back to an acceptable level before the preventive maintenance effort can be applied. Even then, the preventive effort will, for a while, have to be larger than it will be in the long term. Higher management is often resistant to the suggestion of injecting more money into maintenance *in the hope* that, at some future time, it will result in increased output and will therefore need to be presented with a persuasive well-documented case based upon the proposed plan and quantifying in some detail its economic benefits.

A maintenance plan for a local passenger transport fleet

This example has been chosen because the problems it presents are different from those of the paper mill. The ideas of availability outlined in Section 2.4 need modification. The availability of a single bus can be defined, as before, on a *time* basis, i.e.

$$A_{unit} = \frac{T_{up}}{T_{up} + T_{down}} = \frac{\text{Time (a)} + \text{Time (b)}}{\text{Total time}} \quad \text{(see Figure 2.5)}$$

Such a ratio is important in providing a measure of the effectiveness of the maintenance effort for that bus. However, what is more important is a measure of availability for the whole fleet. Because of the way such a fleet is operated, this ratio must in some way relate to the number of buses required during the short peak-demand periods. The level of the peak demand remains fairly constant over relatively long operating periods and the satisfaction of this demand therefore imposes a firm constraint on policy. The size of fleet required so that satisfaction of peak demand can be guaranteed (i.e. allowing for unavailable buses) is one measure of the effectiveness of the maintenance effort for the fleet as a whole. This can be usefully expressed as:

$$\text{Peak demand ratio (PDR)} = \frac{\text{Buses required at peak}}{\text{Total buses in fleet}}$$

In the short term, availability can be monitored in terms of

$$\text{Fleet availability at peak demand} = \frac{\text{Buses in state (a) and (b) at peak}}{\text{Total buses in fleet}}$$

In other words, the availability is measured in terms of 'number of buses' rather than time.

In addition, some measure of the number of in-service failures is required. Such failures do not cause a large *short-term* revenue loss but engender a lack of confidence in the service provided and might result in a serious *long-term* loss of revenue. The best way to measure such failures is by a simple failure count as a function of shift, day, unit number, unit type. Unavailability costs do not occur in the same way with bus fleets as with continuous plant in as much as they have been 'bought off' in the capital cost of the fleet.

The transport authority of this example operates from twenty or so garages located in different parts of a large conurbation, each garage providing transport in its own area and also the necessary parking and maintenance facilities. The garages are divided into three groups and in each group the major maintenance work (overhauls) and reconditioning is carried out at a central works. The system for a single garage and works is outlined in Figure 4.7.

The buses employed are mostly of the double-decker, front-entrance, rear-engine type. The various models are enumerated in Table 4.3, which also shows the peak demand. The difference between these figures provides a small standby pool on which essential maintenance can be carried out.

The existing maintenance plan is based on an inspection and service at 3-weekly intervals (3000 miles). Shorter and longer term maintenance schedules are based on sub-multiples or multiples of this basic period. At the end of the year the bus is prepared for the annual MOT test. Overhauls are carried out at intervals of approximately 3 years. This plan had evolved over a period of time and was in need of review because it was felt that:

1. the Peak Demand Ratio was too low,
2. the incidence of in-service failures (and unscheduled corrective maintenance) was too high,

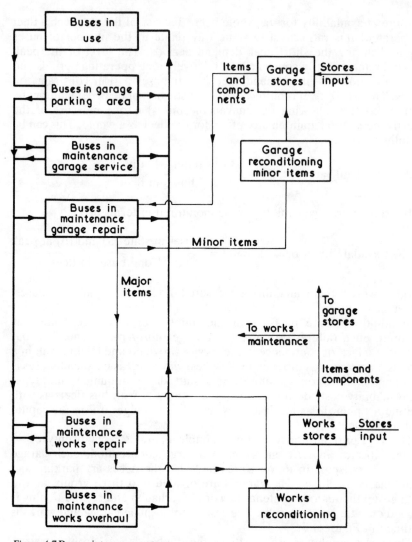

Figure 4.7 Bus maintenance system

TABLE 4.3. Fleet inventory and maximum demand

Bus type	Bus make	Number	Maximum demand
Single deck bus	A	6	4
Double deck buses	B1	1	
	B2	14	
	B3	16	
	B4	13	
	B5	40	
	C1	23	
	Ç2	86	
	D	10	
		203	177
	Total all buses	209	181

3. the existing inspection procedures were too subjective and often omitted altogether.

As in the earlier paper mill example, this maintenance plan will be reviewed in six basic steps.

Step 1

Examination of the pattern of fleet operation (see Figure 4.8) shows that production windows occur

(i)   daily between 9 a.m. and 4 p.m. when fleet demand is 50% of peak demand,
(ii) daily between 7 p.m. and 6 a.m. when fleet demand is 10% of peak demand,
(iii) weekly over Saturday and Sunday when fleet demand is 40% of peak demand.

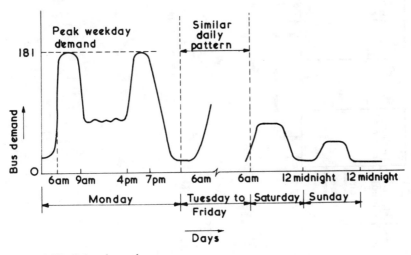

Figure 4.8 Daily bus demand

Because of the difficulties and expense of night and week-end work, the most useful windows are those of type (i).

Although, outside these windows, time for maintenance does occur because of the 16% excess of buses (or a PDR of 84%) over the peak demand, it is clearly advantageous to maximise the use of the windows listed, because this would reduce the need for so many excess buses and hence reduce the capital cost of the fleet.

Step 2

Using Functional Systems Documentation, FSD, (see Appendix 1), the fleet is analysed into its items, the fleet as a whole being regarded as the plant and a bus as a unit of plant. Figure 4.9 shows part of the analysis, the *items* of plant being those indicated by a black triangle in the bottom right hand corner. Typical identified items are listed in Table 4.4

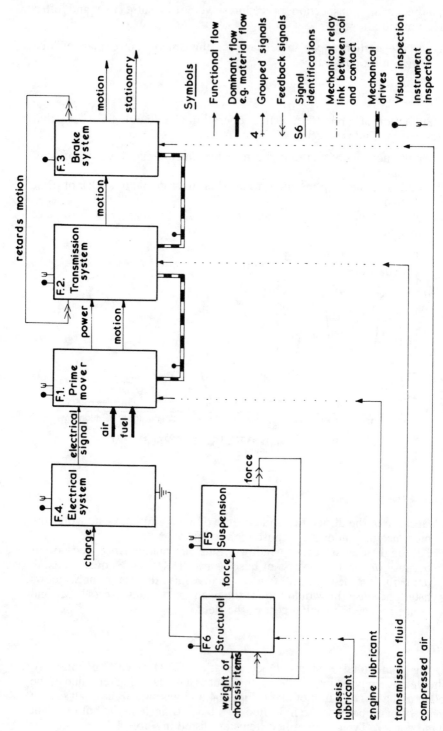

Figure 4.9(a) The complete bus system

69

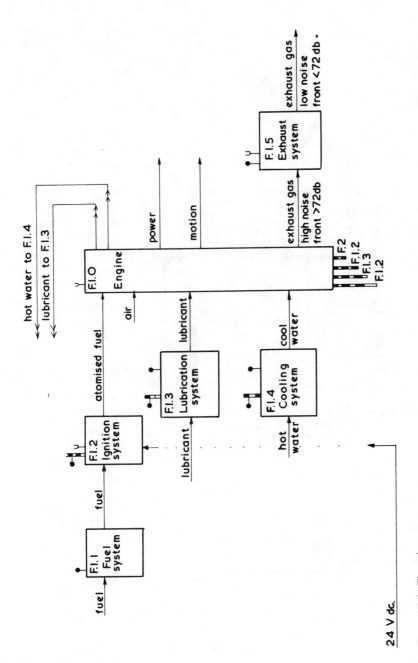

Figure 4.9(b) The prime mover

70

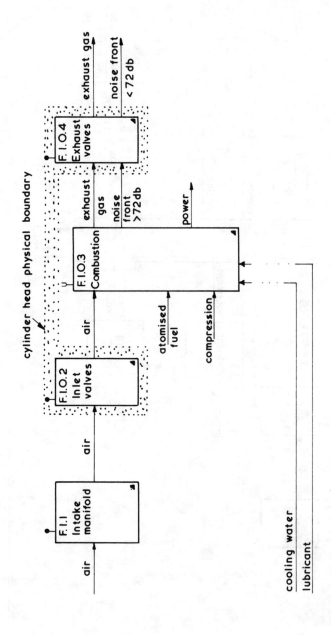

Figure 4.9(c) F.1.0 Engine

TABLE 4.4. Example of identified items (Type B5 double deck)

Function analysis			Items—replaceability at garage level	
1st Level	2nd Level	3rd Level	Complex replaceable items	Simple replaceable items
F.0. bus	F.1 Prime mover	F.1.0 Engine	Engine, Cylinder head	Intake manifold
		F.1.1 Fuel system	Fuel Pump	Fuel filter, Fuel tank
		F.1.2 Ignition system	Fuel injector pump	Air filter, Injector
		F.1.3 Lubrication system		Oil filter element, Filter assembly, Oil pump, Pressure relief valve, Engine oil, Oil pipes
		F.1.4 Cooling system		Water pump, Thermostat, Radiator, Fan, Belt, Bearing, Water, Additives, Hoses, Hose clip
		F.1.5 Exhaust system		Exhaust manifold, Flexible pipe, Down pipe, Trail pipe, Silencer, Bracket, Pipe clips
	F.2 Transmission system	F.2.1 Steering gear	Hydrosteer ram, Power steer pump	Steering wheel, Steering shaft, Steering box, Drag link, Relay lever, Track rod, Power steer reservoir, Filter element, Rubber seal, Steering fluid, Pipe, Hose
		F.2.2 Front axles		Inner hub bearing, Outer hub bearing, Oil seal, King pin, Axle arm bush, Thrust bottom, Shims
		F.2.3 Clutch fluid coupling	Clutch fluid coupling with lock-up	
		F.2.4 Lock-up mechanism		
		F.2.5 Gearbox	Gearbox	Gearbox oil, Oil filter assembly, Oil filter element, Oil seal, O-ring
		F.2.6 Angle drive	Angle drive	
		F.2.7 Propellor shaft	Propellor shaft	
		F.2.8 Rear axle differential	Rear axle differential	
		F.2.9 Perception head	Perception head	

TABLE 4.5. Example of effective maintenance procedures for identified items (Type B5 double deck)

Functional system	Item	Consequence of failure		Maintenance procedure	Frequency	Time	Initial maintenance action	Secondary maintenance action
		cost	safety					
1.1 Fuel system	Fuel filter	2	2	Replace fuel filter and clean filter bowl	12 W	mins	—	—
	Fuel sedimenter	2	2	Drain sedimenter	12 W	mins	—	—
	Fuel tank	1	2	Check for leaks, cracks, damage	12 W	mins	Replace on condition	—
	Fuel feed pump	1	2	Check for leaks	12 W	mins	Replace gasket or replace on condition	Recondition at works
1.2 Ignition system	Air filter	2	2	Check filter and engine performance monitoring	12 W	mins	Replace on condition	—
	Fuel injectors	1	2	Test drive performance monitoring for symptoms, cylinder knocking, engine misfiring, black smoky exhaust, increased fuel consumption, loss of power, overheating. Remove and test	24 W	mins	Replace on condition	Recondition at works

Key

(i) Cost: 1 = High cost. If item fails—cause immediate unavailability with high unavailability cost and secondary damage. Bus must be towed back to repair or replace failed item. 2 = Low cost. If item fails—does not cause immediate unavailability or secondary damage. Bus can be driven back to garage for repair or replacement, or inspectors on mobile van can repair or replace failed item at site or at the last station.

(ii) Safety: 1 = Critical. If item is not repaired or replaced immediately, it can result in accidents or injury to driver, passengers or other road users. 2 = Not critical. Failure of the item will not result in accidents or injury to driver, passengers or other road users.

Step 3

The maintenance characteristics of the items are used to rank the procedures, cost and safety factors, to identify the best of these (see Figure 3.10).

Simple, but objective, methods of condition checking are identified for consideration and, where possible, the period of inspection extended from three to six weeks. The critical question 'would the inspection give confidence in the operation of the items until next inspection?' is always asked.

Where necessary (and if data is available) Weibull analysis is used to determine the MTTF and the mode of failure (see gearbox example, Chapter 11).

Table 4.5 shows some of the identified procedures.

Step 4

A plan for the bus is built up by collecting together all the matching periodicities of Table 4.5 and, if necessary, classifying by trades (see Table 4.6(a)). The six-weekly service and inspection routine is the *basic* service. The other procedures are clustered into multiples of this basic period. Each year after the 48-week service, the bus is required to pass the Ministry of Transport's new Freedom From Defects (FFD) test. At the time of this study the detailed requirements of this have not been released. However, it is felt that the existing service procedure should cover all the necessary work. The major maintenance work (see Table 4.6(b)) is based on the existing 3-year overhaul and, since the 7-year certificate of fitness no longer applies, and the annual mileage of the buses has fallen, the economic life of the bus has been extended to 15 years.

Step 5

The previous step established a maintenance plan for each bus. The scheduling of the application of such plans to the whole fleet, with the objective of smoothing out the workload, has now to be considered.

Servicing and minor repairs—garage maintenance. The daily, weekly and fortnightly services are simple checks which involve little resultant corrective maintenance and therefore little time. Such work may be carried out by a separate service team in the 9 a.m. to 4 p.m. window, or at night.

The 6-weekly maintenance is scheduled by dividing the year into eight 6-weekly periods (5 working days per week). This leaves two weeks for holidays and two weeks for MOT preparation and, since the total number of buses involved is 209, this requires 7 buses to be serviced per day. The estimated time for each service is shown in Table 4.7(a), and the daily loading, which does not take into consideration the resulting corrective maintenance, in Table 4.7(b). In the majority of cases the service plus corrective maintenance time can be completed within the window. Where this is not the case the bus is not available for operating during the peak demand and counts against the PDR. In addition, this planned workload is supplemented by the unscheduled corrective maintenance resulting from

TABLE 4.6(a). The maintenance plan for a bus (Type B5 double deck)

Period	Maintenance procedures	Service and lubrication
Daily	Check and adjust tyre pressure Remove oil, grease and foreign bodies from tyres Secure engine bonnet and side panels Sweep upper and lower saloon floors	Check and top up engine oil Check and top up water coolant using radolarm Check and top up windscreen reservoir Drive bus through washing machine

Weekly	Steering gear performance monitoring: Test drive vehicle
	1. If steering is hard, check to ensure:
	  a. Steering sockets are not too tight;
	  b. Cam and roller not over-adjusted in mesh;
	  c. Steering sockets not short of lubricant;
	  d. King pins not short of lubricant;
	  e. Tyres at correct pressure.
	2. If vehicle wanders, check to ensure:
	  a. Steering socket is not loose;
	  b. Cam roller correctly adjusted in mesh;
	  c. Correct wheel castor;
	  d. Correct wheel alignment.
	3. If wheels shimmy or tramp, check to ensure:
	  a. Steering socket is not loose;
	  b. Cam roller correctly adjusted in mesh;
	  c. King pins are not worn;
	  d. Steering gear is not worn.
	Check road wheel's retaining nuts for tightness
	Check wheel studs for wear around tapered ends
	Check brakes performance—Tapley Test
		Check and top up power steering reservoir
		Check and top up gearbox oil
		Check and top up automatic chassis lubrication reservoir
		Check and top up alcohol evaporation unit

2 Weekly	Clean interior glass windows Clean seats	Check and top up battery Clean and tighten battery terminals
6 Weekly (Basic)	Check all engine mountings and tighten Check and torque cylinder head nuts Check operation of fuel injection pump Drain and refill cambox Check lubrication system for oil leaks Check and adjust radiator fan belt tension	Grease water pump bearing Grease fan shaft joint and splines, and fan centre bearing Grease power steering ram ends Grease propellor shaft splines and joints Lubricate footbrake pedal linkage Top up shock absorber oil level

Check exhaust manifolds for leaks and torque nuts to 25 lbf.ft.
Check front axle ball joints for free play
Check and tighten clutch fluid coupling drain plug
Check engine–clutch fluid coupling–gearbox alignment
Check gearbox-angle drive alignment
Check propeller shaft joints and splines for wear
Check propeller shaft needle roller bearing for wear—lift up propeller shaft and check amount of free play
Check propeller shaft circumferential movement
Check propeller shaft for noise and vibration
Check electro-pneumatic unit for leaks using shock pulse meter (SPM)
Drain away water from electro-pneumatic unit (drain plug)
Check brake and transmission system and items for air leaks using SPM
Check brake liners for wear and damage
Check brake liner-drum clearance using feeler gauge
Check and lubricate automatic slack adjusters
Check starter motor commutator and brushes
Operational test of all electrical items in alarm and warning system, lighting system, trafficator system, start and stop system, and auxiliary items
Check security and rubber buffer of suspension springs
Check shock absorber—fluid level, link rubbers, leaks
Check torsion bar stabiliser for security, damage and distortion
Check body panels for damage and loose riveting
Check chassis frame for damage and security of attachment
Check to ensure all autolube chassis lubrication bearing points are not clogged
Check alcohol evaporation unit strainer (winter only)

Check, clean or replace heater and demister filters

12 Weekly   BASIC plus
Engine magnetic plug debris analysis
Check inlet and exhaust valve clearances
Clean fuel filter bowls and change fuel filter
Drain fuel sedimenter

Change engine oil and oil filter
Steam clean engine

TABLE 4.6(a). Continued

Period	Maintenance procedures	Service and lubrication
	Check fuel tank and fuel pipes for damage and leaks Check air filter—change if loss of engine performance Check and tighten exhaust silencer and pipe brackets Check steering wheel for fracture, tightness and movement Check steering shaft end float play and universal joint Check steering box performance—operate from lock to lock with road wheels off ground and against road resistance Check steering box for oil leaks Check hydrosteer ram performance, alignment and wear on ball end and wear on relay lever, drag links and check for loose joints Performance monitoring on air compressor Clean condenser filter element	
18 Weekly	BASIC plus Check front axle hub bearing adjustment Check gearbox piston travel on all gears and adjust Check brake band automatic adjuster Reshim top speed adjustable push rod to adjust top speed piston travel	Change gearbox oil and filter element Wash debris in paraffin, dry and weigh to trend monitor
24 weekly	12 weekly PLUS Performance monitoring of fuel injectors and injection pump for obvious symptoms—cylinder knocking, engine misfiring, black smoky exhaust, power loss and overheating Check front axle king pin bushes for wear—jack to leave road wheels clear and rock in vertical plane Check gearbox piston seals—remove each gear chamber drain plug and select each gear in turn. If oil is blown out, change piston seal Check angle drive backlash between bevel gear and pinion	Steam clean complete vehicle

Continued in multiples of 6 weeks to 48 weeks and then repeated.
NOTE: When checking the performance of an item, also check its security of mounting and physical condition for cracks, fracture, damage, corrosion, leaks, etc.

TABLE 4.6(b). The maintenance plan for a bus type B5 (double deck). Major work

Frequency	Inspection and corrective maintenance	Timing	Inspection time (hrs)	Repair time (weeks)
3 year	Complete bus inspection and repairs at *works* Thoroughly inspect/replace/repair all items and/or components. On completion bus to undergo a 'Freedom from Defects' test.	(1) time based—(3 years) (2) condition based (3) mileage based (4) regulation based (FFD)	4–5 hours	10
6, 9 and 12 year 15 years economic life of buses	Same as 3 year Fixed by management on a criterion based on a combination of the following factors: economics, obsolescence, condition.	same	same	10

TABLE 4.7(a). Maintenance service type

Service period	6	12	18	24	30	36	42	48
Estimated time (hrs)	½	1½	1½	3	½	1½	½	4
Maintenance class	A	B	B	C	A	B	A	D

TABLE 4.7(b). Daily workload for red group

Maintenance period	Maintenance class (see 4.7(a))	Red group—35 buses				
		Day 1	Day 2	Day 3	Day 4	Day 5
6W	A	✓	✓	✓	✓	✓
12W	B	✓	✓	✓	✓	✓
18W	B	✓	✓	✓		✓
24W	C	✓	✓		✓	✓
30W	A		✓	✓	✓	✓
36W	B	✓		✓	✓	✓
42W	A	✓	✓	✓	✓	
48W	D	✓	✓	✓	✓	✓
Buses per day		7	7	7	7	7
Hrs per day		12.5	11.5	10	11.5	12.5

in-service failure, which can be minor work or work requiring several days of effort. Buses are transferred to the central works for overhauls, major repairs and the FFD test.

 Overhauls and major repairs—works maintenance. As shown in the maintenance plan, the timing of major work is governed by the FFD and the 3-year overhaul. Thus, using similar reasoning to the above, the buses could be scheduled for overhaul and FFD at the central works on a 3-yearly basis. Taking into consideration the time (10 weeks) for overhaul, about 15 buses would be in the works for overhaul at any one time. This once again counts against the PDR.

Step 6

Corrective maintenance guidelines are particularly important because of the extensive inspections which are carried out as part of the basic service and which are designed to identify and rank (according to priority) the necessary corrective maintenance. For this reason, and because of the repetitiveness of much of the corrective work, it is essential that the high-cost areas of garage corrective maintenance should be identified and planned for in terms of spares, methods, fault finding and decision guidelines.

 The FSD system used to functionally analyse the bus comes into its own in this step since it offers a logical fault finding method. Obviously, it is best used in areas where difficulty is experienced in locating faults (see Figure 4.10 and Table 4.8 for an example of FSD applied to the bus starting system).

 Analysis of the maintenance plan of Table 4.6 supplements the historical record of spares usage in providing information for planning future spares usage and reconditioning.

TP   Test points

⅃   Indicates some form of test equipment required

⏚   Indicates that the maintainer can use his own senses or merely operate a built-in facility

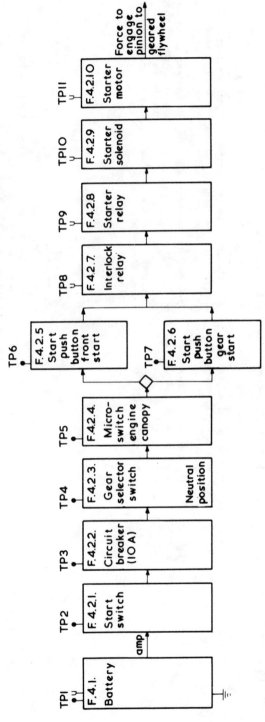

Figure 4.10 F4.2 Starting system (also incorporates F.4.10 Start protection system)

TABLE 4.8. Extract from test and signal data chart for F4.2—starting system for a bus (Type B5 double deck)

TP No.	TP location	TP description	Test equipment/test operation	Condition	Normal indication	Remarks
TP3	Battery	(1) Operational test	Start engine and switch on all headlights with the bus parked stationary	Failing battery	Sluggish starting and failing lights after short period of parking	Charge up battery and check cell conditions with high rate discharge tester
		(2) High rate discharge test	High rate discharge tester—a timed-on voltage applied on each cell	(a) Good cell	Constant readings for 10 sec.	Battery terminals must be clean to ensure smooth operation
				(b) Partially discharged cell	Constant readings for 10 sec. but low	Charge up battery
				(c) Failing cell	Low readings with rapid fall off after 5 secs.	
		(3) Test s.g. of acid	Hydrometer	Depends on condition of cell and temp. At 10°C—fully charged / half discharged / fully discharged. Correction is 0.007 for each 10°C variation, e.g. at 20°C, fully charged condition gives 1.247	1.254 / 1.184 / 1.104	— / — / Charge up battery
TP2	Start switch	Operational test	Turn on start switch —start engine —check output with test pin	Good / Good	Engine starts / Bulb lights	Replace faulty switch

Summary

The main changes proposed involve an extension of the basic service period from three weeks to six weeks and a reduction in the periodicity of a few procedures to one week. The reasoning behind this modification is that investigation of the existing inspection procedure reveals that it is not sufficiently comprehensive or thorough and, in most cases, too subjective. Management will not permit an increase in the number of inspectors—even for a short period. Thus, if a more effective inspecting procedure is to be established, it will have to be carried out by the existing inspectors. The proposed schedule satisfies this constraint.

Would the new plan reduce the combined costs of unavailability and resources used? The daily, weekly and 6-weekly scheduled preventive work would be carried out in the windows and would therefore not affect the PDR or involve an increase in the workload. Since the major preventive work would not change appreciably this also should not affect the PDR or resources used. The most important point is whether the new inspection and service procedures would lead to fewer in-service failures and less unscheduled corrective work. The expected level of such work that would result from the new plan is difficult to estimate. However, the more thorough consideration of the maintenance procedures for each item and the resulting increase in the items covered, coupled with more objective inspection procedures, should result in a reduction of such work. Even a small reduction would result in fewer buses being repaired at any one time, a higher PDR and a smaller workload.

It is suggested that the new plan be adopted for a small number of buses and the results compared with those from a control group of buses maintained by the existing plan. In this way the possible advantages could be evaluated prior to any decision regarding the implementation of the plan for the fleet as a whole. This approach would appear to be a better way of establishing the optimum level of preventive maintenance than a mathematical operational research analysis which is often insufficiently flexible to encompass the complexities of maintenance decision making, where not only periodicities but also the engineering nature of actions has to be considered.

It will be appreciated that the new plan might well need further modification before it could be considered as optimum.

A maintenance plan for a batch chemical plant

The plant manufactures a wide range of similar organic chemicals, some of which are soluble in water and some not. A process flow diagram is shown in Figure 4.11. The plant is made up of six reaction streams, three making soluble products and three insoluble products. Each reaction stream is devoted to its own range of chemicals and is not interchangeable. The finishing streams are also divided into those processing soluble products and those processing insoluble products. The finishing streams are only interchangeable within these groupings. A plant path is a complete path through the plant from the reaction process to packaging.

82

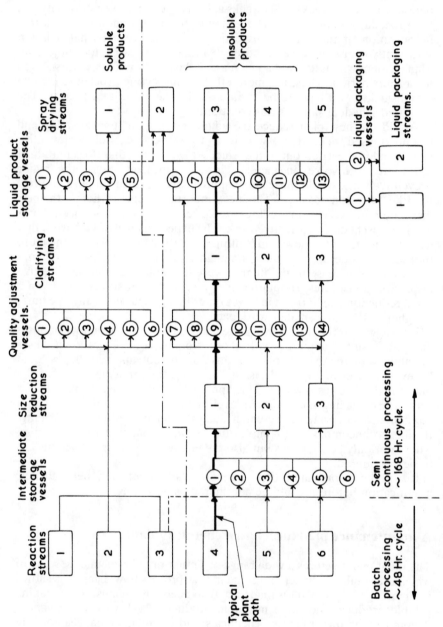

Figure 4.11 Process flow chart of a batch chemical plant

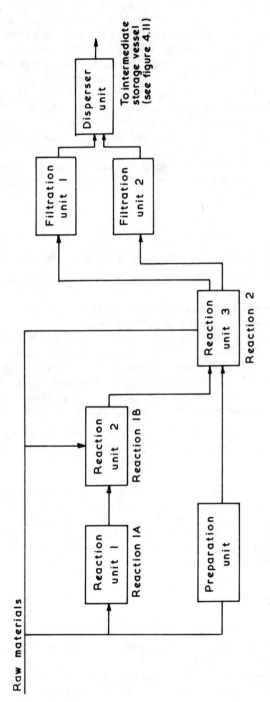

Figure 4.12 Process flow chart of a reaction stream

A typical reaction stream, outlining the inter-relationship of the units, is shown in Figure 4.12. The reaction process operates on a 48-hour batch cycle while the finishing process operates on a 168-hour semi-continuous cycle (see Figure 4.11). A number of reaction cycles are necessary before enough chemical is stored to allow a finishing process to begin.

In addition to the main product flows, the plant is supported by a full range of chemical and engineering services, i.e. primary chemical supply, intermediate chemical supply, salt, flake ice (not shown). The reaction streams are computer controlled and the rest of the plant is remotely controlled so the plant can be operated by a small production staff.

It will be instructive at this point to provide some brief information on some of the typical units making up the plant. The units selected are from the reaction stream since it is this part of the plant that causes the main maintenance problems (see Figure 4.12).

Reaction Unit 3 (see Figure 2.2)

10 000 gallon mild-steel rubber-lined vessel built in ring sections.

Agitation System DC variable-speed motor. Worm reduction gear box. Mild-steel rubber-lined paddle agitator.
Weigh vessel system Mild-steel rubber-lined vessel (300 gal)—not shown. Weighing mechanism. Weigh scale instrumentation.
Pumping System 1 (re-circulation and filter press feed). DC variable speed motor. Mono pump. Pump protection instrumentation. Mild-steel rubber-lined pipework. GRP/PVC lined pipework. Valves and fittings.
Pumping System 2 (filter press feed) As for Pumping System 1
Instrumentation and Controls DP cell (level). Thermocouple in tantalum-clad pocket. Steam injection posts (temperature). pH probe (chemical)

The main work is associated with the pumps, pipework and reactor rubber lining. Considerable information is available on pumps, motors, gear-boxes, etc., but only limited information on the failure and deterioration characteristics of the rubber lining. It appears from the information at hand that the rubber lining has a life which can vary from 6 to 10 years and the only method of monitoring the deterioration is by a combination of visual examination and touch. The time to commencement of deterioration and the deterioration rate are also uncertain but it is known that the rate of deterioration is slow and the lead time exceeds one year.
A lining inspection/repair takes 4 days and a replacement 8 days.

Reaction Units 1 and 2

1500 gals mild-steel, glass-lined with welded jacket.

Agitation System AC motor. Worm reduction gearbox. Agitator Gland. Agitator (stainless steel anchor).
Weigh Vessel System As for Reaction Unit 3.
Pumping Systems (Cooland re-circulation) AC Motor. Centrifugal pump, pipework, valves and fittings.
Instrumentation and Controls Temperature dip pipes, steam injector posts

These vessels are considered as pressurised vessels due to the steam injection and are subject to a two-year pressure vessel inspection. Other maintenance is associated with pumps, valves, motors, pipework and the glass lining. The glass lining fails randomly and the approach of failure is not monitorable. The lining is repairable with tantulum plugs, requiring 2½ days off-line. After numerous repairs over many years the vessels are replaced, requiring 8 days off-line. The rate of lining failure is low.

The existing policy is to perform essential lubrication on an on-line basis and to shut down the plant (one plant path at a time) for about 7 days each year. In addition, there is a considerable level of unavailability due to unexpected corrective work. The 7-day shutdown is used for internal inspection of the vessels, replacement of certain valves on a rotational basis and overhaul of the pumps as necessary. The shutdown is also used for rehabilitation work, and for the implementation of modification work. It may be extended to allow for the replacement of vessels or vessel sections.

The six-step method of determining an alternative plan will again be used.

Step 1

The plant is operated on a full-time basis, i.e. 168 hours per week, 51 weeks per year. During the Christmas period the plant is not used by production but the chemicals are held in process to minimise the effect of the holiday loss. The production plan is complex because of the many products manufactured, but there is a balance throughout the plant which means there is little, or no, spare capacity on the finishing stream if all the reaction streams are in use. A simulation model of the plant has been built to study multi-product schedules and this can also be used for examining the scheduling of maintenance. Therefore there are no production windows for long-term maintenance scheduling. The existing one-week shutdown is an agreed maintenance shutdown (state (c) of Figure 2.5).

Closer investigation shows that over any monthly period all the units in a plant path become available for maintenance, at short notice, for periods of between 2–8 hours. These random 'production windows' occur because of the batch nature of the process and the various washing-out procedures that are required between different products. Such windows can be used for small off-line jobs if there is good communication between production and maintenance.

It will be instructive at this point to consider how the batch nature of the process influences the scheduling of the major off-line maintenance. Because of the short cycle time of the reaction process (48 hours) each reaction stream has to be considered as a whole when major maintenance work needs to be carried out. In other words, if one reaction unit is taken off-line for one day, then the whole reaction stream is taken off-line. This is not the case with the units in the finishing stream because the cycle times are much longer. Thus, if a reaction stream is taken off-line for, say, three days, this maintenance window moves down the finishing stream by unit—the 'knock-on' principle. The interchangeability between finishing streams makes the scheduling of maintenance in this window a straightforward exercise.

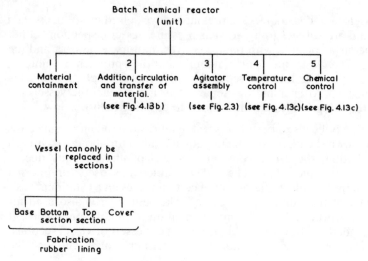

Figure 4.13(a) Classification of reactor items

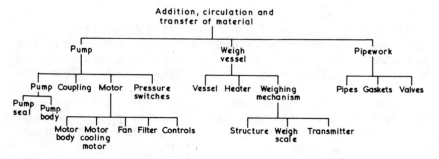

Figure 4.13(b) Classification of reactor items

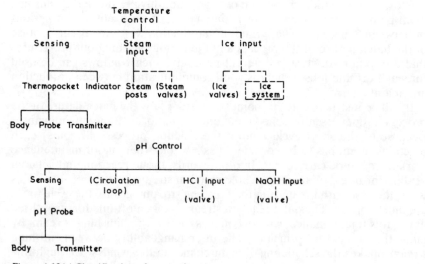

Figure 4.13(c) Classification of reactor items

Since there is little interchangeability between reaction streams, and no spare capacity in a normal sales market, failure of the plant means a downtime cost of approximately £50 per hr. The existing maintenance plan has already been outlined.

Step 2

An example of a detailed classification for a reactor is given in Figure 4.13.

Step 3

Analysis of effective procedures is well illustrated by an examination in this respect of the chemical reactors.

Example (a) Reaction Unit (3) (including Preparation Unit)

The main maintenance needed on these vessels is the repair (4 days) or replacement (8 days) of the rubber lining. This is subject to permeation by chemicals which can eventually deteriorate to failure. Since the deterioration can be accelerated by accidental damage it has been found that the life of the rubber can vary from about 6 to 10 years. The deterioration rate of the rubber is slow and can give about a year's notice of failure. It is important not to allow the rubber to deteriorate too far for the following reasons. If the steel vessel is penetrated there is considerable risk to safety as well as a long and expensive repair. Early detection of rubber deterioration involves only a repair lasting 4 days rather than a replacement lasting 8 days. Extensive deterioration can contaminate the product causing a diminution in customer confidence in product quality.
The range of procedures to be considered is as follows:

(a) Operate to failure.
(b) Fixed-time internal inspection (a combination of visual inspection and touch to detect rubber degradation).
(c) Fixed-time external visual inspection (through the manhole via fibre optics or television).
(d) Electro-chemical monitoring.
(e) Product sampling for contamination (at levels below the unacceptable-product level).

From what has been said above option (a) is clearly not acceptable. Option (d) relies on penetration of the rubber to allow a current to flow and again this is not acceptable other than as a safety device to give warning of such penetration. Option (e) has been investigated but rejected because of the high rate of deterioration once contamination has begun. This again could be used as a device to shut down a reaction unit but each batch would require to be sampled. The choice is between external and internal inspection. There are clear advantages in external inspection because of the time taken to isolate and wash the reactor before internal inspection can take place. However, external inspection is limited to visual inspection via optical aids since it is impossible to see or touch enough of the lining area from the manhole. Fibre optics have been tried out but are of limited use due to their small field of vision. Television proved better but was not considered sufficiently effective without the back-up of 'touch'. External inspection is still being investigated but in the meantime fixed-time-internal inspection and repair or replace on-condition remains the selected procedure. Using the limited data available the best period of inspection appears to be 12-monthly, but this can be reviewed as more data is collected.

Item	Timing	On-line or Off-line	Perio-dicity	Time and Labour	Maint. action	On-line or Off-line	Expected Period-icity	Time and Labour	Further maint. action
Reaction Vessel–rubber lining	Fixed time visual inspect. and touch	OFF	12 M at agreed shut-down	3 days 2 fitters	Repair as necessary	OFF continu-ation of inspection shutdown	2 Y	1 day 2 men	Replace in situ 8 days 4 fitters 2 men

Example (b) Reaction Units 1 and 2

These present a different problem because they are glass-lined and the lining fails randomly following rapid deterioration—in other words, there is no inspection technique to detect the approach of failure. Electro-chemical techniques can be used to detect failure of the lining and prevent steel penetration. The best procedure would appear to be operate-to-glass-lining failure and repair as necessary.

Item	Timing	On-line or Off-line	Perio-dicity	Time and Labour	Initial maint. Action	On-line or Off-line	Expected Period-icity	Time and Labour	Further maint. action
Reaction Vessel–glass lining	Operate to failure indicated by electro-monitoring	ON Monitor-ing of glass lining to failure	Contin-uous	Operator monitor-ing	Repair lining as necessary	OFF on failure	2 Y	2 fitters 2 days	Replace vessel on condition Contract labour

This is an example of the need to give careful thought to a corrective maintenance policy to ensure that the repair is done as quickly as possible and that other opportunity maintenance is carried out as necessary during the shutdown.

Similar reasoning is used to establish the best procedures for the other items in a plant path.

Steps 4 and 5

Due to the complex structure of the plant and the batch nature of the process, the approach previously outlined required modification. In this case it is useful to list the identified maintenance procedures for the whole plant against the stream and unit to which they belong. (This is similar to Idhammer's Main List of Figure 8.15.) Table 4.9 shows part of such a list, the maintenance procedures for a Reaction Unit. From the full listing the work can be further sub-divided and extracted as necessary for scheduling into on-line maintenance, window-maintenance (off-line work of less than

8 hours duration) and shutdown work (off-line work of more than 8 hours duration).

On-line maintenance is classified by area, trade and frequency and is scheduled over the year. The production department is not involved in this scheduling. Such work is often planned through the use of simple check lists (for an example see Idhammer's Check List 8.14).

Window maintenance is clustered at unit level and scheduled into weekly loads (with considerable tolerance) over a complete year. A bar chart of the type shown in Figure 7.4 is often used. The short-term scheduling and work planning requires close liaison between production and maintenance at first line supervision level. Such work is often planned via the use of multi-trade job packages which include the job methods, tools, requirement and drawings.

Shutdown work involves the major off-line maintenance work which is scheduled for a complete plant path by utilising the knock-on section-by-section shutdowns. In order to operate such a schedule a maintenance plan for each major section, or unit of plant must be established. A maintenance plan for a reaction stream (established in a similar way to the plan for the Paper Machine) is shown in Table 4.10. It can be seen that the plan is based on the annual inspection and repair of the rubber lining of Reaction Unit 3. The remaining work is fitted into this maintenance window on an opportunity basis.

The periodicity of shutdown for a complete plant path is based on the plant section or unit with the shortest maintenance period—in this case the annual shutdown of the reaction stream. The shutdown work for a plant path is therefore scheduled annually and starts with, say, a 4-day shutdown on a reaction stream. The maintenance work on the remaining plant sections and units is carried out as the window is knocked-on down the path. The plant is made up of six plant paths and in order to spread the maintenance load evenly over the year (to minimise the use of contract labour) there should be a major shutdown of a plant path every two months; the flexibility of the finishing stream aids this scheduling.

Step 6

From the point of view of corrective maintenance it is important to identify those units that are either operated to failure or those that, in spite of preventive actions, might still fail unexpectedly and cause serious disruption. Repair and replacement techniques for such units (e.g. the glass-lined reactor) must be studied for effectiveness, job method and organisation.

Summary

The general observations made about the plan for a paper machine, in particular those made about the economics of the plan, apply also in this case. This example also illustrates the approach to determining a maintenance plan for a large complex plant where there are random production

TABLE 4.9. Extract from maintenance procedure listing for batch chemical plant (Reaction unit 1)

Item	Timing	On-line or off-line	Periodicity	Time and labour	Initial maintenance action	On-line or off-line	Expected periodicity	Time and labour	Further maintenance action
Reaction vessel glass lining	Operate to failure-indicated by electro-monitoring	ON	continuous	Operator monitoring	Repair lining as necessary	OFF	2Y (R)	1 day 2 Fitters	Replace vessel on condition—contract labour
Steel casing (pressure vessel)	Statutory inspection	OFF	2Y	2 days 2 Fitters 1 Inspector	Repair jacket and joints as necessary	OFF	4Y (WO)	2 days 2 Fitters	Replace vessel on condition
Agitation system									
A.C. motor bearings	SPM trend monitoring	ON	2M	mins. 1 Inspector	Replace motor on condition	OFF	4Y (R)	1 hr. 1 Fitter 1 Electrician	Recondition motor
grease	fixed-time lubrication	ON	2M	mins. 1 Greaser	—	—	—	—	—
Gearbox bearings	SPM trend monitoring	ON	2M	mins. 1 Inspector	Replace box on condition	OFF	4Y (R)	4 hrs. 2 Fitters 2 Riggers	Recondition gearbox
oil	fixed time lubrication	OFF	2M	mins. Greaser	—	—	—	—	—
gears	lubrication, oil trend monitoring	OFF	2M	mins. 1 Inspector	Replace box on condition	OFF	?	4 hrs. 2 Fitters 2 Riggers	Recondition gearbox
Gland	visual inspection	ON	1M	mins. 1 Inspector	Adjust gland	ON	6M	1 Fitter mins.	Repack gland on condition
Weigh vessel system									
weighing mechanism	Visual condition checking	OFF	6M	1 hr. 2 Inspectors	Calibrate mechanism	OFF	1Y	30 mins. 1 Inspector	Recondition mechanism on condition
powder feeder	Visual condition	OFF	6M	1 hr. 1 Inspector	Calibrate mechanism	OFF	1Y	30 mins. 1 Inspector	Recondition mechanism on condition

	Lubrication, oil trend monitoring	OFF	2M	mins. 1 Inspector	Replace drive unit	OFF	3Y	1 hr. 1 Fitter	Recondition drive unit
hydraulic drive									
Valves Type A (5 off)	Fixed time replacement	OFF	2Y	1 hr 1 Fitter					Recondition valves
Type B (10 off)	Fixed time replacement	OFF	5Y	1 hr 1 Fitter					Recondition valves

R—Random. WO—Wear-out

TABLE 4.10. Maintenance plan for the shutdown work on a reaction stream

Item	Timing	On-line or off-line	Periodicity	Time and labour	Initial maintenance action	On-line or off-line	Expected periodicity	Time and labour	Secondary maintenance action
Rubber lining (unit 3)	Fixed time visual inspection & touch	OFF	Y agreed* shutdown	3 days 2 Fitters	Repair lining as necessary	OFF	2Y	1 add. day (4 days total) 2 Fitters	Replace in situ on condition
Rubber lining (preparation unit)	Fixed time visual inspection & touch	OFF	Y at agreed shutdown of unit 3	3 days 2 Fitters	Repair lining as necessary	OFF	2Y	1 day 2 Fitters	Replace in situ on condition
Steel casing (unit 1)	Statutory inspection	OFF	2Y at agreed shutdown of unit 3	2 days 2 Fitters 1 Inspector	Repair jacket and joints as necessary	OFF	4Y	2 days 2 Fitters	Replace vessel on condition
Steel casing (unit 2)	Statutory inspection	OFF	2Y at agreed shutdown of unit 3	2 days 2 Fitters 1 Inspector	Repair jacket and joints as necessary	OFF	4Y	2 days 2 Fitters	Replace vessel on condition

*Schedule other maintenance work (window and deferred) into this shutdown as convenient

windows and batch production. The main thrust of the plan involves three inter-related schedules:

i)   an on-line maintenance schedule (based on plant area);
ii)   a production window schedule (based on units);
iii) a plant path shutdown schedule.

Where there is evidence of a high level of unexpected failure, the plan might be better based on operate-to-failure and opportunity maintenance. However, such a plan is difficult and expensive to operate and it is the author's opinion that such a predicament should not be allowed to develop—the cause of unexpected failure should be designed out. In this case only the glass-lined reactors present such a problem and the failure incidence is low. This can therefore be tolerated and advantages taken (where possible) of the resultant occasional outage.

The final point is more general and related to all three examples. In Chapter 3 (see Figure 3.1) the distinction was made between maintenance plan and replacement strategy. It was pointed out that replacement strategy was reserved for the replacement of major units or sometimes of the plant itself (e.g. a paper machine, a bus, a chemical reactor). Many factors other than maintenance costs and availability levels affect replacement strategy, e.g. obsolescence, product demand, tax structure. The life of the paper machine and the chemical reactor was long (up to 25 years) and relatively little historical information was available on maintenance resource costs and unavailability levels. Thus, it was impossible to have a static strategy of replacement every 'X' years. Such replacement decisions must take into consideration the *trend* in maintenance resource costs, unavailability levels and the various other factors mentioned above.

In the case of the bus considerable historical data *was* available. This is hardly surprising since there were some 2000 buses in operation, the basic design of which had not changed for many years. An economic replacement period could therefore be calculated[2]. Table 4.6(b) gave the replacement period for the buses considered as 15 years. In this case it was not that overhaul was uneconomic, it was more a response to the passengers' dislike of riding in old buses. The author feels that in future even these decisions will have to respond to economic dynamics.

References

1. Idhammar C. *Notes from the course on Maintenance Management for Developing Countries*. Ali Rati, Lidingo, Sweden.
2. Jardine A.K.S. *'Unit Replacement'*, Terotechnica 2 (1981), 51–58.

Chapter 5

Maintenance organisation

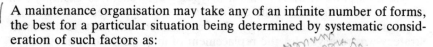

A maintenance organisation may take any of an infinite number of forms, the best for a particular situation being determined by systematic consideration of such factors as:

(i) maintenance work load and its pattern,
(ii) amount of emergency work,
(iii) cost of unavailability,
(iv) location of plant,
(v) production organisation,
(vi) maintenance resources.

In many cases the problem is one of achieving the *optimum balance between plant availability and maintenance resource utilisation*. For example, decentralised repair teams would probably experience a lower utilisation than centralised teams but would be able to respond more quickly to breakdowns and would therefore achieve a higher plant availability. Unavailability cost is the dominant factor in the design of a maintenance organisation. If this cost is high then the design should aim at producing a rapid response to production requests for maintenance; if it is not, the aim is the achievement of high resource utilisation in order to reduce the direct cost of maintenance.

A maintenance organisation can be considered as being made up of three necessary and inter-related components i.e. :

(i) *Resources* : men, spares and tools, of a particular size, composition, location and movement.
(ii) *Administration* : a hierarchy of authority and responsibility for deciding what, when and how work should be carried out.
(iii) *Work planning and control system* : a mechanism for planning and scheduling the work and feeding back the information which is needed if the maintenance effort is to be correctly directed towards its defined objective.

The totality of the maintenance/production system is a continuously evolving organism in which the maintenance organisation will need continuous modification in response to changing requirements. *Since the primary objective of the organisation is to match resources to workload it will be necessary to consider the characteristics of both of these before enlarging on the three basic components listed above.*

The workload

The primary division here is into corrective work, preventive work and modification work. The last, although strictly not maintenance, is included because the maintenance department is often involved in carrying it out.

Corrective work

For the plant as a whole, corrective jobs occur with almost random incidence and it is often found that the distribution of the times needed for such jobs approximates quite closely to the log-normal[1]. The consequent daily workload varies as shown in Figure 5.1. In the absence of condition monitoring, scheduling cannot be carried out until the work-demanding event has already occurred.

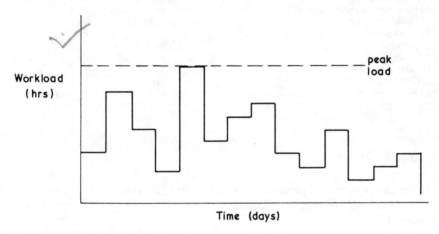

Figure 5.1 Fluctuation of corrective maintenance work load

Part of the corrective load, the emergency work, occurs with little or no warning and requires urgent attention. The remainder, the deferred work, is of varying degrees of urgency and can be scheduled accordingly, often being used to smooth the emergency work load. Emergency work and other high-priority low-warning work is difficult to plan for. At best, only the average incidence can be forecast, and individual jobs demand attention during the shift in which they occur. This work is sometimes called the unplanned work, a term which, in the author's opinion, is a misnomer since such work must be planned for in terms of men, spares and equipment. The difficulty centres on the *amount of time available* for scheduling and planning such work. If less than a shift is available then such planning and scheduling must be carried out at the location of the job since it is not feasible to direct it through a centralised planning office.

Corrective maintenance can be sub-divided, according to priority, as follows:

(i)   Emergency work—high priority, off-line (less than 24 hours notice).
(ii) Deferred work—lower-order priority, off-line.
(iii) Removed-item work—reconditioning (further divided into major and minor items).

The use of condition-based maintenance results in a shift in the workload from emergency to deferred work. In other words a smaller proportion will be unplanned.

The procedural steps of a corrective job are listed in Table 5.1. For each corrective job numerous decisions need to be taken that might involve both

TABLE 5.1. Procedural steps for corrective maintenance

Procedure	Department involved	Main functions involved
a) Locate malfunction	P, M	C
b) Record malfunction	P, M	Pg
c) Diagnose fault	M	C, T
d) Prescribe corrective action	M	C, T
e) Decide priority	P, M	Pg
f) Plan resources	M	F, C
g) Schedule work	M, P, S	Pg
h) Assign work	M	Pg
i) Carry out work	M	Pg
j) Check work	M	C, T
k) Record necessary information	M	Pg

Key
P—Production
M—Maintenance
S—Stores
C—Craft
Pg—Planning
T—Technical

the maintenance and production departments (see column 2 of Table 5.1) and might require inputs of technical, craft and planning information (see column 3).

Preventive work

This can be planned in detail and scheduled well in advance with time tolerances for slotting and work-smoothing purposes. Such work is best classified according to the ease with which it can be scheduled, i.e.

(i)   *Routine* Short periodicity work carried out mainly on-line.
(ii) *Minor off-line* Services and other minor work involving short and medium periodicity off-line work. Often carried out in production windows.
(iii) *Major off-line* Overhauls and other major off-line work involving long periodicity, multi-task, multi-craft work. Mostly requires a scheduled shutdown.

In general the first two categories can be scheduled evenly over the year, the major off-line work being planned and scheduled as a separate exercise.

The main difference between preventive and corrective work is that the level and type of preventive work is decided within the maintenance department rather than being generated from the plant. A number of departments are involved in the decision-making process and various information inputs are necessary.

Project and modification work
This, although not maintenance, often involves maintenance manpower and therefore must be included in the maintenance load. Such work can be planned and scheduled some considerable time ahead, the smaller jobs (modification work) being carried out exclusively by internal labour, while the larger jobs are carried out mainly by contract labour and demand a separate planning exercise (see Chapter 9). In either case the work tends to have a low priority and may be usable for work smoothing.

Total workload and the maintenance organisation
Since each type of maintenance work has different characteristics (see Table 5.2), the nature of the maintenance organisation will depend very much on the relative proportions of preventive, corrective and modification work (see Figure 5.2). An organisation for a workload containing 80% planned work (mainly preventive and modification) would be totally different from that for a workload containing 80% unplanned work (mainly emergency). The latter presents the most difficult and potentially costly organisational problem.

Considerable operating experience is required if the expected level of corrective work consequent upon a given input of preventive work is to be correctly assessed. The relationship between preventive and corrective work is always unclear. There is always a time lag before the unplanned

TABLE 5.2. Characteristics of the maintenance work load

Work type	Priority	Plannability	Comments
Corrective	HIGH	LOW	
—emergency			Off-line work incurring production loss.
—deferred work			Off-line work that can be scheduled for a production window or some other stop
—removed item work (reconditioning)			Either carried out in specialised workshop or used for work smoothing (where possible)
Preventive			
—routines			Mainly on-line work carried out as running maintenance
—minor off-line work			Carried out as far as possible in production windows
—major off-line work			Carried out in production windows and via arranged plant shutdowns
Modifications			
—minor work	LOW	HIGH	Either independent of existing plant or scheduled in production windows
—major work			Usually independent of existing plant Mostly carried out by contract labour

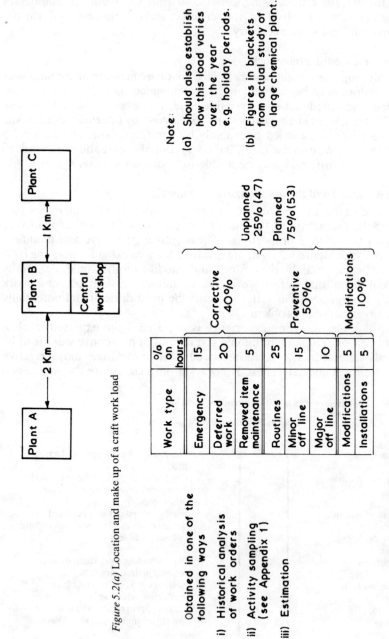

Figure 5.2(a) Location and make up of a craft work load

Obtained in one of the
following ways

i) Historical analysis
   of work orders

ii) Activity sampling
    (see Appendix 1)

iii) Estimation

Work type	% on hours		
Emergency	15	Corrective 40%	Unplanned 25% (47)
Deferred work	20		
Removed item maintenance	5		
Routines	25	Preventive 50%	Planned 75% (53)
Minor off line	15		
Major off line	10		
Modifications	5	Modifications 10%	
Installations	5		

Note:

(a) Should also establish
    how this load varies
    over the year
    e.g. holiday periods.

(b) Figures in brackets
    from actual study of
    a large chemical plant.

Figure 5.2(b) Typical weekly workload

corrective load is brought under control and this must be allowed for in the organisation of resources.

The variation of the workload with time (the workload pattern) is very much a function of the type of plant. If this consists of small independent units (i.e. the bus fleet) the workload is very much as above. If it consists of a few, large, continuously operating production lines then the work (excluding emergency work) occurs in large bouts at periodic intervals (see, for example, the paper machine). Obviously this has a considerable influence on the nature of the maintenance organisation.

Considerable attention should be given to establishing a clear priority coding system (see Table 5.2) and to establishing which work is to be used for work smoothing. Smoothing is particularly important where the workload contains a high level of emergency tasks or, as pointed out above, where the load comes in large packets at periodic intervals.

Resource characteristics

Manpower

This may be classified according to the technical area in which it is employed (mechanical, electrical, instrumentation, building), further divided according to craft (fitter, welder, electrician, etc.) and, if necessary, still further sub-divided into specialisations (boiler fitter, turbine fitter etc.). Maintenance jobs mostly tend to require more than one craft so the above classification is done on the basis of the *main* craft content of each job.

The quality of labour available will depend mainly on the environment within which the company operates. It will depend on the technical and craft training system, on the availability of retraining and specialist training, on the availability of contract labour and on the influence and attitudes of trade unions. These factors differ enormously from country to country.

Spare parts

The objective of spares organisation[2] is to achieve the optimal balance between the cost of holding (depreciation, interest charges, rental, etc.) and the cost of stockout (unavailability etc.). The main difficulty in this simple-stated task arises from the variety and complexity of the many thousands of different items (of widely varying cost and usage rates) required to sustain a typical operation. In a sense, each spare part presents an individual problem of control. To facilitate such control and also cataloguing, identification and storage, spares can, and usually are, classified according to function, (abrasives, bearings, etc). However, a most important classification is according to usage rate and other associated characteristics which assist the ability to forecast (see Figure 5.3). Thus the easiest problem is presented by Group 2 of Figure 5.3 and the most difficult problem by Group 3. In any given situation the proportion of Group 2 items, as opposed to Group 3, can be increased by designing-in greater interchangeability of items.

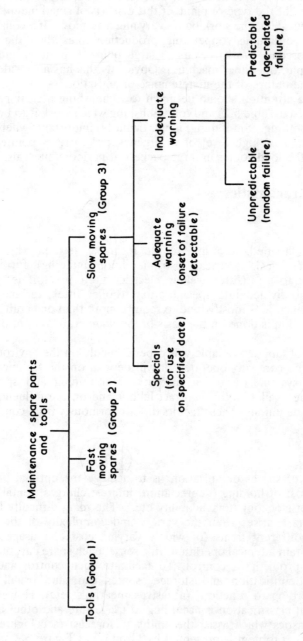

Figure 5.3 Classification of spares by usage rate

Tools

The objective of tools organisation is similar to that of spare parts organisation but the control problem is different because tools are not, in the same sense, consumable. The main problem with returnable tools is the development of a system to monitor their loan and to maintain them (and replace as necessary) when returned.

Resource structure

The aim here is to match the size, mix and location of the resources to the expected workload. It is, therefore, essential to have as full a picture as possible of the latter workload (see Figure 5.2).
Such a picture should include:

(i)   The location of the load (at a power station essentially centralised at an oil refinery well distributed).
(ii) Calculation, for each trade, of the expected preventive maintenance load, its nature and pattern over a given period. Such a calculation is aided by the maintenance plan.
(iii) Estimation, for each trade, of the expected corrective maintenance load, its nature and pattern over a given period and its categorisation. Where a work order system is in operation such an estimate can be made with some confidence. At a new plant considerable uncertainty exists until operating experience has been built up.

Tradeforce mix

(The number of the different trade groups making up the maintenance tradeforce).

In general, the greater the division of work the greater the skill of the individual trades. On the other hand, many maintenance jobs require inputs from several different skills and this renders the achievement of high labour utilisation particularly difficult. In theory, the aim should be to achieve a reasonable balance between individual skills and labour utilisation. In some countries, notably the UK, this may be severely constrained by trade union demarcation rules, flexibility being limited to the establishment of areas of special skill to match sophisticated plant, or to the establishment of functional groups (e.g. inspectors, although even an inspection force may have to include more than one trade).

Labour flexibility, particularly with regard to simpler work, can be improved in two principal ways. Firstly, through productivity agreements and other management-workforce bargains, thus reducing demarcation disputes, and secondly through formal training programmes, both internal and external, to broaden tradesmen's skills. An excellent example of such work is the scheme, negotiated over a period of three years, at the Redcar Works of the British Steel Corporation[3]. This was called the Group Working Practice (GWP) Scheme and included both skilled and non-skilled maintenance workers. The proposals were founded on the premise that tradesmen have a fairly wide range of natural skills. What was needed

TABLE 5.3. Redcar flexibility training programme

Fitters		Electricians		Boilermakers	
Days	Module	Days	Module	Days	Module
3	Flame cutting	3	Flame cutting	5	Use of m/c tools
5	Arc welding	5	Arc welding	10	Electrical appreciation
10	Electrical app.		Use of m/c tools		
5	Use of lifting gear	5	Use of lifting gear	5	Use of lifting gear
23	Total	18	Total	20	Total

was for these natural abilities to be developed, by formal training, so that tradesmen would have a working knowledge of each other's skills. The formal training course used was modular, and based on the programme shown in Table 5.3. The advantages to the Corporation in terms of utilisation and planning are illustrated in Figure 5.4. The example shows a job which required seven trades before the implementation of GWP and only two trades afterwards. The scheme was extended to cover first-line

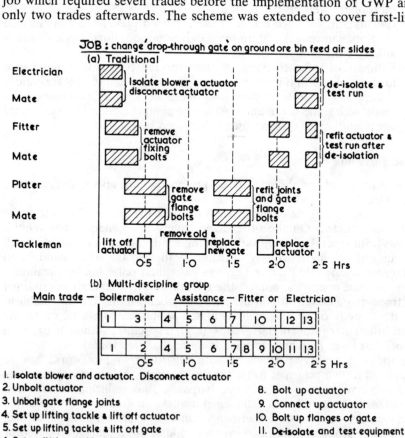

Figure 5.4 Comparison of traditional working practice (a) and multi-discipline group concept (b)

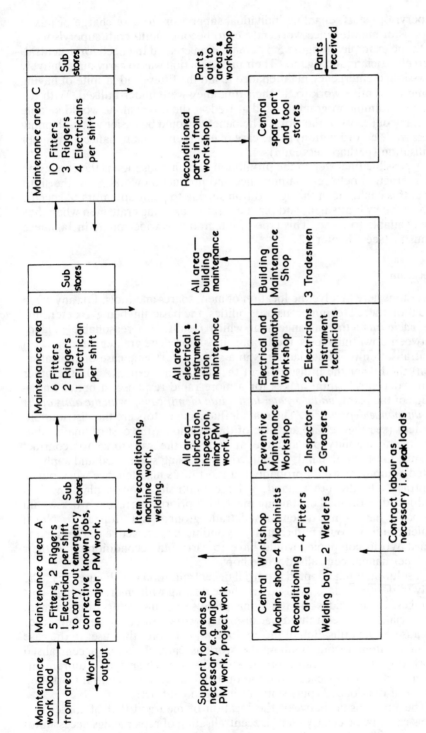

Figure 5.5 Resource structure for a decentralised production system

supervisory staff, enabling individual supervisors to take charge of mixed groups of maintenance workers, i.e. to become multi-craft supervisors.

In the example of Figure 5.5 demarcation created the need for decentralised electricians and riggers. Their main function was to carry out relatively low-skilled emergency maintenance to aid the fitters and in spite of having some preventive work to fill their time they were under-utilised. With the type of training programme used at Redcar the fitters alone would be able to carry out most of the work. The benefits would be easier work-planning (less trade co-ordination) in the case of emergency maintenance and higher utilisation (perhaps less men).

A possible final step in the promotion of high utilisation is the expansion of interaction between maintenance and production workers. In the short term this could mean the agreed transferring to plant operators of specific jobs done by craftsmen, and plant operators assisting craftsmen when they are available to do so. This type of integration is wide-spread in Japanese industry (see Chapter 12).

Location

Decisions here involve the location of men, spares and tools. For any given situation there are numerous possibilities, the basic aim being to determine *for each trade* that arrangement which results in a reasonable balance between downtime costs and labour utilisation. The greater the degree of centralisation (contract labour is in a sense an extreme case of centralisation) the higher the utilisation but the slower the response. On the other hand, decentralisation makes for a more rapid response, a better knowledge of the plant, *and a greater individual identification with the aims of the maintenance department.* The main influencing factors are the distribution, content (see Figure 5.2) and size of the workload, the cost of unavailability, the availability of, and the attitude of the workforce to, contract labour. On the one hand, a small company using specialised and sophisticated equipment would probably put most of its maintenance work out to contract. On the other hand, a large multi-site process plant, with a multi-trade workload containing much high priority corrective work would probably have some decentralised trade groups. A European or North American firm would find contract reconditioning attractive whereas many Third World companies would have to carry out reconditioning at their own permanent centralised workshops.

A solution often adopted is partial decentralisation (see Figure 5.5). The only trades to be decentralised are those dealing with emergency high-cost outages. Other trades and functional groups (e.g. inspectors or instrument technicians) are centralised because their work can easily be planned or because of the utilisation of the equipment and stores they use. In the case of major-item reconditioning, the work is carried out in a centralised workshop, mainly because of the specialised machine tool requirement. Such work cascades back from the outlying areas to the central workshop which, if overloaded, puts some of it out to contract.

The relationship between the location of men and that of spares and tools can now be clearly seen. Decentralisation of repair gangs necessitates corresponding decentralisation of spares and tools. However, this brings additional problems of control and increases holding costs (because of duplication). Clearly, there is a strong case for the central holding of slow-moving expensive spares and tools. Thus, in the example of Figure 5.5 the spares and tool system is based on a central administrating and controlling stores and a number of satellite stores located in each production area.

Tradeforce size

The requisite size of each craft group is a function of the workload and its variation with time, of the performance of the men and of the efficiency of maintenance planning. If the incidence of the workload is deterministic (as in the case of the preventive maintenance) it is not difficult to decide the best size. However, in the case of the repair team its main function is to respond rapidly to high-priority corrective maintenance the incidence of which is quite random (see Figure 5.1). If such was the sole work undertaken by the team, determination of the optimal team size (that which would minimise the total cost of labour and unavailability) would be difficult. A simple 'queueing theory' model of this problem is illustrated in Figure 5.6. If the team size is set at a level below peak demand then the

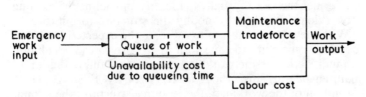

Figure 5.6 Queueing model for corrective maintenance work

cost of labour is small but of unavailability high. Conversely, if it is set at a level above peak demand then waiting cost is zero but the labour cost is much greater. Clearly, the main factor is the cost of unavailability; where this is high, low tradeforce utilisation may have to be accepted as a feature of the optimal solution (see Appendix 3 for a further description of queueing theory).

Other work, of lower priority, can be used to smooth the workload of the repair team (see Figure 5.7). In addition, utilisation can be improved by allowing the peak loads on the repair gang to be transferred to the workshop, and then, if necessary, to contract.

Even from this simple example it is clear that the problems of mix, of location and of size are closely inter-related. Determination of the most suitable resource structure involves a clear understanding of the workload and a logical analysis to decide:

(i)   the mix location and size of each trade group,
(ii) the mix, location and size of the total trade force (using the information from (i)
(iii) the location and logistics of movement of the spares and tools (to suit the structure established in (ii).

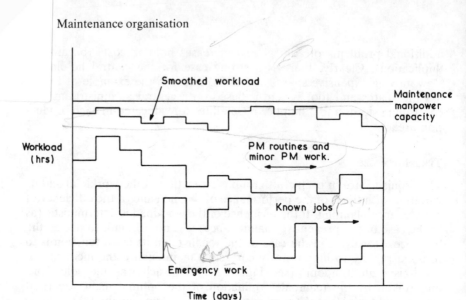

Figure 5.7 The use of low priority work to smooth high priority work

For an existing plant such an analysis will be different from that for a new plant. With the former the task is usually to identify and define the existing structure and workload and then to modify the structure to improve its effectiveness. With the latter the task is to estimate the expected workload and then to develop a structure to cope with it. In both cases the solution might require modification as the workload changes. (A full definition of an existing maintenance organisation A MAINTENANCE SNAPSHOT includes a description of the workload, the resource structure, the administrative structure and maintenance work planning and control.) Management control systems should monitor those parameters (e.g. emergency maintenance response time) which measure the need for changes in resource structure.

As indicated, operational research techniques, such as queueing theory and simulation, can be used to establish optimum structures. Such techniques are, however, of value in only a limited number of cases. More often than not a clear understanding of the maintenance problem and of the principles of economics and management will enable a sound resource structure to be developed and adjusted as required (see the example at the end of this Chapter).

The administrative structure

The second step in designing a maintenance organisation is the formulation of an administrative structure. Before examining this particular problem it will be instructive to look at administration in general.

Administrative structure and decision making

An administration can be considered as a decision making system[4], the aim of which is to direct the available resources towards the achievement of the organisational objective. The various tasks carried out by each individual in the hierarchy are comprised of two elements, *deciding* and *doing*. Thus there is horizontal division of the hierarchy into the various work functions (doing) i.e. mechanical, electrical, etc., and also vertical division into levels of authority (deciding) over the commission of such functions. The higher levels are more concerned with deciding than doing, while the lowest, shop-floor, level may have only minimal powers for decision. The top of the hierarchy will be concerned with the determination of the company objective and policy and will focus mainly on the non-recurrent issues of capital expenditure many of which are at best non-quantifiable and at worst outside the organisation's control. It is at this level that the administrative structure is designed and established, a task which necessitates:

(i) determining the task areas and responsibility (decision making bounds) of each member of the hierarchy,

(ii) establishing the relationships, both vertical and horizontal, between these areas,

(iii) ensuring that the company objective has been interpreted for, and understood by, each member of the hierarchy,

(iv) establishing effective communication and information systems.

Traditional view of administrative structure

Figure 5.8 shows the relationships between the functions and responsibility levels of the management team and its relationships with the shop floor. A link between levels, like that shown between manager and foreman, is the key *manager/subordinate relationship*. The essence of this is that the foreman has the *responsibility* for ensuring that his own and his teams's work achieve a desired result. In order to carry this reponsibility the foreman must have the *authority* to make or veto decisions within his responsibility area. The manager delegates work to the foreman and with it the authority for the foreman to use the necessary resources. The manager remains responsible for this work to higher management, ie. authority should be delegated as far down the line as possible but responsibility is not shed by doing this.

One man can only effectively manage a limited number of subordinates. It has been suggested that this number lies somewhere between four and eight depending on the complexity of decision making. Because of the constraints imposed by this *span of control* most organisations are made up of a number of management/subordinate levels. In the example of Figure 5.8, the *chain of command* passes down through six management levels, from Managing Director to shop floor. Since there are clear advantages in having a short chain of command, some compromise must be reached between the length of chain of command and the span of control.

The above discussion refers only to *line relationships* (the transmission of decision-making power down the hierarchy into the various work areas) but relationships are also necessary for the horizontal transmission of information and, in certain cases, of decision making power. The three main relationships here are:

(i) *Collateral*—those in which the work carried out in one area impinges on that of another independent area (i.e. between workshop foremen and area maintenance foremen of Figure 5.8).

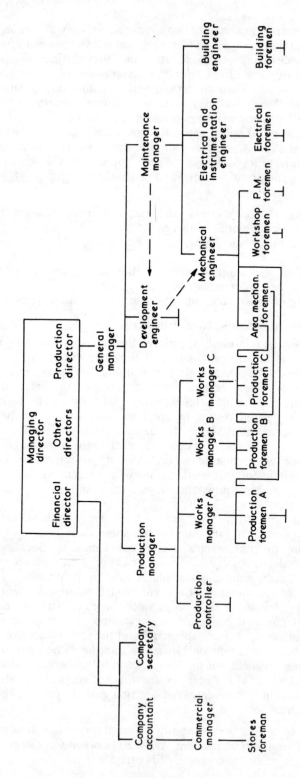

Figure 5.8 An example of a maintenance administrative structure to suit the resource structure of 5.5

(ii) *Staff*—those in which the occupant of a managerial role has authority in a defined area of another manager but does not have line authority (managerial authority) over this manager. In the example of Figure 5.8 the Maintenance Manager gives the Development Engineer the authority to make decisions and give instructions to the Mechanical Engineer in the limited area of design-out-maintenance. Managerial authority remains with the Maintenance Manager.

(iii) *Matrix*—these differ in structure rather than class of relationship. Classical theory dictates that each individual should be responsible to one person only, this principle, '*unity of command*', is the basis of the line relationship. However, a number of structures contravene this by dividing an individual's work so that he is responsible to different managers for different areas of it. This is shown in Figure 5.9 in the relationship between the Production Manager, Maintenance Manager and Works Manager. In order to avoid confusion and conflict the former two must communicate closely about their instructions to the latter.

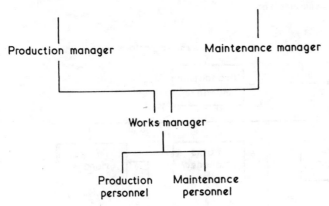

Figure 5.9 A matrix relationship

Even small organisations involve numerous complex relationships and it is therefore essential that there is a *job description* for the work of each individual in the hierarchy. This should set out in clear, unambiguous terms, giving his main functions, his limits of responsibility, and set bounds on his authority, bot financial and with regard to personnel. It should state to whom and for whom he is responsible; including staff and matrix relationships. In addition, because of the interdisciplinary nature of most work it is necessary to:

(i) establish *committees* and *working parties* for joint decision making.
(ii) establish *standing orders* for the handling of large repetitive jobs which cross functional boundaries.

To conclude this survey of the traditional approach to administrative theory it is necessary to say something about management control. The basic system by means of which a manager controls his team is shown in Figure 5.10 and that for a large organisation in Figure 5.11. The Production Manager is concerned with work and decisions which involve a much

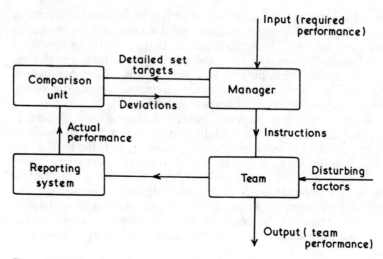

Figure 5.10 Basics of management control

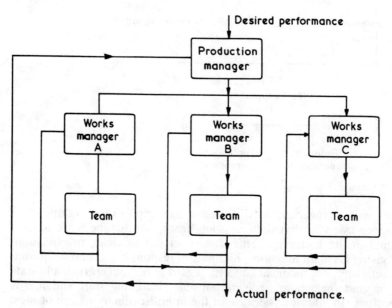

Figure 5.11 Management control system for large administrative structure

longer time-scale than his Works Manager. The former carries out his task
by communicating the necessary instructions, and the aim of the work, to
one or more of his subordinates. They in turn instruct their team on how to
complete the work. Information feedback to the Works Manager enables
him to control the completion of the work in the short term and
information feedback to the Production Manager enables him to control
his subordinates and hence the completion of the work in the long term.

The effect of groups

The traditional view of administrative structure considers managers and supervisors as individuals and structured hierarchical groups. However the natural instinct of people is to form into groups of their own choosing with common interests or characteristics (work or social). A natural group size consists of about six people and can form within or between departments. Such groups have their own objectives, leaders, and communication systems and can have considerable influence on the operation of the formal organisation. Thus within an existing organisation there is both a formal and an informal structure. It is important that the existence of the informal organisation be recognised and, as far as possible, manipulated in the interest of the organisational objectives. Where this is not possible and where the objectives of the informal group are not compatible with those of the organisation then an attempt should be made to modify the group in

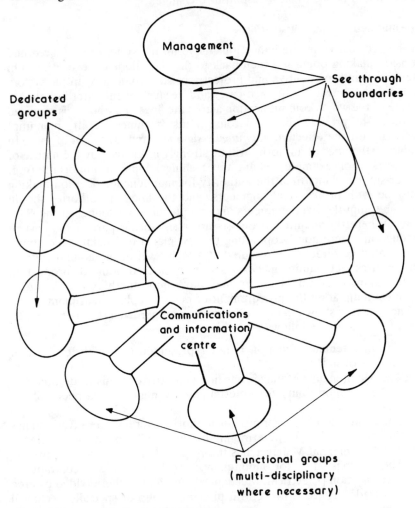

Figure 5.12 An organisation based on groups

order to minimise its influence. For example, at shop-floor level, maintenance trade-groups can become so strong as to threaten a supervisor's authority and influence his judgement in their favour; work planning can be used to separate the group and to keep them apart until a more permanent solution is found. The influence of groups on maintenance organisation and motivation is discussed in more detail in Chapter 12.

The concept of groups can be built into the structure. A model[5] of this is shown in Figure 5.12. The structure is designed around groups or sub-groups which each have a clearly defined function and objective and are allowed a degree of autonomy. The communication system allows each group to see and communicate with the other groups. Such a structure allows a large organisation to be broken up into smaller interactive and responsive parts. This arrangement is an attempt to overcome the tendency of the traditional structure to over-formalisation of the decision-making function and hence to slow response to change.

The maintenance administration

In this, corrective maintenance jobs move up the system to the accepted decision-making point and then back to the shop floor for execution. On the other hand, preventive and project jobs start some way up the system and move downwards. In each case, and because of the interdisciplinary nature of the work, communication across the lines of authority is required in order to provide the numerous inputs (technical, craft, planning) necessary for the effective *planning*, *assignment* and *execution* of jobs. In addition, the lines of authority will be strongly influenced by the nature of the work. For example, where the technical input is important (e.g. power-station plant) then the authority for maintenance decision-making must be with professional engineers, and the lines of authority should continue unbroken via engineers and maintenance personnel to the shop floor. Where the maintenance costs are a significant part of the cost of production (continuously-operating process-plant) the maintenance function should be directly represented at a high level of the administration. This ensures that maintenance is properly considered alongside production when making operating decisions and, more importantly (see Chapter 1), when contemplating the procurement of new or replacement plant.

The structure shown in Figure 5.8 might be regarded as traditionalist. Its main features are as follows :

(i) The maintenance function is not represented at a high level either directly or indirectly.

(ii) The Maintenance Manager has line authority over his tradeforce and has the responsibility for determining the maintenance needs of the plant.

(iii) The Production Manager has line authority over his operatives and has the responsibility for determining the production needs of the plant.

(iv) The Commercial Manager has the responsibility for spares control.

(v) The responsibility for maintenance work is divided according to specialisation (Electrical, Mechanical, etc) and further divided by area and trade. There is no central planning group or specialist technical group.

(vi) The responsibility for production work is divided by area with a separate function for production planning.

(vii) Because of the division of responsibility for the plant, numerous collateral relationships, committees and communications systems are used for maintenance decision making.

Difficulties have been encountered with this traditional structure and various industries have modified it, some, for example, to ensure that the maintenance function is represented at a high level (see Figure 5.13).

A major difficulty is the division of responsibility for the *plant operation* between production management and maintenance management. In spite of clearly defined job descriptions, stating that maintenance management is responsible (after consultation with production) for the maintenance of plant, what tends to happen in practice is that maintenance dictates what is done, and production dictates when. Therefore, unless there are excellent communications, and team spirit, considerable friction is generated and production gets its own way. This is particularly so in a large organisation. In order to avoid friction, and realising that team spirit is easier to engender in small groups, some companies have modified the structure as shown in Figure 5.13. The Maintenance Department is now used in an advisory and service capacity to production. In other words, production controls the plant and the maintenance resources in its area and asks for additional maintenance assistance or technical help when required. The Works Manager in each plant budgets for all the expenditure on his own plant and is responsible for operation *and* maintenance. Maintenance management then has a staff relationship with production management. The danger is the lack of technical expertise available in-line with the Works Manager. This, coupled with production pressure and a poor Works Manager, often results in the abuse of plant to achieve short-term production objectives. Large organisations overcome this problem by introducing a professional engineer and planning expertise in each area, the so-called Ship System. This is an example of the idea of groups discussed in the previous section.

In a matrix structure the technical authority (the setting of standards, procedures etc) for maintenance work could come via the maintenance line, and the managerial authority (the planning input) via production. This would alleviate some of the problems of the former structure but would introduce others because of the dual authority.

The additional difficulty of the traditional structure is that maintenance managers are often expected to carry out every one of the following functions :

(i) setting objectives, determining the maintenance plan, organisation and budget,

(ii) controlling the maintenance department,

(ii) supplying professional, technical and craft help as required,

(iv) assisting in long-term work planning,

(v) dealing with day-to-day industrial relations.

Clerical or back-up planning assistance is frequently inadequate. Consequently managers become so involved with short-term supervisory tasks

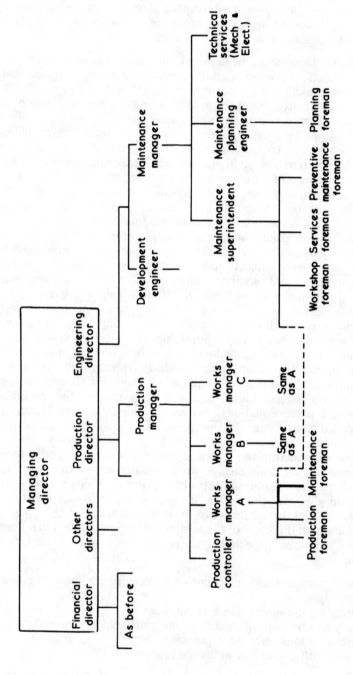

Figure 5.13 Modified administrative structure for resource structure of Figure 5.8

that they neglect their main functions. They are being controlled by the plant rather than controlling the plant. Some larger companies, appreciating this, have reorganised their structure along the lines of Figure 5.13.

Work, its planning, scheduling and control

The third and final step in the design of a maintenance organisation is the formulation of the work planning and maintenance control systems. The previous sections have dealt with the problem of ensuring that the appropriate resources are available, correctly located and properly administered. This can be called the *statics* of maintenance organisation. Now the *dynamics* of maintenance must be examined; this means the process of ensuring that the right resources with the right information arrive at the right place, at the right time, to do the right job in the right way.

The work planning system

The design of this must take account of the basic principles of work control, i.e.

(i) The right information about the work load and the resources must be available to the work-planner at the right time.
(ii) The work planner must have the authority (or access to it) to take the decisions (i.e. the allocation of priorities) which affect the work load and resources.

The major issue is the extent to which work planning should be centralised. The advantages of centralising this function are similar to those already put forward for centralising resources—there is better utilisation of manpower, planning aids and documentation and better co-ordination of those resources that are dispersed. The disadvantages are the difficulty of maintaining detailed knowledge of the latter and slowness of response. The planning system will therefore depend very much on the resource structure. Because of the dynamic nature of the workload, and the complexity of co-ordinating partly decentralised resources so as to match this load, it is inevitable that planning should also be partly decentralised. This leads to the third principle:

(iii) Where the resource structure is decentralised into various levels it is advisable to have corresponding levels of work planning.

The following additional principles should then be observed:

(iv) The areas of responsibility of, and lines of communication between, the planning levels must be clearly defined.
(v) The priority of work (see Table 5.2) determines the level at which its initial planning takes place; the higher the priority the lower the initial planning level (e.g. emergency corrective maintenance is dealt with, directly, at the lowest level).
(vi) The plannable (low priority) work can start at a high planning level and move down the planning levels to assignment at the lowest level. The scheduling time-scale decreases, and the detail of planning

116

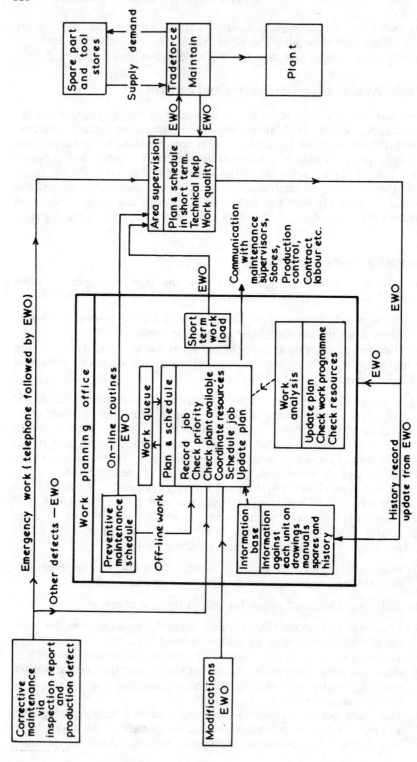

Figure 5.14 Maintenance work planning system

increases, with descending level. Low priority work is often used for smoothing the high priority work, at the assignment level (Figure 5.7).

Further insight may be gained by examining a model (see Figure 5.14) of a work planning system suitable for the resource and administrative structure of Figures 5.5 and 5.8. Two levels of planning are indicated (three if charge-hands are taken into consideration), A *Central Planning Office* and *Area Supervision* (for simplicity only one foreman and area have been shown). Also shown is the organisation of the work (divided into corrective, preventive and modification work). The corrective work occurs randomly and originates either from inspections or from production-indicated defects, the priority of such work being agreed between area maintenance and production supervision. The preventive work originates from a previously agreed maintenance plan and schedule, such work usually carrying a time tolerance. The modification and project work originates from production or upper management and requires inputs from a number of sources to determine its priority from the point of view of demand on maintenance resources.

The vehicle for the flow of work through the planning system is the *work order*. This is the key document for the planning and control of maintenance work. Depending on its design, such a document can perform a number of functions. The work order shown in Figure 5.15 acts as a work request, a planning document and a conveyor of work and failure data.

Responsibility for work is based on priority and therefore on plannability. Emergency corrective work, and deferred work needing to be completed within two days are the planning responsibility of the area foreman; all other work is the planning responsibility of the central office.

The main function of the work planning office is planning and scheduling of maintenance workload, in the medium and long term, for the area foremen. The planning horizon can therefore extend from as little as 48 hours to a year and will encompass all work other than high priority deferred jobs and emergency maintenance. The office is responsible for providing the maintenance foreman with the short-term workload to be carried out over the next production period of, say, one week and which, before the period begins, is to be allocated an agreed time before the period start date. Within this responsibility is included the initial co-ordination of multi-trade work, the provision of maintenance information such as drawings or manuals, the checking of availability of major spares and the checking of the availability of critical plant. The degree of detail involved depends on the nature of the work. A major scheduled overhaul, involving both internal and contract labour to be completed within a time limit, may need planning on a detailed time scale (shift by shift, say) and may demand the application of Critical Path Analysis (see Chapter 9).

Detailed planning and assignment of jobs are the main planning functions of first-line supervision and must be left to them to carry out at the location of the work. In the case of area supervision this is particularly important because emergency work is reported directly to them and its occurrence can alter priorities and, therefore, short-term scheduling.

In addition to planning, scheduling and assignment, there is also the need for work control, the number of levels of which will depend upon the

MAINTENANCE WORK ORDER NO.		Mt'ce Code	Plant	No.
Plant Description	Date			
Plant Location	Time			
Work Requested by	When Requested			
Defect/Work Required	JOB PRIORITY			
	Emergency	1		Tick 1 box
	M/c Running	2		
	Not Applicable	3		

Cause

Action Taken

Trade Code		Tradesman's Signature	Date	Time On	Time Off	Total Hrs.	Hours Mins.	Clock Number		

Maintenance Foreman's Signature	Date Completed	Week No.		
For Office Use		Total Repair Time	Hours	Mins
		Down Time		

Figure 5.15 Work order

number of levels of work planning. At supervision level the feedback of information regarding resources is continuous, as is the input of corrective work requirement. The supervisor is, therefore, continually updating his schedule and re-assigning his tradeforce. Where possible he uses low-priority work to smooth the high-priority corrective work. At planning office level the time scales are longer. Information received via the Work Order (see Figure 5.15) allows the long-term schedule for each area and work-type to be updated and priorities modified. Analysis of Work Orders can provide forecasts of the expected average level of non-plannable work for each area, trade group and period so that for each of these divisions

workload plannable by = workload capacity of − average
Central Office   available resources   non-plannable
                                                                workload

Efficient communication is of the essence if such a work planning system is to function effectively. The short-term workload is decided at weekly meetings in the planning office, involving maintenance, production and stores supervision. This workload can be dealt with effectively only if there is good communication between planning office and stores, transport services, production supervision, maintenance engineers (for technical input) and maintenance supervision (for detailed planning). Maintenance supervision itself communicates directly with these various functions, its most important contact being with area production supervision (for priorities) and maintenance engineers (for standards and safety).

An additional function of the work planning office is ensuring that its own information base (drawings, manuals, parts list etc.), and those of the design office and stores control, are updated in the light of modification work.

Maintenance control

So far, only the control of resources has been discussed. If there is also to be monitoring and control of maintenance effectiveness, systems such as those outlined in Chapter 2 (see Figure 2.10) for the control of (i) maintenance costs and (ii) plant condition must be implemented. Figure 5.16 shows the incorporation of these systems into the planning system of Figure 5.14. Before going into this in more detail, however, the related topic of budgeting should be examined.

Maintenance budgeting

The need for this arises from the overall budgeting need of corporate management. It involves estimation of the cost of the resources that will be needed to meet the expected maintenance load. It must therefore include a quantitative statement of the maintenance plan, itself a function of the level of production activity.

The type of maintenance budget required by corporate management will depend upon the administrative structure. If maintenance authority is centralised a company-wide budget will be required. This can be built up from the budget for each plant and workshop. The mechanical maintenance for each area can be estimated from the maintenance plan, translated into resources needed, costed and added to similar estimates from other trades and areas (see Figure 5.17). Budgeting of preventive and project work is usually relatively straightforward. Corrective work, however, presents a far more difficult problem. Nevertheless, if a record of the costed experience is available it is often possible to estimate, with reasonable accuracy, the level of corrective work to be expected for a given

120

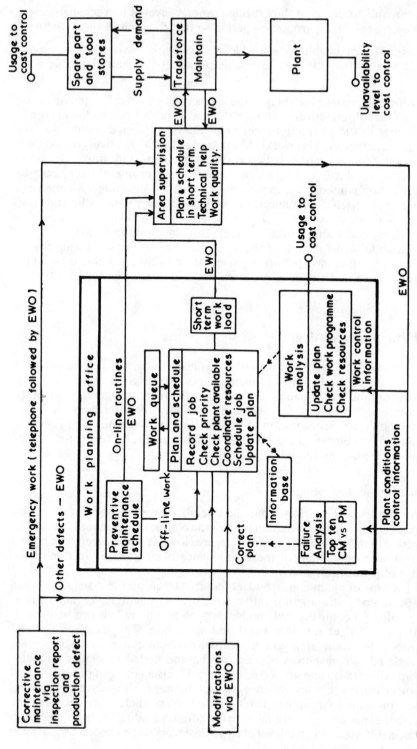

Figure 5.16 The maintenance system

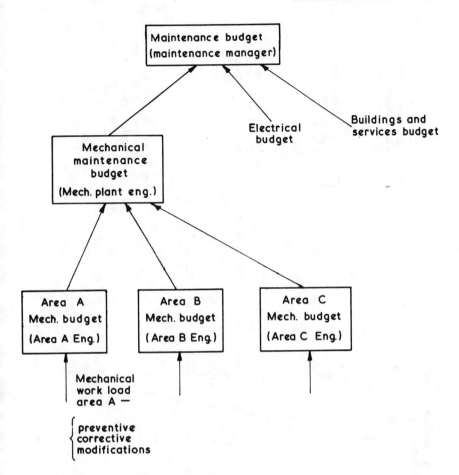

Figure 5.17 Build-up of a maintenance budget

level of preventive effort. Without such experience little confidence can be placed in the estimate and this must be made clear in the budget statement.

In practice, budgeting is rarely as rational as above. At best, the manager might add or subtract ten per cent from last year's budget after a glance at the production programme for the forthcoming year. At worst, the maintenance budget is prepared by someone in the accounts office without any consultation with the line managers concerned. This is no form of budgeting, it is an attempt to forecast what is likely to be spent in the absence of any management intention to deviate from what has gone before. The resulting figures are useless as a basis of control.

Many difficulties arise because of the incorrect assignment of responsibility areas. Thus, a maintenance manager may find it impossible to budget for those resources which are outside his control. He is often responsible, for example, for the *usage* of steam, electricity and water, rather than the efficiency and quality of the service. In a structure such as that outlined in Figure 5.8 he would be responsible for the maintenance of plant but not for the way in which it is used. Consequently, he would often be budgeting for

122

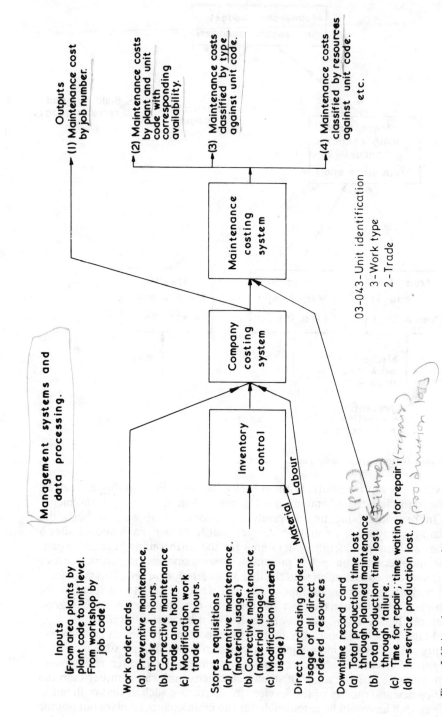

Inputs
(From area plants by
plant code to unit level.
From workshop by
job code)

Work order cards
(a) Preventive maintenance,
trade and hours.
(b) Corrective maintenance
trade and hours.
(c) Modification work
trade and hours.

Stores requisitions
(a) Preventive maintenance.
(material usage.)
(b) Corrective maintenance.
(material usage.)
(c) Modification (material
usage)

Direct purchasing orders
Usage of all direct
ordered resources

Downtime record card
(a) Total production time lost
through planned maintenance
(b) Total production time lost
through failure.
(c) Time for repair; time waiting for repair (repair)
(d) In-service production lost. (production logs)

(failure)

Material   Labour

Inventory
control

Company
costing
system

Maintenance
costing
system

Outputs
(1) Maintenance cost
by job number.

(2) Maintenance costs
by plant and unit
code with
corresponding
availability.

(3) Maintenance costs
classified by type
against unit code.

(4) Maintenance costs
classified by resources
against unit code.
etc.

Management systems and
data processing.

03-043-Unit identification
3-Work type
2-Trade

Figure 5.18 A maintenance costing system

resources in the hope that production will use the plant correctly. A structure along the lines of Figure 5.13 would avoid this difficulty. The production manager is responsible for the plant and budgets (with the necessary professional advice) for production and maintenance.

Cost control

A basic system is outlined in Figure 5.18 (see also the Case Study of Chapter 10). The hardware is classified into cost centres at plant level and further divided and classified at unit level. Maintenance work carried out on a particular unit is classified by type (preventive, corrective, or project) and the labour used classified by trade. An example of a typical cost code is given in Figure 5.18. The input information comes principally from work orders (or time cards), stores requisitions and downtime record cards.

The outputs from the system are maintenance resource costs and availability performance, provided at plant and at unit level. The costs can be divided according to work type and further divided according to resources used. Such information can be used —

(i)   for maintenance budgeting,
(ii) to monitor trends in the usage of resources and in unavailability,
(iii) to control the level of preventive work by monitoring its influence on the level of corrective work and on downtime.

Plant condition control

This requires the monitoring and recording of all failures so that those which cause recurrent or major plant breakdown can be identified and diagnosed.

The basic system for doing this is shown in Figure 5.19. Information which is usually collected at item level, because that is where the maintenance plan is established, is usually recorded on a Work Order and typically[7] includes

(i)   the time of occurrence of the failure
(ii) the nature of the failure (e.g. bearing seized, valve failed closed, etc)
(iii) the nature of the repair,
(iv) total downtime, manhours and spares.

The *first level of control* is at first line supervision where the more obvious recurring and major failures are identified by the number of work orders (or jobs) generated by a particular area.

The *second level of control* is at the planning office where, a centralised record enables recurrent-failure items to be identified on a company-wide basis. Spare inventory control can aid this by identifying abnormal spares usage.

A possible *third level of control* lies in the contact between the various users of all such plants and the plant manufacturer. This offers the opportunity for maintenance information to be collected from a much larger amount of equipment. However, since more than one user company will be involved it is, in practice, the least effective level of control. It is the

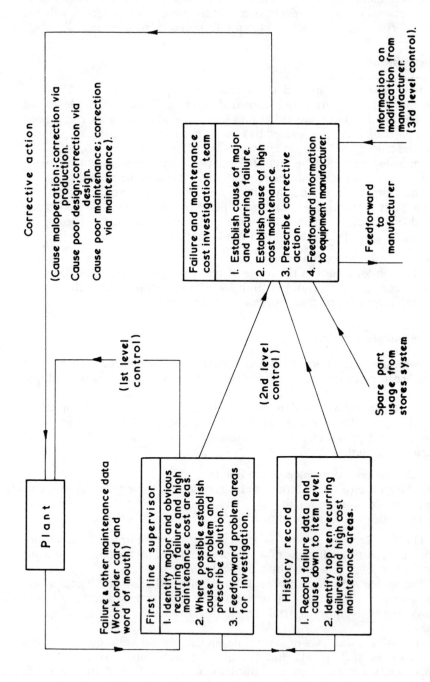

Figure 5.19 A basic plant condition control system

author's view that the onus for the success of such an activity rests with the plant manufacturer[8].

Since investigative effort is necessarily limited, only a small number of problem items can be looked into at any one time. The criteria for selection of those to be studied will depend upon the nature of the information input and can be based upon one or more of the following : frequency of failure, cost of resultant lost production, cost of resultant maintenance resources used.

Having identified the problem item, the next step is to diagnose the cause of the problem and then to take action either to eliminate it (e.g. design it out or change operating procedure) or to minimise its effect (e.g. by better maintenance procedures). Since the cause of failure may be complex and interdisciplinary, it is important that the investigation personnel be either inter-departmental or independent. Investigation could even be by one engineer with access to internal and external help.

The control system described would provide management with the information needed to best direct resources towards achievement of the maintenance objective. It will be recalled (see Figure 2.5) that maintenance management's main mechanism of control is the adjustment of resources to achieve optimum preventive maintenance (which, of course, includes design-out-maintenance). Without information on costs and failures, such optimisation would be impossible.

Illustrative example

Long-established paper manufacturers have decided to expand their paper making operation into a new area. Eight machines of the type shown in Figure 4.2 have been acquired. Availability of buildings requires their location to be as shown in Figure 5.20. The machines are operated for 24 hours, split into 3 shifts, each day.

Senior management have decided to adopt the maintenance plan of Table 4.2 for each of the machines. The additional maintenance work considered necessary is summarised in Table 5.4.

The necessary manpower resource structure is to be established from analysis of the workload and the plant layout.

Mechanical workload

Planned wire belt stops : this causes periodic work peaks.
Resource requirement per machine (from Table 4.2)
monthly work : 2 fitters, 3 riggers
two-monthly work : 4 fitters, 7 riggers
six-monthly work : 4 fitters, 7 riggers, 1 welder
Add to this the resource requirement for deferred work (see Table 5.4).

$$\frac{4 \text{ manhours/week} \times 4 \text{ weeks}}{8 \text{ hours each stop}} = 2 \text{ fitters}$$

So, maximum mechanical gang for a planned stoppage = 6 fitters, 7 riggers, 1 welder.

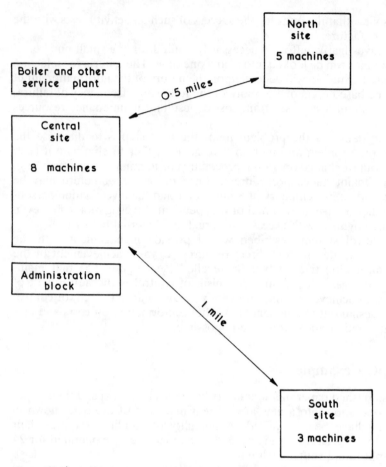

Figure 5.20 Plant layout for a paper manufacturing company

The machine stoppages (eight per month) can be scheduled to occur during the day shift and at not more than one per day. Where possible the stoppages are spread evenly over the month.

Emergency work : this gives rise to the need for shift cover.
In order to determine the cover required it is necessary to consider this as a queuing problem (see Appendix 3).
Furthermore, because of the travelling time between sites it would appear that a decentralised structure should be used.

Central site

One-gang policy

Failure rate $\lambda = \dfrac{1 \times 4}{168}$ failures/hour

Repair rate $\mu = \dfrac{1}{4}$ repairs/hour

TABLE 5.4. Additional maintenance work for each paper machine

Mechanical Maintenance Work—for each machine unless otherwise stated
  Corrective Maintenance
    Emergency work: times between breakdowns are exponentially distributed, with a mean value of 168 hours. Repair times are likewise distributed, with a mean value of 4 hours. Each job requires a fitter and a rigger. Machines are repaired on a first-come first-served basis.
    Deferred work: its incidence is random but it can be scheduled into the planned stops for wire-belt change. Each job requires a fitter. No jobs take longer than 8 hours. The average load is about 4 man-hours/week.
    Removed item maintenance: all work can be scheduled and amounts to 5 man-hours/week of fitting, 10 man-hours/week of rigging and 4 man-hours/week of welding.

  Preventive Maintenance
    Lubrication: 10 man-hours/week
    Inspection routines: 5 man-hours/week of fitting work
    Boiler plant: 10 man-hours/week of fitting work

Electrical and Instrumentation Work—for each machine unless otherwise stated
  Corrective Maintenance
    Emergency work: negligible
    Deferred work: its incidence is random but it can be scheduled into planned stops for wire-belt change. The average load is about 4 man-hours/week of electrical work and 8 man-hours/week of instrument work.
    Removed item maintenance: all can be scheduled and amounts to 4 man-hours/week of electrical work and 8 man-hours/week of instrument work.

Preventive Maintenance
    Electrical inspection: 3 man-hours/week of electrician work
    Instrument inspection: 5 man-hours/week of instrument technician work.
    Boiler plant: 6 man-hours/week of instrument technician work *in total*.

NOTE: The cost of unavailability is £1500/hr and the cost of labour £5/hr. The travelling time between sites is about 30 minutes. Assume 8 hour shifts at a maximum of 40 hours per week per man.

$$\text{Mean number of machines in queue} = \frac{\lambda^2}{\mu(\mu - \lambda)} \simeq 0.011$$

Production-loss cost $\simeq 0.011 \times £1500$ = £16/hr
Labour cost   = £10/hr
Cost of policy   = £26/hr

Two-gang policy
Queueing time effectively nil
Labour cost only = £20/hr
Consider employing two gangs.

Other sites

Failure per site is only half that at central site so employ one gang per site.
    It would appear that a good solution for the plant as a whole would be to use one gang at each site and to cover the exceptional situation of two failures at one site by transferring from another.

Removed-item and preventive work : this load is relatively light and schedulable with considerable time tolerance.
Fitting and rigging can be used for work smoothing the shift-gang load

Fitting $(5 + 5) \times 8 + 10 \simeq 90$ manhours/week
Rigging $10 \times 8 \simeq 80$ manhours/week
Other work needs separate trades; schedulability demands centralisation.

Lubrication $\dfrac{10 \text{ hours/machine} \times 8 \text{ machines}}{40 \text{ hours per man week}} = 2$ greasers

Welding $\dfrac{4 \times 8}{40} = 1$ welder

Electrical and instrumentation workload

Planned wire belt stops :

Electrical work $\dfrac{4 \text{ manhours/week} \times 4 \text{ weeks}}{8 \text{ hours each stop}} = 2$ electricians

Instrument work $\dfrac{8 \times 4}{8} = 4$ technicians

So, maximum electrical gang = 2 electricians, 4 technicians for planned stoppage

Removed-item and preventive work : same comments as for mechanical work but in this case the situation is less complex because no shift requirement. The 4 technicians and 2 electricians can be centralised on day shift and this work used to smooth their workload.

Electrical work $(4 + 3) \times 8 = 56$ hour/week
  Since the two Electricians have 64 hours available this can be fitted in.
Technician work $(8 + 5) \times 8 + 8 = 109$ hours/week
  This can also be fitted into the 4 technicians' workload.

Human resource structure

1st attempt

	Central Site	North Site	South Site
Days	6 Fitters	—	—
	7 Riggers		
	1 Welder		
	2 Greasers		
	4 Technicians		
	2 Electricians		
	(To carry out planned stopwork, reconditioning, and preventive routines)		
Shifts	4 Fitters	4 Fitters	4 Fitters
	4 Riggers	4 Riggers	4 Riggers
	(1 Fitter 1 Rigger each shift to cover emergency maintenance over 168 hour week)		

This structure is unsatisfactory because of the low utilisation of the mechanical work force—in particular of the shift cover. However, the response time for emergency work should be very short. The electrical resource structure appears satisfactory.

2nd attempt

	Central Site	North Site	South Site
Days	1 Welder		
	2 Greasers		
	4 Technicians		
	2 Electricians		
	1 Fitter (preparation for planned stops and reconditioning)		
	1 Rigger ,,	,, ,,	,,
Shifts	4 Fitters	4 Fitters	4 Fitters
	4 Riggers	4 Riggers	4 Riggers

(Shift cover to carry out emergency repairs, reconditioning and preventive routines and in addition, to cover jointly the planned machine-shutdowns.)

It can be seen that the mechanical manpower utilisation is improved considerably. The success of this structure depends on some overtime working and good work planning. The plan could be adopted at the start of the operation and be modified as experience is gained.

The practice is not usually as simple as in this illustration because of uncertainty about the level of the workload and it is essential, initially, to be cautious about this, starting with a small workforce which can be augmented as experience indicates—it is more difficult (and expensive) to shed than to recruit manpower.

References

1. McKinnon, R., *Maintenance Repair*, Business Administration, 44–47, Apr (1971).
2. Harris, M.J., *An introduction to maintenance stores organisation and spares inventory control* Terotechnica 1, (1979).
3. Macleod, R.A., Flegg, D.A. and Prout, R., *Minimising the cost of maintenance in a large integrated steelworks* Terotechnica 2 (1981) 89–104.
4. Simon, H.A. *Administrative Behaviour*, Macmillan Co. New York, (1950).
5. Mayers, D. *Power Station Organisation*, E.S.B. Course notes, Dublin, March (1982).
6. Darnell, H. *The Ship System*, Proc. of the conference of the Metals Society, London, May (1980).
7. Steedman, J.B., and Treadgold, A.J., *Collection and Analysis of Data on Chemical Plant*, Conference Pub. 11, I.M.E. (1973).
8. Riddell, H.S. *Life-cycle costing in the chemical industry*, Terotechnica, 2 (1981), 9–22.

Chapter 6

System operation and documentation

The documentation necessary for the operation of a system such as that of Figure 5.16 is outlined in Figure 6.1. Such documentation can be manual or computerised. It can be seen that the Preventive Maintenance system feeds information into the Work Order system which in turn feeds into the Maintenance Control Systems. A key document is the Work Order (see Figure 5.15) because it is this that both initiates work and conveys maintenance control information back to the planning office.

In order that the planning systems can function effectively a number of other information systems (the information base) must provide planning and maintenance personnel with technical data, job specifications, spares records, plant history and documents and manuals.

A Plant Inventory Number or Code should be the key to this information base.

Plant inventory

This is a list of all the equipment making up a particular plant. Each entry is given a unique identification number or alpha-numeric coding and also contains the most basic information about the equipment e.g.

Plant Inventory Number	Unit Description	Location Drawing	Manufacturer, Type & Year	Cost
Water 03-043	014C53 Discharge System	Smith	76W,1971	£10,000

The list would normally differentiate between equipment down to at least unit level and, as in the above example, may be complemented by a set of plans/machine-drawings indicating the location of each unit (i.e. of each entry in the list). A typical number or coding system would be constructed as follows:

Plant Serial No./Unit Serial No./Assembly Serial No.

An example of this coding system is shown in Figure 6.2. The unit number 03-002 is used for the on-site identification of the unit; this is essential for work planning and for the collection of cost and unavailability

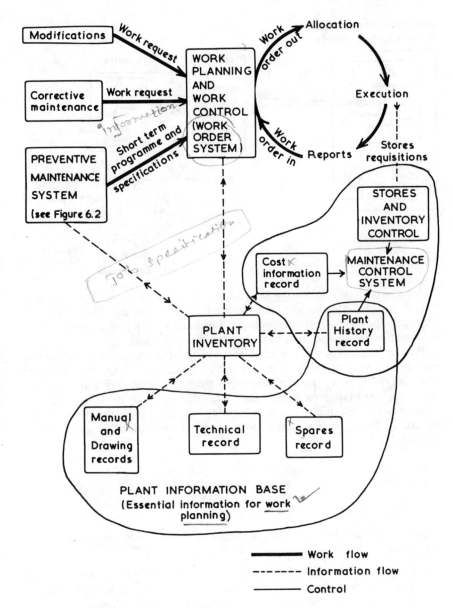

Figure 6.1 Maintenance documentation model

data. The *unit number* should indicate whether the unit is mechanical, electrical or instrument (e.g. all mechanical units might be numbered in the range 001 to 499, electrical 500 to 699, instrument 700 to 999) and within each of these divisions the most straightforward way of numbering is probably to do so in the order in which the units occur along the route of the process (sometimes a separate coding for identifying process flow or electrical flow may already exist, but it will probably not be suitable for maintenance purposes).

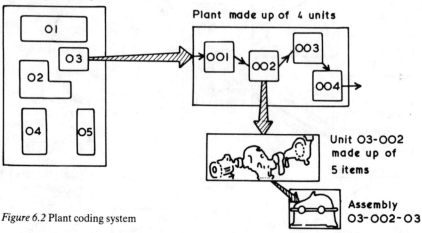

Manufacturing company made up of 5 plants

Plant made up of 4 units

Unit 03-002 made up of 5 items

Assembly 03-002-03

Figure 6.2 Plant coding system

An *assembly number* may be added (as in the example) for accessing data from the information base or for failure recording. This degree of differentiation between equipment is normally only possible, however, if information filing and data handling are computerised.

Where large expensive assemblies, e.g. gearboxes, are re-conditioned off-site and very possibly re-installed on a different site, or on a different unit, an additional number, *separate from the inventory number*, and uniquely identifying the particular piece of equipment must be assigned. This aids the planning of reconditioning and enables a separate history record to be kept. Thus, gearboxes and motors could be identified as follows :

G	XX	XX	XXX
Gearbox	Type	Size	Serial No
EM	XX	XX	XXX
Electrical Motor	Type	Size	Serial No

Regarding numbering/coding systems in general, Idhammer[1] gives the following advice for ensuring system flexibility :

(a) Keep the Spare Part Code separate from the Plant Inventory Code. The Inventory Code should facilitate access to the information base at the point where the coding of the relevant spares is listed.
(b) Keep the Drawing Code separate from the Plant Inventory Code (but inter-connected as in (a)).
(c) Keep the Accountancy Code separate from the Plant Inventory Code. All jobs require an Accounting Coding, but only site jobs need a Plant Coding for maintenance cost control.
(d) If there are several factories, do not over co-ordinate the coding system.

This is only advice, however, The numbering/coding system should be designed to suit the particular plant. For example, where a company has many groups of similar units, such as conveyors, it might be advantageous to adopt an alpha-numeric system. e.g.

XX	CV	XX	XX
Plant	Conveyor	Type of Conveyor	Serial Number

This would facilitate scheduling instructions (e.g. lubricate all conveyors in area XX). With a flow process, plant identification of the sub-system in which the unit functions might be desirable.

Information base

Figure 6.1 shows the headings under which information might be filed. The amount of information held, and its format, will depend on the type of plant and on the method of data storage. In a small machine shop information would be held on a single filing card for each machine tool; in a large integrated chemical plant much more detailed information, differentiated down to assembly level, might be held on computer magnetic disc.

Technical data

This is an expansion of the basic information in the Plant Inventory. With a manual system, such data is usually filed by unit and often subdivided into electrical, mechanical and instrumentation. Its function is to supply the planner with essential information (e.g. outside service engineer, manufacturers and manufacturer's number, unit specification) in times of need.

Spares Record

This should list, for each unit, all spares and their stores coding against the unit's Plant Inventory Number.

Other information, useful in an emergency, could also be included such as the location of identical or similar parts. In some systems only the Stores Code is given and, in this case, further information would then be obtained from the spares control documentation.

Manuals and drawing records

The Drawing Record should list users' drawing-numbers and manufacturers' drawing-numbers against the Plant Inventory Number. In paperwork, as opposed to computerised form, an entry might be as follows:

Plant Inventory No.	Own Drawing No.	Drawing Description	Manufacturer's Drawing No.	Date Prepared	Last Revised
03-043	0363843	Assembly Drg.	2941/1973/350	73.01.06	
	3373735	Pully Det. Drg.	2951/1973/387	73.04.06	

Drawings can be held in drop-leaf files or, better still, on micro-film. The Manual Record would be similar.

PSS

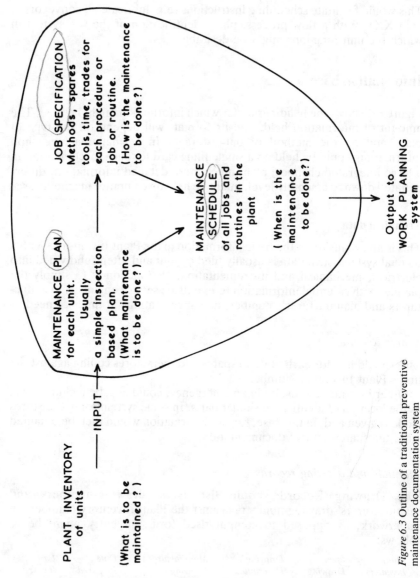

PLANT INVENTORY
of units

(What is to be
maintained?)

INPUT →

MAINTENANCE PLAN
for each unit.
Usually
a simple inspection
based plan.
(What maintenance
is to be done?)

JOB SPECIFICATION
Methods, spares
tools, time, trades for
each procedure or
job or routine.
(How is the maintenance
to be done?)

MAINTENANCE
SCHEDULE
of all jobs and
routines in the
plant

(When is the
maintenance
to be done?)

Output to
WORK PLANNING
system

Figure 6.3 Outline of a traditional preventive
maintenance documentation system

Preventive maintenance documentation

Most preventive maintenance documentation systems are based on similar principles but differ because of the nature of the process and the size of the plant. The principles involved are best discussed with reference to the traditional manual system shown in Figure 6.3. This is based on the plant unit and is suitable for small machine shops or transport fleets where the unit is clearly identifiable, can be scheduled separately *and the plan is mainly inspection based.* The system is made up of three main parts, a *plan* for each unit, *specifications* for each job (or routine) and a *schedule* for the

TABLE 6.1. Maintenance plan for a crane

Maintenance plan		*Inventory No: 73-103*

Plant description
  5 ton crane
		Site
		  warehouse (73)

	Mechanical	Electrical
Weekly inspection	General Check long travel drive motor for noise, vibration and abnormal temperature. Check cross travel drive motor for noise, vibration and abnormal temperature. Hoist unit Check motor for noise, vibration and abnormal temperature Closely examine rope sheave and hook for damage. Establish correct operation of top and bottom limits Check security and condition of pendant control.	NONE
Three- monthly inspection	Long travel Check security of motor mountings Test track for correct operation and check lining wear. Check security of drive shaft bearings Inspect condition of reduction gears Cross travel Check security of motor mountings Test brake for correct adjustment and check lining wear Hoist unit Test brake underload for correct adjustment and check lining wear Check gear case for oil leaks Inspect rope for wear and fraying General Report on condition of lubrication Report on general cleanliness of machine	Long travel Check security and condition of motor leads and earthing Inspect downshop leads for correct tension and slippers for wear. Cross travel Check security and condition of motor leads and earthing Inspect catenary assembly for damage and check free operation Hoist unit Check security of motor leads and earthing Check conditions of wiring to top and bottom limits Check wiring and push buttons on pendant control Controller Check condition of all wiring and security of connections Check for correct and free operation of all relays Check setting of overloads at 10.8 amps

plant. The *Maintenance Plan* is a list of the identified maintenance procedures, for a *unit* of plant, classified by trade and frequency (see Table 6.1). *Job Specification* can be written for:-

an individual procedure— if the procedure contains a large work content or some particular technical difficulty (see Figure 6.4),

a job   — a set of off-line procedures on one unit and to be carried out on one occasion (see Figure 6.5),

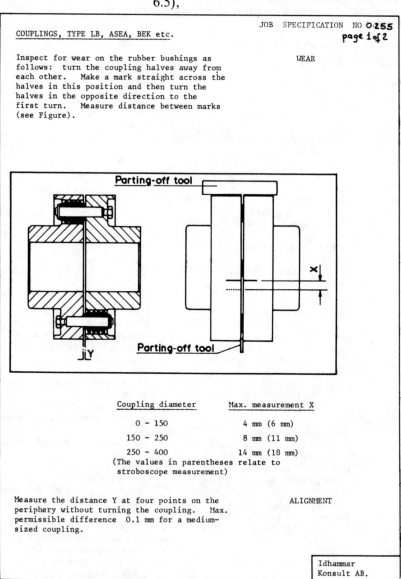

Idhammar
Konsult AB.

Figure 6.4 Job specification for coupling inspection[1]

Job specification	Plant No.	73 103				
Plant description	Maintenance code	11				
	Job code	Mech/ 3 monthly (M3)				
Site	Week Nos.	8	24	37	1	

Spares required
Drawings and manual refs.
Special tools.

Long travel

1. Check security of motor mountings.
2. Test brake for correct operation and check lining wear.
3. Check security of drive shaft bearing.
4. Inspect condition of reduction gears.

Cross travel

5. Check security of motor mountings.
6. Test brake for correct adjustment and check lining wear.

etc.

Figure 6.5 Job specification (from *Figure 6.3*)

a routine	— a set of on-line procedures (usually simple inspection or lubrication) in one area and involving one trade and carried out on one occasion.

The *Maintenance Schedule* is arranged with the aid of a bar chart (see Figure 6.6) and with the aim of achieving a balanced workload. Jobs of short-term periodicity (less than a month) are not included and are scheduled separately, usually by first-line supervision. The great advantage of the bar chart is that *the total preventive load for a plant can be seen* and smoothed to the required profile.

In most of the traditional preventive documentation systems the bar chart is used mainly for scheduling jobs into some form of card index, sometimes called the 'job tickler file'. The index, made up of 52 slots, can then be used directly for the scheduling and control of preventive work i.e. each week it feeds a weekly load of job specifications, plus a summary, into the work planning system. Each specification is accompanied by a Work Order on its way to the shop floor. The index can be updated and re-scheduled as necessary on the return of the job specification cards.

Unit description	Unit No / Week No	1	2	3	4	5	6	7	8	9	10
Plant description					Malleable iron foundry						
5 ton crane	1 03								3 M / 3 E		
Mould con.	1 04				AM						
Shake out	1 05				IM / IE				I M / I E		
Sand belt	1 06				6E						
Hopper	1 08	IE			3M / IE				IE		
M. M/c	1 11	IE / IM			IE / IM				3E / 3M		

Job specification No.

Figure 6.6 Maintenance schedule on a bar chart

Resulting corrective work is noted on the completed Work Order and stays in the work planning system. A manual documentation system based on these ideas is described on page 149 and a computerised version on page 205.

In the case of large process plants, e.g. the batch chemical plant or the paper machine of Chapter 4, scheduling of preventive work is much more complex and not always inspection-based. There is a need to integrate the scheduling of maintenance work on many units of plant and, if a manual system is being used, a bar chart must be used for the initial schedule *and to control the completion of work*. The work load is read off the bar chart and the specifications are then selected from their file and sent, as before, to the shop floor. Such a system is described on page 170.

A simplification of the traditional system is to use a work manual containing coded job specifications (see Figure 6.4) which is made available to the maintenance tradeforce. The Work Order from the Planning Office will contain a brief job description and a job specification code. Such a system is described on page 161.

The main variation on the foregoing traditional ideas is the extension of the job tickler file into a maintenance job catalogue. The latter includes all preventive jobs (frequency jobs) and as wide a range of corrective jobs (non-frequency jobs) as possible. Each job, and routine, in the catalogue is listed under the relevant Plant Inventory Number and the specification includes job method, standard time, frequency, trade(s), spares, tools and an indication of whether it is on-line or off-line. If it is off-line, the plant that has to be shut down in order to complete the job as indicated. Such information, stored in a computer file, can form the basis of a preventive maintenance scheduling programme which can also take into account resource constraints, the possibility of multi-unit scheduling, opportunity maintenance and deferred work. This is a more detailed and flexible approach than that of the traditional systems and is appropriate for large complex process plants where a computer is already being used for data processing. On page 182 a simple manual version of a job catalogue is described and on page 188 a complete computerised system.

Documentation for work planning and control

The flow of this documentation, for a non-computerised system, is shown in Figures 6.7 and 6.8. The main documentation and planning aids used are as follows :

Work Order—   'A written instruction detailing work to be carried out' (BS 3811). The information this might carry is summarised in Table 6.2. When used to its fullest extent it can act as a work request (see Figure 5.15), a planning document, a work allocation document, a history record (if filed) and as a notification of modification work completed.

A typical work order (raised in triplicate and in this case not acting as a work request) is shown in Figure 6.9.

TABLE 6.2. Information carried by a Work Order

Planning Information
    Inventory number, unit description and site
    Person requesting job
    Job description and time standard
    Job specification and code number
    Date required and priority
    Trades required and co-ordinating foreman
    Spares required with stores number and location
    Special tools and lifting tackle required   } usually carried on
    Safety procedure number   job specification
    Drawing and manual numbers

Control Information
    Cost code for work type and trade
    Downtime
    Actual time taken
    Cause and consequences of failure
    Action taken

Work Request :   'A document requesting work to be carried out' (BS 3811). It usually carries such information as person requesting, plant number, plant description, work description, defect, priority, date requested.

Job Catalogue :   A file of job specifications (preventive and corrective) as previously described.

Planning Board :   For planning preventive work a bar chart as already described. For planning corrective work a Work Order loading board covering a horizon of up to 12 weeks, in units of 1 week and having pockets to allow the Work Orders to be scheduled into the appropriate week.

Allocation Board :   A short term planning board showing men available on each day of one week which allows jobs to be allocated to men. This can be supplemented by the allocation board shown in Figure 6.10.

JOB ORIGINATION	PLANNING	SCHEDULING	SCHEDULING	PLANNING
Request to planning office or supervisor. Add plant description, location, requestor, date, priority and defect description.	Check priority. Check if job is on file and update file as necessary. Raise W.O. Add job no., plant no., cost codes, job specifications, Check spares	Schedule WO on long term programme. Update programme according to planning meetings.	Schedule weekly load of W.Orders.	Check and bond spares and tools. Raise safety request. Check and supply manuals and documentation. Add this information on W.O.

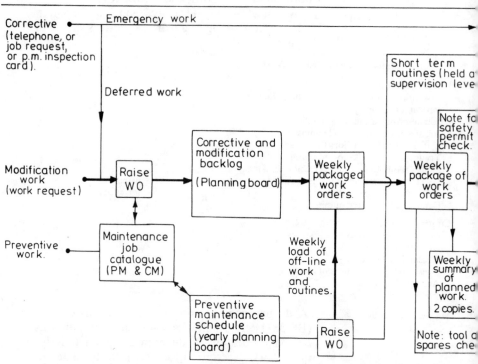

Figure 6.7(a) Work order system for planning and scheduling

Other Documentation : Safety permit, stores and tool note, weekly work programme, stores requisition, top ten report, cost report, history record.

Work planning (see Figure 6.7(a))

Requests for *emergency work* are made verbally to area supervision who raise Work Orders.

Requests for *deferred corrective work and modifications* are made to the Planning Office on Work Request Forms. A Work Order is raised directly

PRODUCTION	SUPERVISOR	STORES	TRADEFORCE
Raise safety permit. Complete separate downtime record.	Raise emergency WO and perform all planning checks. Allocate WO's to men.	Bond and issue spare parts. Compile requisition.	Complete work

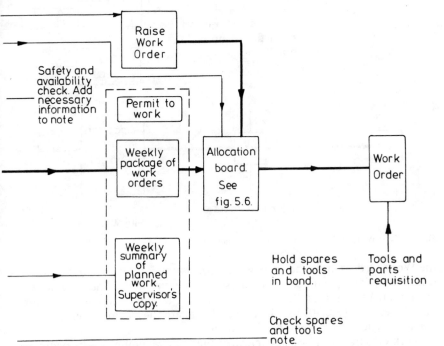

Figure 6.7(a) Cont.

or by reference (if held) to the Job Catalogue. The priority of such work is decided at a weekly Plant Meeting and the jobs loaded into the corrective maintenance Planning Board.

Preventive work is planned and scheduled as explained in the previous section. The preventive maintenance system feeds a weekly load of work into the work planning system to be considered for the weekly programme alongside the corrective and modification work. Work Orders are raised (by reference to the job catalogue) and work not to be carried out is rescheduled using the Planning Board.

The complete weekly programme for each area or plant is planned in terms of resources, plant availability, and opportunity maintenance and entered in a weekly work summary. This is sent to the area supervisor with

TRADEFORCE	STORES	SUPERVISOR
Add cause of failure, time taken, action taken, downtime.	Complete stores requisition for parts usage. Stores requisition to stores control and cost control.	Checks work satisfactory. Issues new request of work arising. Update allocation board. Completes WO and returns to planning office. Cancel safety permits. Consider causes of failure.

Requisition to stores and cost control
Return parts unused and parts for scrap and reconditioning.

Cost report

Top ten

WO → WO → Allocation board (update) →

Return tools

File W O copy

Figure 6.7(b) Work order system for maintenance control

the Work Orders and other necessary information i.e. manual and drawing references, job specification codes, spares requirement. The area supervisor then uses a short term planning board and/or a simple allocation board (see Figure 6.10) to schedule and allocate the planned jobs and the emergency jobs that come to him direct.

Work Orders are raised in triplicate, one copy remaining in the planning office, one with the supervisor and one sent as the order to the tradesman. As the Work Order is returned through the system the copies can be filed or destroyed. An important point is that for effective control the execution of all work should be covered by a Work Order and a copy of all completed Orders should return to the planning office.

Control (see Figure 6.7(b))

The main information necessary for control comes from the completed Work Order and Stores Requisition Forms. The main information necessary to complete the Work Order (job completed, cause, hours taken, action taken etc) comes from the tradesman and is checked and augmented by the supervisor.

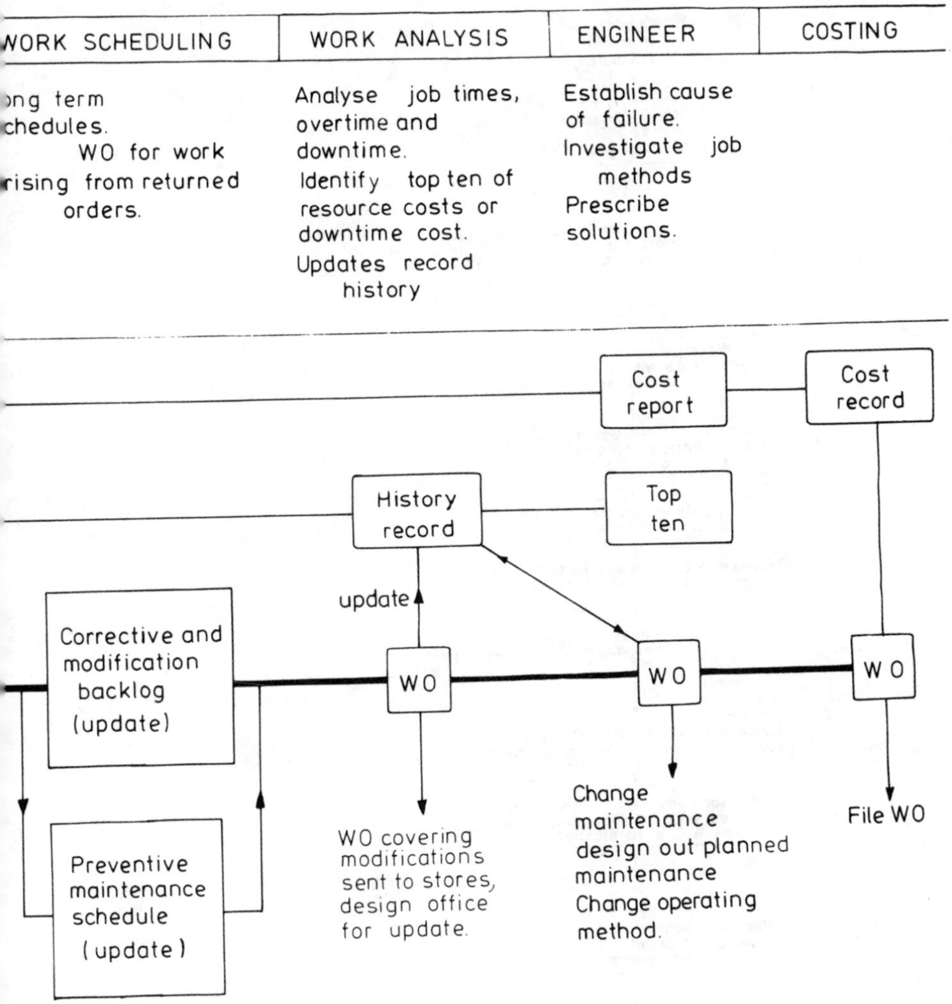

WORK SCHEDULING	WORK ANALYSIS	ENGINEER	COSTING
ong term chedules. WO for work rising from returned orders.	Analyse job times, overtime and downtime. Identify top ten of resource costs or downtime cost. Updates record history	Establish cause of failure. Investigate job methods Prescribe solutions.	

Figure 6.7(b) Cont.

Work Control is completed by the daily updating of the Allocation Board and the weekly updating of the Planning Boards via the return of the Work Orders. In addition the Work Orders are classified by trades and analysed to establish overtime hours and the proportion of time spent on planned and unplanned work (see page 115). If a work measurement scheme is in operation the work analysis can extend into performance calculation for the consequent report.

As illustrated in Figure 5.19, the first level of *plant condition control* operates via information passed from the tradesman to the supervisor either verbally or through the Work Order. The supervisor is responsible for seeing that the cause and consequences section of the Work Order is completed by the tradesman and, where this is not the case, for establishing the reason. The second level of condition control operates through the planning office and depends partly on an effective History Record. This in turn depends on the information on causes, costs and work

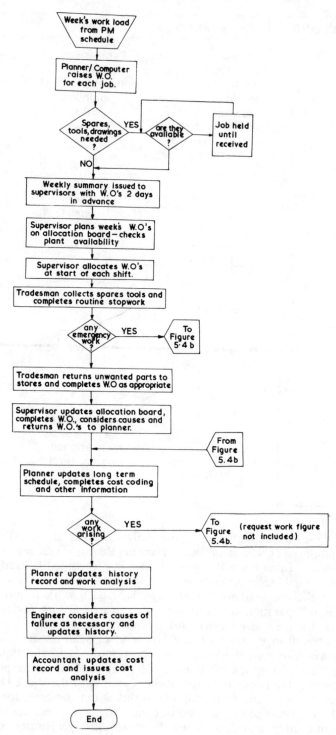

Figure 6.8(a) A flowchart for preventive maintenance jobs

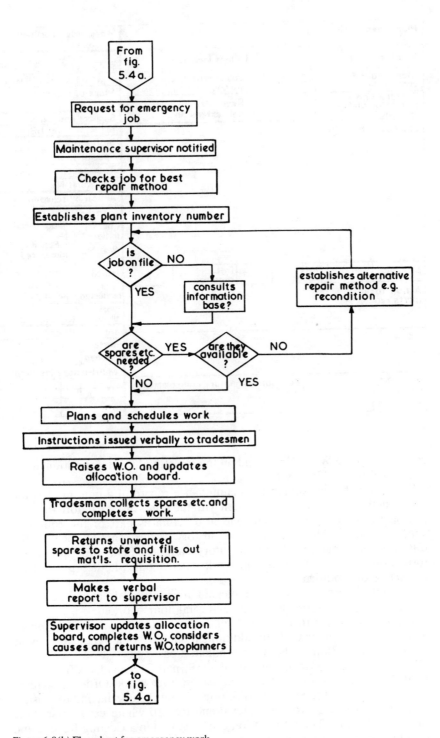

Figure 6.8(b) Flowchart for emergency work

Plant description:				Work order number			
Plant number		Plant location		**Permits**			
				P.T.W.	S.F.T.	L.O.A.	S.F.S.
Maintenance cost code		Job specification number		M	L.V.	H.V.	None
Coordinating supervisor and extension		Requested by and extension		Place of issue:			
Job / defect description:				Support and services			
				M	R	C	L	E	HP	W
				Stores check			
				Special tools			
				Transport			
				Check list No.			
				Action by scheduler			
				Stores		Work	
				Check initiated		programmed	
				Available		Permits requested	
				Note issued			
Priority		Date issued		Date required		Tools requested	Transport arranged
Action taken (parts replaced)				Work allocated to			
Cause				Job	time	date	
				Started			
				Finished			
				Multi-trades involved			
Downtime (if any)		Foreman's signature and comments:					

Figure 6.9 Work order form

conveyed on the Work Order and on the transfer of this information at the right level to the History Record.

The latter should contain the maintenance record of a unit and has the dual function of providing tradesmen with the unit's history before the next job on the unit is carried out, and also acting as part of the condition control system. Thus, a complete history record should include the following information : Plant Inventory Number; Plant description; Information on, and dates of, all work carried out whether preventive, corrective or modification.

The information should also include item affected, components replaced, possible causes, downtime and total hours worked.

If the history record is to perform both its functions it must be easily accessed and interrogated. In addition, it should be designed to provide automatic indication of the main problem areas.

The *cost control system* relies on the information provided against each Unit Number, on the three main cards, the Work Order providing manpower usage, the Stores Requisition providing material and tool usage and the History Record (or a Downtime Record where used) describing the unavailability. The information can be stored in a Costing Record and should consist of total maintenance cost per production period per plant

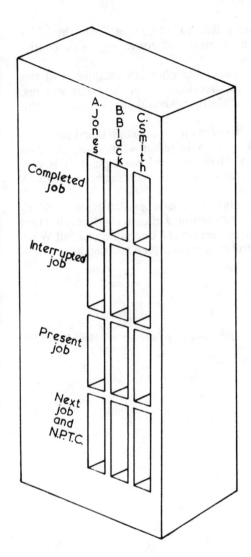

Figure 6.10 Allocation board

and per unit (i.e. per process line, per workshop, per vehicle etc.) with the achieved availability for that unit. A cumulative record should also be kept. This information can be further analysed into mechanical, electrical, instrumentation costs and also into materials and manpower costs. The system should provide a monthly summary for engineering management, the planning and supervision.

Comments

The documentation system that has been outlined does not have to be used in its totality. Any part, or parts, can be used as needed. For example, many companies use only the Preventive Maintenance system plus a limited Plant Inventory and History Record. Others use only the Work Order system and that mainly as a means of conveying work control information for incentive schemes.

The information base takes considerable effort to establish and this should not be allowed to inhibit the development of the other systems. Where possible the equipment manufacturer should supply much of this information.

Manually-operated preventive maintenance and work scheduling systems have been shown to work effectively, even with large, complex plants, e.g. offshore oil platforms. However, with such plant, it is very difficult to operate an effective manual system of maintenance control. A computer based system is essential.

Although maintenance can be planned and scheduled without Work Orders for *every* job, it cannot then be *controlled* effectively. If it is felt that the workforce and supervision will not accept the discipline of a full Work Order system then the loss of control must be accepted and the documentation designed to suit.

References

1. Idhammar, C. *Maintenance course notes for Developing Countries* Ali Rati, Fack 1213, Lidingo, Sweden.

Chapter 7

Some manually operated documentation systems

A complete manual documentation system, and several part-systems (directed particularly at preventive maintenance), will be examined in the light of the general model described in the previous chapter.

A complete system

A system in use in many plants in the UK is that devised by the Production Engineering Research Association (PERA) and described in some detail by Corder[1]. The essential difference between this system and the general model of Chapter 6 is that the documentation for preventive work is separate from that for corrective and modification work.

Plant inventory and information base

The plant inventory lists equipment at unit level (e.g. lathes). A minimum of four digits classifies and identifies each unit, e.g.

Main class	Sub-class	Make or type	Serial Number
4	1	1	5
(Moulding plant)	(Moulding machines)	(Wallwork)	(Machine No. 5)

Each unit has one main Record Card (see Figure 7.1) which acts as the inventory entry and the information base, file numbers indicating the location of separately held drawings and manuals. The cards are stored in visible-edge files (see Figure 7.2) the visible-edge acting as the inventory index. Information on spares is not on this card.

Preventive maintenance system

This is essentially the system of Figure 6.3. An inspection-based plan consists of a basic service at regular intervals with additional services at various multiples of this interval. For example, the plan for the Rhodes Press is made up of three-monthly and yearly inspections. Each job (or routine) for each unit is entered onto a Job Specification Card (see Figure 7.3) and separated, where necessary, into mechanical, electrical and

INSTALLATION		DIMENSIONS				LOCATION				VALUE			
DATE	Sept 1972	WEIGHT	9 Ton			COMPANY	XY - Tools Ltd			PURCHASE	£6005=00		
ORDER No.	664/E	FLOOR AREA	4'.1"x8'.0"			SITE	Spade Forge			DATE	14/8/72		
A.C. No.	-	MAX. HT.	10'-0"			SECTION	Spade 1	CC14		PRESENT			
DATE MANF'D	August 1972	MOUNTING	2'.0" Thick Concrete			DATE	Sept/72			DATE			

DESCRIPTION & REFERENCES   MANUFACTURERS No.

"Rhodes" Special RF 100 Geared Upright Open Front Fabricated Press

Pressure Capacity 100 Ton 1" From Bottom of Stroke

90 Ton $\frac{1}{4}$" " " " "

MANUAL & CATALOGUES

Rhodes RFP 703 (Modified)

FILE No.

DRAWINGS   Modified Ram Rhodes Drawing No. 17117

All Other Drawings Retained by Rhodes

Prints Supplied   Modified Ram Guides JRS 2048

"   "   "   "   AYH 289

Bed Plate   Print   AYH   99

PLANT DESC. AUX. EQUIPT.

Fixed Stroke 4" Ram Adjustment 4" by Hand Ratchet Lever

Speed 80 S.P.M.

Pneumatic Friction Clutch & Brake. Single Stroke & "Inch" Cycles Foot Control

Tecalemit One Shot Lubrication

PLANT DESCRIPTION   PLANT No. 1650

100 Ton Rhodes C Frame Press (Socket Swaging)

Figure 7.1(a) Record card (mechanical plant)

ELECTRICAL EQUIPMENT			DISTRIBUTION BOARD No. OVERHEAD TRUNKING		
	1.	2.	3.	4.	5.
DRIVE	MAIN				
ITEM	MOTOR				
MAKER	CROMPTON PARKINSON				
SERIAL No.	EA 46791				
DATE	1972				
TYPE	HIGH TORQUE/HIGH SLIP				
CAT. REF. No.	–				
VOLTS/ph/CYCLES	440/3/50				
AMPS	21.5				
R.P.M.	1400				
H.P.	15				
RATING	CONT.				
FRAME	D160 M				
MOUNTING	FOOT				
COIL No.	–				
O/L SETTING	35 AMP				
INSULATION	CLASS E				
FUSE CAPACITY	50 AMP				
BEARINGS D.E.	1$\frac{1}{4}$" x 2$\frac{7}{8}$" x $\frac{3}{4}$"THRUST				
BEARINGS N.D.E.	1$\frac{1}{4}$" x 2$\frac{7}{8}$" x $\frac{3}{4}$"BALL				
SHAFT DIA/LENGTH	1$\frac{1}{2}$" x 4$\frac{1}{2}$"				
KEYWAY SIZES	$\frac{3}{8}$" x $\frac{1}{4}$" x 4"				
DRG. No.	–				

PLANT DESCRIPTION
100 TON RHODES C FRAME PRESS (SOCKET SWAGING)

PLANT No.   1650

Figure 7.1(b) Record card (electrical plant)

Figure 7.2 Record cards stored in visible edge file

E.T. Ltd.	JOB SPECIFICATION		Week No.					

Company	XY TOOLS LTD.	4						
Location	SPADE SECTION ONE							
Description	RHODES PRESS							

Spec. No. MA/1650

Report other defects NOTICED
ANNUAL INSPECTION MECH

A/c No.

Plant No. 1650

Operation No.

Labour req'd.

Plant status off-line **Time** 4hrs apr

1.	GENERAL	Check operation and control of gears.
2.	SLIDES	Check security of slides.
3.	AIR FILTER	Clean out filter.
4.	LUBRICATOR	Check operating efficiency
5.	DRIVE	Check condition and tension of belt. Adjust if required.
6.	LUBRICATOR LINES	Check for leaks or damaged pipes.
7.	BRAKE AND CLUTCH	Check condition of brake and clutch linings.
8.	GEARS	Remove top cover and check condition and security of gears.
9.	MAIN CRANK	Check security of retaining bolts.
10.	DAMPER CYLINDER	Check efficiency of seals.

Figure 7.3 Job specification card

Location Spade Section 1	Week Commencing																															
			Week No.																													
		Spec. Frequencies			1	2	3	4	5	6	7	8	9	10	11	12	13	14	15	16	17	18	19	20	21	22	23	24	25	26	27	28
Unit	Plt. No.	Mech.	Elect.	Lub.																												
MOTORISED CONVEYOR 20'-0"	0210	M 3 6		6				6			M			M							3		M			M			6
MOTORISED CONVEYOR 20'-0"	0211	M 3 6		6 M	M		6			M			M			M				3		M		M			M		M
MOTORISED CONVEYOR 14'-0"	0212	6		6				6		M			M			M		3			M		3		M		M		M
MOTORISED CONVEYOR 14'-0"	0213	6	3	6		M			6	M		M			M	3		3		M		M		M		M		3
RHODES PRESS	1650	M 3 A 3			M			A	A	M	A		M		M		3		M		M		M		M		3
RHODES PRESS	1651	M 3 A 3				M		A	M	A	M		M		3		3		M		3		M		M	
RHODES PRESS	1652	M 3 A 3				M	A	A	M		M		M		3		3		M		M		M	
RHODES PRESS	1654	M 3 A 3					M	A	A	M	M		M		3		3		3		M		M	
RHODES PRESS	1655	M 3 A 3					M	A	A	A	M		M		M		M		3		3		M	
RHODES PRESS	1656	M 3 A 3					M	M	A	A		M		M		M		M		3		3		M	
RHODES PRESS	1657	M 3 A 3						M	A	A		M		M		M		3		3		M	
									HOLIDAY PERIOD																			
ROLLING MILL	2019	6					6	6					M								3			6	
WATER COOLING UNIT	3008	6	6				M		3			M			M		M		3		M		M		6
L.P.G. FURNACE	0710	3	M									M								M		M		M

Figure 7.4 Extract from preventive maintenance schedule

lubrication. The work is then scheduled, using a bar chart (see Figure 7.4) which allows the weekly work load in terms of inspections, etc, to be read down any one column.

Each Job Specification Card is then held in the appropriate part of a file having a section for each week of the year. This Card Index (see Figure 7.5) represents the work load for the year and is used to trigger the

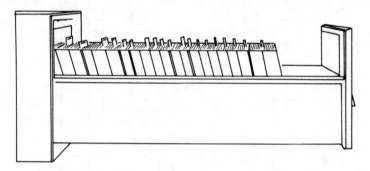

Figure 7.5 Job specification card index

LOCATION: SPADE SECTION I.			WEEK NO. 4.		
Job Spec. No.	Description	Plant No.	On-Line Off-Line	Time* req'd. (hrs)	Day plant* available
M 6M	Motorised conveyor 20'-0"	0201	Off-line		
M A E 3M	Rhodes Press	1650	Off-line	8	
M M	Rhodes Press	1655	On-line		
M 6M E 6M	Water Cooling Unit	3008	Off-line	8	
E M	L.P.G. Furnace	0710	Off-line		
M	L.P.G. Furnace	0714	Off-line		

* Mostly left to area supervisor

Figure 7.6 Weekly summary of preventive maintenance

notification of work to the work planning system. Preventive work enters the planning system as a weekly load of job specifications, arranged into packets of work for a machine or plant area and accompanied by a weekly summary of preventive work (see Figure 7.6). The Job Specifications are enclosed in a plastic envelope with a blank Inspection Report (see Figure 7.7) which acts as a work order for preventive work.

INSPECTION REPORT		Spec.No. MA1635		Week No.		Class.		
				4		0	1	4
Description RHODES PRESS				Main Code		Plant No.		
Plant Location SPADE SECTION ONE				1	1	1	6	5	0

Op. No.	Item	Defect	Cause	Action/Repair

Tradesman's Signature	Clock No.	Date	Time ON	Time OFF	Total		Rate	£	p
					Hrs	Dec			
					Total R/T Hours				

Figure 7.7 Inspection report

Work order system

This is similar to that of Figure 6.7. Work Orders due to production defects are raised in triplicate (Figure 7.8) by the production supervisor who completes the top part of the order and thus requests maintenance work. In the case of an emergency the top copy passes direct to the maintenance supervisor (generally following a verbal request) and the second progress copy is sent to the planning office. The bottom copy is retained until the job is completed, and then destroyed. For all other work both top and progress copies are sent to the planning office.

Work Orders arising from inspection reports are raised in triplicate by the maintenance supervisor. With emergency jobs the top copy is passed to the tradesman and other copies held until job completion. In the case of deferred work, the top and progress copies are sent to the planning office who integrate the work into the corrective backlog schedule. Information from this latter schedule, from the preventive work schedule, and from priority-assessment meetings is used by the planning office to provide maintenance supervision with

(1) the weekly summary of preventive work plus job specifications and blank inspection reports,
(2) a weekly summary of corrective maintenance plus the relevant work orders (also included is an indication of those corrective jobs that should be carried out while a machine is down for preventive work).

MAINTENANCE WORK ORDER	0351		Week No.	Cost Centre		

Plant Description Rhodes Press	Date 27.1.81		4	0	1	4

Plant Location Spade Sec. 1	Time	a.m. p.m.	Maintenance Code		Plant No.	

Requested By Required By	1	2	1	6	5	0

Defect/Work Required	IS PRODUCTION STOPPED?	YES NO	Tool BDN	1	
Attention to Scrap Remover			M/c Running	2	Tick one box
			M/c Breakdown	3	
			Not Applicable	4	

Cause Cylinder Rod Broken		Wear and Tear	1	
Arm connecting		Accident Misuse Neglect	2	Tick one box
badly worn		Component Failure	3	
		Job Report	4	
		Not Applicable	5	

Action Taken
Made and fitted new cylinder rods replaced worn parts

with parts from spare scrap remover

Tradesman's Signature	Date	Clock No.	Time ON	Time OFF	Total Hours		Rate	Amount	
					HRS	DEC		£	p
L. Gaskell		7907			0 4	5 0		14	41

Maintenance Foreman's Signature	Date Completed	Total R/T Hours		HRS	DEC	
	27.6.81	4.5	Repair Time	0 4	5 0	
For Office Use Only			Down Time	0 4	5 0	

Figure 7.8 Maintenance work order

For all the listed jobs the planning office carries out the necessary planning checks, on availability of spares, special tools, plant etc.

The maintenance supervisor plans the work over the week and allocates the jobs by passing job specifications, blank inspection reports, work orders etc. to the appropriate tradesmen. If a particular job requires the assistance of other trades, the supervisor raises additional work orders. Tradesmen collect necessary spares and tools (completing, in conjunction with the storeman, Stores Requisitions, see Figure 7.9) and on finishing each job, complete the central part of the Work Order and return it to the supervisor.

Control

Work control is achieved through the return of the Work Orders and Inspection Reports and the updating of the allocation board and planning

STORES REQUISITION

Unit description	Date	Unit No.		1	6	5	0
RHODES PRESS	27.1.81	Maintenance cost code			1		2

Part No.	Description	Qty.		Price		Bin location
		Reqd	iss	part	total	
013414	Cylinder Rod					

Tradesman's. sig.	Foreman's sig.	Storekeeper's sig.	Stock control

Figure 7.9 Stores requisition

Description				Plant No.	
Date	Item	Defect	Cause	Repair action	Time taken
8.11.79	C4152	SOLENOID REPAIRED (7907)		0.5	0.5
24.11.79	C6356	SCRAP REMOVER REPAIRED (7907)		18.0	18.0
26.11.79	C4169	SOLENOID REPLACED (7907)		1.0	1.0
12.1.80	C6611	SCRAP REMOVER REPAIRED (7907)		17.0	17.0
14.1.80	C4199	FAULTY SOLENOID (7907)		2.0	2.0
26.1.80	C7077	FILTERS CLEANED ON AIRLINE (7910)		4.0	6.0
8.4.80	C5172	SCRAP REMOVER REPAIRED (7907)		6.0	6.0
14.4.80	C5191	SOLENOID REPLACED (7922)		1.0	1.0
3.6.80	C4140	REPAIRS (7909)		3.0	3.0
28.6.80	C9625	NEW GAUGES M/F (7923)		3.0	3.0
22.7.80	C5066	SOLENOID CHANGED (7907)		8.0	8.0
28.7.80	C5072	" " (7907)		1.5	1.5
20.10.80	C5210	SCRAP REMOVER REPAIRED (7907)		1.0	1.0
13.4.81	C7814	NEW SOLENOID FITTED (7907)		1.0	1.0
23.5.81	D1583	SCRAP REMOVER REPAIRED (7920)		12.0	12.0
11.6.81	D2210	MADE & FITTED NEW CYLINDER ROD, REPLACED WORN PARTS WITH PARTS FROM SPARE SCRAP REMOVER (7907)		4.5	4.5
27.6.81	D2106	SOLENOID VALVE CHANGED (7920)		1.0	1.0
17.8.81	D2392	JAWS ON SCRAP REMOVER NOT CLOSING - SHUTTLE VALVE BLOCKED— DIRTY AIR LINE CLEANED OUT		1.0	1.0
17.8.81	3MINSP	NO DEFECTS			
22.8.81	D1001	SCRAP REMOVER OVERHAULED (7926)		32.0	32.0
Mechanical history record		RHODES PRESS		1650	

Figure 7.10 History record

TABLE 7.1. Maintenance cost code

Department	Preventive	Emergency	Deferred	Recond.	Modifications	Installations
	Work class			*Corrective*		
Mechanical	11	12	13	14	15	16
Electrical	21	22	23	24	25	26
Instrumentation	31	32	33	34	35	36
Civil	41	42	43	44	45	46

office schedules. The maintenance supervisor checks and signs the Work Orders and Inspection Reports (entering the maintenance cost codes, see Table 7.1) before returning them to the planning office. The Job Specifications are returned to their file for future issue.

Analysis of the Work Orders establishes the proportion of maintenance being spent on planned and unplanned work in each area of the company. Such information is used by the planning office to decide how much planned work to pass through to the maintenance supervisors each week.

Plant condition control is achieved through the information obtained on causes of failure, corrective action and downtime entered on the work orders. Such information is subsequently recorded in the History Records (see Figure 7.10). Control of the first level is facilitated by the weekly summary of emergency maintenance (see Figure 7.11) issued to the Engineers and to the Maintenance Supervisor for on-site follow-up and investigation. Control at the second level is achieved by 'top ten' analysis

SUMMARY OF EMERGENCY MAINTENANCE			Area 04 Week No. 4		
Unit No.	Unit Description	Defect, Cause, Action	Repair time M	E	Down time
1650	Rhodes Press	Remover Cylinder-Wear-Replaced Rod Broken	5.0	1.0	6.0
1655	Rhodes Press	Solenoid-over-replaced valve load defect		1.0	1.50
2019	Rolling Mill	Bearing-Poor-Replace seized seal seal.& Bearing	8.5		10.0

Figure 7.11 Weekly summary of emergency maintenance

MONTHLY TOP-TEN RANKING ON TOTAL DOWNTIME

Unit No.	Unit description	Unit location	Mechanical hrs.	Electrical hrs.	Total hrs.
1650	Rhodes Press	Spade Section 1	19	3	22
3205	HOIST	Main Shop H.P.	7	8	15
0211	Motorised Conveyor	Spade Section 1	6	1	7

Figure 7.12 Top-ten analyses

MONTHLY UNIT GROUP ANALYSIS

Group	No. in Group	Description	Repair hrs.	Down time hrs.	Comments
021	4	Motorised conveyor	12	9	Bearing problem now overcome
165	7	Rhodes Press	52	36	Main problem associated with scrap remover

Figure 7.13 Plant group analysis

(see Figure 7.12) and 'Grouped Unit' analysis (see Figure 7.13). These analyses give a monthly indication of problem units and areas. These are investigated by the engineer both on-site and through the History Record.

Maintenance cost control is achieved through the Work Order and the Stores Requisition. Each document contains both Plant Inventory Number and Maintenance Job Code, allowing the cost of manpower, spares and downtime to be recorded against each area, unit or group or smaller units.

Comments

The author observed this system in operation in two companies. In practice only the preventive maintenance system worked in the way described. The other systems either did not exist, or were only in part operation.

In neither company was the Plant Inventory Record card completed and only very simple plant inventories were employed. Being small companies, they felt that simple files for drawings and manuals were sufficient and there was no need to use a Record Card to find such information. Because the companies were working shifts, these files were located in area supervisors' offices and not in planning offices. A similar attitude was taken on spare parts information which was held only in stores.

Shift working also meant that only preventive work was planned and scheduled from the planning office. Corrective jobs were almost always planned and scheduled, in the area of their origin, by the maintenance supervisor.

From the point of view of planning and control, Work Orders were used in a disciplined way because the times recorded on the orders were used in calculating tradeforce pay. From the point of view of collecting information on failures and repairs, however, the same could not be said. Often such information was omitted or did not refer to the real cause of failure. One company kept no History Record but filed all Work Orders, the manner of doing this, however, rendered analysis impossible. The other company did use a History Record (shown in Figure 7.10). Neither analysed work orders to identify the more troublesome plant, so condition control was non-existent. Work analysis was more or less limited to a listing of weekly emergency maintenance. There was little maintenance cost control other than a monitoring of costs arising from the companies' overtime payment schemes.

A preventive maintenance system based on a job specification manual

This is intended for use in small plants (e.g. an asphalt production plant[2]). It is outlined in Figure 7.14.

Plant inventory and information base

Each unit of plant is numbered and has a Plant Inventory Record Card (see Figure 7.15) stored in a visible edge file, the edge acting as an inventory index. The front of the card gives the maintenance plan for the unit, the

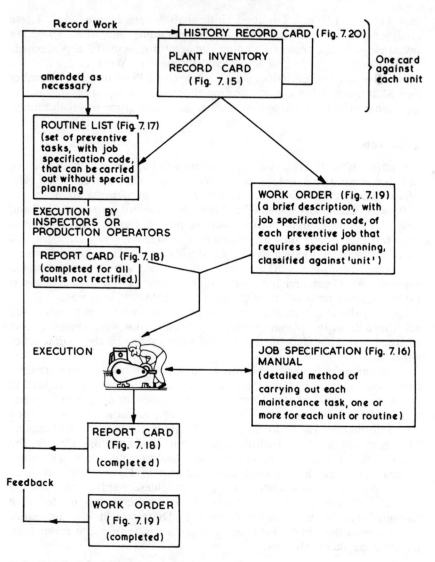

Record Work

amended as
necessary

One card
against
each unit

HISTORY RECORD CARD (Fig. 7.20)

PLANT INVENTORY
RECORD CARD
(Fig. 7.15)

ROUTINE LIST (Fig. 7.17)
(set of preventive
tasks, with job
specification code,
that can be carried
out without special
planning

EXECUTION   BY
INSPECTORS OR
PRODUCTION OPERATORS

REPORT CARD (Fig. 7.18)
(completed for all
faults not rectified.)

WORK ORDER (Fig. 7.19)
(a brief description, with
job specification code, of
each preventive job that
requires special planning,
classified against 'unit')

EXECUTION

JOB SPECIFICATION (Fig. 7.16)
MANUAL
(detailed method of
carrying out each
maintenance task, one or
more for each unit or routine)

REPORT CARD
(Fig. 7.18)
(completed)

Feedback

WORK ORDER
(Fig. 7.19)
(completed)

Figure 7.14 Outline of Idhammer system

reference number of the Job Specification and an indication of whether the work is to be carried out on-line or off-line. The back of the card gives technical data, drawing and manual reference numbers and the stores code of main spares held. The Job Specifications (see Figure 7.16) are held in a manual to which tradesmen have direct access.

Planning and scheduling

The scheduling of preventive work is based on its division into off-line and on-line work, the latter consisting of on-line maintenance routines.

Interval	No.	Activity
1 week	11	Service as per routine list
4 weeks	12	Check V-belt drive as per routine list
2000hrs	24	Inspect valves, clean, change oil, check V-belts.

Spare part card no.:

	Jan 77	Febr	March	April	May	June	July	Aug	Sept	Oct	Nov.	Dec
Activity no				24	24		24		24			
Date				2-1-74	29-1-75		3-1-76					
Oper time				2056	4103			6320				
Activity no												
Date												
Oper time												
Activity no												
Date												
Oper time												

Compressor, instrument air No. 1

5-20

IDHAMMAR KONSULT AB
Viksängsvägen 10, 151 57 Södertälje, Sweden, 0755/874 50

Figure 7.15(a) Plant inventory record card (front)

164

TECHNICAL DATA

Card no.:

Spare parts card no.:

Component:

Manufacturer	Phone:
Agent	Phone:
Type	
Manufacturing no.	
Manufacturing year	
Weight	
Placing	
Reference to manuf. instr. and drawings	
Technical data	
Technical data	
Technical data	
Bearing data	
Bearing data	
Notes	

Figure 7.15(b) Plant inventory record card (back)

COMPRESSOR ATLAS COPCO KE4, KT6	
Spec. No.	Job description
24	INSPECT VALVES, CLEAN, CHANGE OIL, CHECK SAFETY VALVES
	NB: Check compressor is depressurized.
1	Check and clean suction and pressure valves. Replace defective valves. Replace packings. Clean valve chambers.
2	Check and clean pressure surge damper and pressure pipe.
3	Clean crankcase and change oil.
4	Check whether cleaning system is working. satisfactorily. For higher discharge pressure, screw in regulating screw towards valve seat. For lower discharge pressure, unscrew regulating screw.
5	Check that safety valve opening pressure is 50–100 KPa (7–14 lb/in^2) above compressor working pressure. To change opening pressure Turn clockwise to increase opening pressure. Turn counter-clockwise to reduce opening pressure.

Figure 7.16 Job specification

A list of routines is drawn up for each area and, if necessary, for each trade. Each list is then further divided into routines that are to be carried out each shift, every one to four weeks, and every one to twelve months. The shift routines are detailed on a simple check list which is held by the supervisor. The weekly to four-weekly tasks are listed on four cards, one for each of four weeks. Weekly work is listed (see Figure 7.17) on all four cards, two-weekly on two cards and monthly on one card. The work is distributed so as to even out the workload over the month. Monthly to twelve-monthly work is dealt with in the same way.

Card No.	Description	Interval	Job Spec. No.	Procedure
9-1-2	Sulzer Compressor I	1 w	12	Check temperature of bearings, motor, not above 75°C
				Clean intake filter and oil sparingly.
				Check V-belt tension.
				Drain air tank.
				Check compressor oil level.
				Test safety valve
9-1-9	Sulzer Compressor 2	1 w	12	As above.
2-1-4	Dilution water pump 2	2 w	2	Check temp. of bearings, pump and motor not above 75°C
				Check for noise, vibration and leakage.
2-1-1	Dilution water pump 1	2 w	2	As above.
6-1-2	Level control	4 w	2	Check oil level in control.
				Check wire and pulley wheels.
				Check motor. Must not be hot to touch.
2-4-7	EXP-pump 1	2 w	6.7	Check temp. of bearings, pump and motor, not above 75°C
				Check for noise, vibration and leakage.
				Check oil level in bearing housing.

Figure 7.17 Mechanical weekly routine list

Unit No. 5-20	Description Compressor, instrumentation air, No.1	
Observation		
V-belts worn	**Date reported** 1 Jan. '77	
Should be replaced	**Reported by** BT	
Activity	**Date completed**	
	Sign.	
Spare parts used		

Figure 7.18 Report card

The lists are held in simple dropleaf files and issued with blank Report Cards (Figure 7.18) to tradesmen. Defects that cannot be dealt with directly are indicated on the Report Card and the necessary work initiated via the Work Order System.

Jobs which can be scheduled which necessitate stopping the plant are listed on the Plant Inventory Record Card. The 2000 hr service (Specification No. 24) for the Atlas Copco compressor of Figure 7.15 was scheduled for January '77, the previous service having been in January '76. Each month the planner determines from the Record Cards the off-line jobs that are scheduled for the following month and initiates a Work Order (see Figure 7.19) for each. Since this contains the job specification number, the tradesman can readily consult the specification if he so wishes. The deferred corrective jobs (each initiated by a Work Order) are scheduled to coincide with the preventive jobs, wherever possible. Emergency defects are handled directly via the Work Order system.

Control

Work control is achieved by using the information on the Routine Lists, Report Cards and Work Orders to update short-term planning-boards. Condition control is achieved through the information contained in the Work Order Card, under the heading 'Job Report'. This information is recorded on a History Record Card (see Figure 7.20), which is filed behind the Plant Inventory Record Card.

Comments

The main features of this system are the division of work into on-line and off-line schedules, and the use of a job specification manual. This is typical of an Idhammar Konsult[2] design (see page 205 for the computerised version). Its advantage is that it minimises the flow of paperwork between planning office and shop floor. It is suitable only for relatively small maintenance departments because of the considerable clerical effort required for the updating of the Record Cards.

WORK ORDER	Plant Description Compressor instr. air No. 1	No. 5-20
		Instr. No.
Planned month Jan. 77	Activity No. 24	
Planned place 8300		
Planned op. time		
Performed date 5 Jan. 77	Work report Completed. Pressure valves replaced	
Operation time 8360		
Sign AB		
spare parts 1 set pressure valves HP A2 72033		

E 140

Figure 7.19 Work order card

Date	Notes about repairs cause of defects, clearances, special remarks, etc.
2 Jan 74	Pressure valve changed
29 Jan 75	Discharge pipe changed LP-side
3 Jan 76	All suction and pressure valves changed.

E174

Figure 7.20 History record

A preventive maintenance documentation system for a large process plant

The previous two systems are not sufficiently flexible for the complexities of scheduling work on a large process plant (e.g. an oil refinery or a batch output chemical plant). The system to be described[3] was designed for an offshore oil platform where unavailability cost could amount to millions of pounds a day.

Plant inventory and information base

Each unit (termed 'equipment' in this system) is identified by a coding, of which the following is an example:

PD	10	GM	10	01	A
System	Sub-system	Equipment	Sub-system	Sequence No.	Line
(Production)	(Produced oil)	(Pump, Elect. Motor)	(Produced oil)	(No. in line)	(Line identification if several in parallel)

It will be noticed that the code for produced oil occurs twice. This is because within the sub-system only the latter part of the code is used i.e. GM 1001 A in this case.

An Inventory Index manual, a page of which is shown in Figure 7.21, references Equipment Record Cards (Figure 7.22), and Technical Record Cards (Figure 7.23) which are held in simple drop-leaf files. The Equipment Record Card carried the basic information needed by maintenance management should they wish to obtain information from outside. For example, the purchase order number indicates the original specification which is also drop-leaf filed. The drawing numbers refer to the operational and general arrangement drawings for the sub-system and the equipment. The Technical Record Card carries references to drawings, manuals, and the relevant entries in the spare parts catalogue.

Preventive maintenance system

This is built around a set of job specifications for each piece of equipment. Figure 7.24 shows one such specification and is not untypical in that most of the procedures listed are some form of inspection. The specifications are classified by equipment, trade and frequency, (e.g. Separator Product Pump PD 10 G 1003, Electrical, 6 monthly) and include references to tools, instruments, drawings and spares required to carry out the work. Minor maintenance tasks (e.g. oil checks, cleaning duties) are performed by the plant operators and are initiated by Operator Service Check Sheets (see Figure 7.25) issued by the Supervisor of the particular Plant Area who himself plans this short-term work.

Because the job specifications are the basis of this system, considerable time and information is needed for their formulation. Some of the information comes direct from the manufacturer, some from mandatory

SUB-SYSTEM		EQUIPMENT/PACKAGE		EQUIPMENT TITLE	INVENTORY REFERENCE		CRITICALITY
Title	Ref. No.	Number	Location		Vol.	Page	
Produced Oil	PD10	C1001	M04	First Stage Separator	2	PD10-1	Primary
		C1002	M04	Second Stage Separator	2	PD10-2	Primary
		C1003	M04;MZ	Third Stage Separator	2	PD10-3	Vital
		C1004	M04;MZ	Test/Clean UP Separator	2	PD10-4	Vital
		C1006A/B	CD	Oil Surge Tanks	2	PD10-5	Vital
		E1001A1/B1 A2/B2	M04;MZ	Interstage Oil Coolers	2	PD10-9	Primary
		E1002A1/B1	M04;MZ	Test/Clean UP Separator Oil Cooler	2	PD10-10	Vital
		E1003A-F	M05	Lube Oil Cooler for G 1002A-C	2	PD10-11	Secondary
		E1004A-F	M05	Lube Oil Heater for 1002A-C	2	PD10-12	Secondary
		G1001A-C	M04	Pipeline Booster Pumps	2	PD10-13	Primary
		G1002A-C	M05	Pipeline Pumps	2	PD10-15	Primary
		G1003	M04	Test/Clean Up Separator Product Pump	2	PD10-17	Vital
		G1004A/B	CD	Oil Surge Tanks Transfer Pumps	2	PD10-19	Primary
		G1006A-C	M05	Lube Oil Pumps for G 1002A-C	2	PD10-21	Primary
		G1010A/B	M05	Pipeline Hi-Flo Booster Pumps	2	PD10-38	Vital
		Y1001-10	M02/M03 MZ	Production Wellheads	2	PD10-38	Vital
		Y1013/14	M02/M03 MZ	Production Wellheads	2	PD10-38	Vital

SYSTEM PRODUCTION (PD)   SUB SYSTEM REF.   SUB SYSTEM REF. PD 10

Page No.   PD10 - 1

Figure 7.21 Inventory index

172

LOCATION		EQUIPMENT NUMBER		TITLE	VENDOR(A)-MANUFACTURER(B) TYPE AND/OR CAPACITY		PURCHASE ORDER NUMBER	DRAWINGS Ref Documentation Register		CRITICALITY
								Vol	Number	
PD	M 04	G 1001	3	Pipeline Booster Pump	A+B	Weirs Pumps Ltd. Size/Type OK 1B 45 Capacity 35.3/460.8 m^3/HR Serial Nos. A 11556-001 B 11556-002 C 11556-003	10200 GO1LAC	2 5 5 5 5 5	10200 EA 208 10200 GO1 04 10200 GO1 18 10200 GO1 22 10200 GO1 34 10200 GO1 41 10200 GO1 42	Primary
PD	M 04	GM 1001	3	Motor	B	Brook Crompton Parkinson Frame: E 280Mb Enclosure:1P54Ex'd' 11AT3 Rating 82kW Supply 415V 3ph 50Hz Serial Nos. A L910425 B L910426 C L910427		5 5	10200 GO1 04 10200 GO1 26	Primary
			3	Coupling	B	Type: Metastream TSP 60 Flexible		5	10200 GO1 04	Primary

SUB SYSTEM   PRODUCED OIL (PD10)   TDC CODE   PD10 G 1001A-C   Page No.   PD10-13

Figure 7.22 Equipment record card

SITE	MURCHISON		
EQUIPMENT	G1002A - PIPELINE PUMP		
LOCATION	M 05	AREA CLASSIFICATION	HAZARDOUS 2
COMMISSIONING DATE		PURCHASE ORDER NO.	10200 G01 LAC
SUB SYSTEM	PD10 - PRODUCED OIL		
CRITICALITY	PRIMARY		

DRAWINGS/MANUALS

EDR 10200EA208	EFD Pipeline Pump and Pig Launcher
EDR 10200 G01 - 15	General Arrangement
EDR 10200 G01 - 03	Outline of 2 Pole Induction Motors
EDR 10200 G01 - 43	Sectional Arrangement Induction Motor
EDR 10200 G01 - 38	Sectional Arrangement Pipeline Pump
EDR 10200 G01 - 21	Mechanical Seal Layout
EDR 10200 G01 - 35	Mechanical Seal Assembly
EDR 10200 G01 - 52	Arrangement of Flange Motors with Single Shaft Extension

EQUIPMENT Pipeline Pump

SPARES REFERENCE

VENDOR (A) MANUFACTURER (B) LOCAL AGENT (C)

A. & B. Pump

Weir Pumps Ltd.,
Cathcart,
Glasgow ,
Scotland.
G44 4EX

Telephone 041-637-7141

Telex 77161/2

B. Motor

Parsons Peebles,
Motors and Generators Ltd.,
Edinburgh,
Scotland.
EG5 2XT

Telephone 031-552-6261

Telex 72125

CODE PD10 - G1002A

PIPELINE PUMP	WEIR PUMPS LTD.	G1002 A
Year Built		
Type	OK 6D 38	
Serial No.	11565-004	
Speed	2960rpm	
Pressure/Temperature	100.3 bar abs @ 20°C	
Capacity	375.3 to 460.8m^{3}/hr	
Weight	3587 kg	
Power Consumption	1306 kw	

Figure 7.23 Technical record card

Bearings - (Type)	Radial: Sleeve Glacier 090-KSA-065	Thrust: Tilting Pad Glacier M8190-2P-2P
Seals	Borg-Warner (Mechanical) Glacier GB267-100	GU5250-5125- 5J4H-5N4A
Lubricant	Turbo 29	
Hydrostatic Test Pressure (Max)	150 bar g	

COUPLING   FLEXIBOX LTD

Type   Metastream M600S Flexible

DRIVER	PARSONS PEEBLES	GM1002 A
Year Built	1978	
Type/Frame No.	MC63011J	
Serial No.	256109/1	
Speed	2975 rpm	
Weight	8200 kg	
Power Supply	11000V 3ph 50Hz	
Rating	Continuous (1306kW output)	
Full Load Current	81.5 amp	
Insulation Class	F (With Class B (80°C) rise)	
Enclosure	CACW	
Bearings	Sleeve: 4in dia x 5½in long white metal lines	
Lubricants	Turbo 29	
Specification	BS5000 Pt/99	

CONTROL GEAR   B/GEC SWITCHGEAR LTD

Starter/Isolator-

Type   MX51S

Rating   630 amp

Serial No.   61517D

Figure 7.23 Cont.

safety requirements and some from the experience of the users and consultants.

The maintenance plan and schedule can best be described by reference to the *Five-year Master Schedule* of Figure 7.26. It can be seen that the Produced Oil System has been divided into a number of identifiable sub-systems (e.g. the Pumpdown Tool System which is made up of seven pieces of equipment). A separate maintenance plan and a set of instruction booklets is prepared for such a sub-system either because it can be isolated for maintenance purposes or because it presents a workload of convenient size. Thus, Package No. 201 contains all the specifications for the jobs carried out monthly on the Pumpdown Tool System. Likewise, Package No. 204 contains the specifications for the twelve monthly work. For convenience, only one job instruction booklet, containing all the job specifications for the Pumpdown Tool System, is issued. The master

EQUIPMENT	SEPARATOR PRODUCT PUMP			JOB NO	
TDC CODE		CRITICALITY	CRAFT	JOB SHEET NO	
SYSTEM	EQUIP.NO.	Vital	Electrical		
PD10	G 1003				
LOCATION		EST. M/HOURS	FREQUENCY	TASKS	
M 04			6 Monthly (6M)	01 – 09	
REFERENCES Mechanical Equipment Catalogue Vol. 10200 DP 053 Insulation Resistance Log Lubrication Schedule				BS4683-1971 BS5405-1976 BSCP1011-1961 BSCP1003-1964	
MATERIALS REQUIRED Bridge Megger Megger Tester Portable Vaccuum Cleaner Grease Gun					

TASK NO.	JOB INSTRUCTIONS	TASK COMP.
	MOTOR INSULATION RESISTANCE TEST	
	NOTE 1 Before commencing ensure full Electrical Lock Out Procedure has been completed	
	NOTE 2 Report any defects found.	
6M 01	Check the balance of the Stator resistance between phases.	
6M 02	Examine security and rightness of all connections, do not overtighten. Examine for evidence of overheating or tracking. Clean and blow out interior of terminal chambers, using portable vacuum cleaner.	
6M 03	Measure insulation resistance of motor and anti-condensation heater. Log results and whether Hot or Cold, then compare with previous readings. Any marked decrease is to be investigated immediately and value restored to a minimum acceptable figure.	
6M 04	Confirm cleanliness and security of motor earthing arrangements. Measure continuity resistance between motor frame and earth.	
	ISOLATOR/CONTACTOR – SWITCHBOARD PS 4008 PANEL M7	
6M 05	Operate several times to ensure that it is in good working order	

INFORMATION, REMARKS, PARTS USED – USE REVERSE SIDE		
AMENDMENT STATUS Rev. June 1979 0	TOTAL M/HOURS	COLD WORK PERMIT NO

Figure 7.24 Job specification form

176

Operator Service Check Sheet

MONTH _____ 19__

EQUIPMENT	S_T V_S	O_P S	1	2	3	4	5	6	7	8	9	10	11	12	13	14	15	16	17	18	19	20	21	22	23	24	25	26	27	28	29	30	31	$T_{A_{S_K}}$	SERVICE

FP 5151A/B EMULSION BREAKER No. 1 DOSING PUMPS — AE OP1

- S2: See Page 1.
- 5D1: Turn shafts of idle pumps (minimum 2½ turns).
- T1: See Page 1.
- T2: Check gearbox oil level correct (Mobilgear 629) Change over duty pumps.
- M1: Observe operation of local controlling instrumentation:- LSLL 5800) Pump auto-stop from CT 5009A/B via LSLL 5803) selector switch HS 5800

CT 5009A/B EMULSION BREAKER No. 1 TANKS — AE OP1

- D1: Monitor and record tank level. Refill on low level. Record usage.
- T1: See Page 1.

Page No. 5

Module   C17

Notes: 1 Each Shift Cross-tick tasks completed   ● SHIFT 1 0000-1200
       2 Each Tour Supervisor Countersign   O SHIFT 2 1200-2400
       3 Use reverse side for remarks as necessary

Supervisors   1 _____ Date _____
Signature   2 _____ Date _____
              3 _____ Date _____

Figure 7.25 Operator check sheet

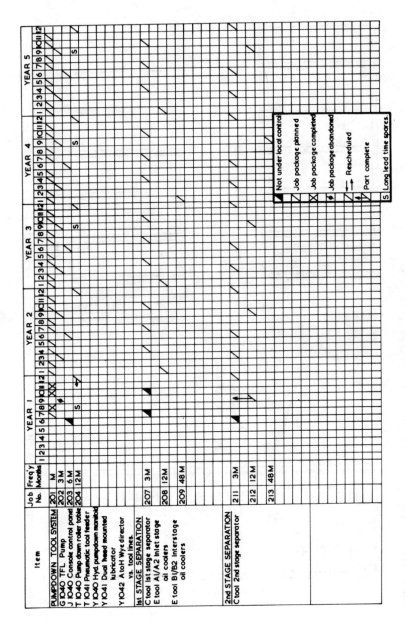

Figure 7.26 Extract from five-year master schedule

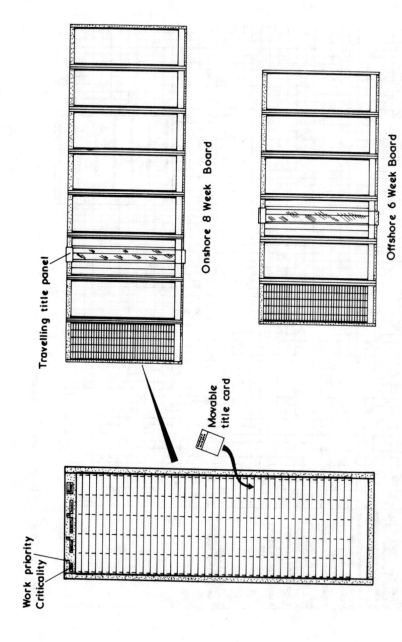

Figure 7.27 Short term planning boards

schedule facilitates smoothing and control of the total workload, for the whole platform, over a 5-year period.

The *Long-Term Onshore Schedule* covers a period of 12 months and is an extract of the relevant section of the master schedule. It goes into more detail, scheduling and smoothing the weekly workloads, with the aid of a magnetic planning board. One of its main functions is to ensure the ordering and availability of spares with long lead times.

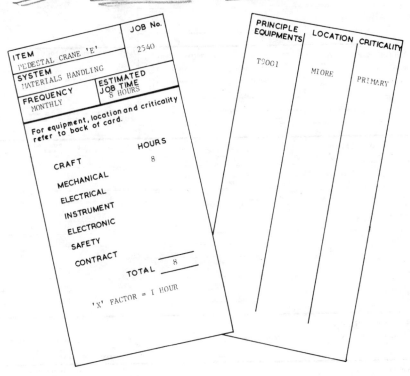

Figure 7.28 Planning cards

The *Short-Term Onshore Scheduling* covers a period of eight weeks and is constructed with the aid of a deep-slot planning-board (see Figure 7.27) into which planning cards for each job package (see Figure 7.28) are mounted. Each planning card represents a package of work (e.g. Package No. 201) and a different colour is used for cards representing monthly, three-monthly, six-monthly frequencies. This schedule identifies the platform workload for the month ahead so that the necessary resources and information can be sent.

Work Order System—Planning and Scheduling (Offshore)

Offshore preventive maintenance planning is carried out with the aid of deep-slot six-week planning-board and planning cards, (see Figure 7.27). The board is updated, in the light of the onshore board, once each month. The preventive work is planned by the week and the daily workload is

WORK ORDER
(COLD WORK PERMIT)

SERIAL № 30

SECTION 1 DESCRIPTION OF DEFECT/WORK		
	PRIORITY	PM JOB No.
	EQUIPMENT	
	EQUIPMENT No.	LOCATION
	ORIGINATOR	DATE

SECTION 2 SAFETY REQUIREMENTS

BREATHING EQUIPT ☐ PROTECTIVE CLOTHING ☐

HOT WORK/ENTRY PERMIT No _____ LIFE LINE ☐ LIFE JACKET ☐

ELECTRICAL WORK PERMIT No _____ EYE PROTECTION ☐ EAR PROTECTION ☐

PLANT/SYSTEMS/DRILLING SUPVR. DATE

ASSIGNED TO (No. of Men_____)

I HAVE READ AND UNDERSTOOD THE WORK INSTRUCTIONS AND SAFETY REQUIREMENTS

_____ SIGNED

SECTION 3 DEGREE OF ISOLATION

A ELECTRICAL

	REQ'D	OPERATIONS LOCK	MAINTENANCE LOCK
Main Breaker Locked Open			

B MECHANICAL

Valve/Blind Status

C SYSTEMS

SECTION 4 ISOLATION AND APPROVAL

THE EQUIPMENT IS ISOLATED AS ABOVE AND IS NOW SAFE TO WORK UPON _____ OPERATIONS SUPERVISOR

_____ OPERATIONS AND MAINTENANCE SUPERVISOR

SECTION 5 ACTION TAKEN _____

MATERIAL VOUCHER No

TOTAL MANHOURS

ELECTRICAL_____ MECHANICAL_____

INSTRUMENT_____ ELECTRONIC_____

CONTRACT_____ SAFETY_____

SECTION 6 DE-ISOLATION AND COMPLETION

I CERTIFY THAT THE EQUIPMENT IS READY FOR DE-ISOLATION AS FAR AS MY WORK IS CONCERNED AND I HAVE REMOVED MY LOCKS _____ ELECTRICAL _____ MECHANICAL _____ SYSTEMS

OPERATIONS LOCKS REMOVED AND PLANT MADE AVAILABLE _____ OPERATIONS

ACCOUNT	DEPT	COST CENTRE	SUB CODE	FEATURE	LABOUR	MATERIALS	OS	TOTAL

Figure 7.29 Example of work order

drawn off the planning board at daily meetings that take into consideration plant availability, resource availability and the corrective and modification work on hand. The onshore board is updated from the platform each day via telex reports.

Before it can be carried out, each preventive or corrective job requires a safety permit which also acts as a work order (see Figure 7.29). The flow and function of this work order system is similar to that of Figure 6.7. The information on Work Orders is also used by the Operations Supervisor to keep a record, on his Manpower Deployment Board, of the location of maintenance personnel.

Control

The work control system is similar to the systems already described and need not be discussed. Plant condition control is achieved through information feedback via entries on work order cards and also via tradesmen's entries on the back of the individual job sheets which are part of the job instruction booklet. This information is sent back to the onshore planning office, recorded in the equipment's History Record and acted upon as necessary. Where decisions have been taken on-shore as a result of this, a preventive maintenance report detailing the actions to be taken is sent to the platform.

Comments

This is a large system and considerable effort is involved in establishing the information base and preventive maintenance system. In addition, considerable clerical effort is needed for operating and continually updating the planning boards and information base. The History Record analysis is prohibitively time-consuming. It is no surprise, therefore, that it has been decided to computerise the system.

Documentation system based on a job catalogue

A unique electro-mechanical method of card storage and selection has been developed by Kalamazoo[4] (see Figure 7.30). This, coupled with photocopying, allows a maintenance documentation system to be developed around a catalogue of these jobs, the majority of which can be covered by individual job specifications. The following description will concentrate on this feature since the other parts of the system are similar to those already described.

Plant inventory and information base

Each unit of plant is numbered, using a method similar to that of the PERA system. Plant Inventory Record Cards and History Record Cards are held in visible-edge files.

Figure 7.30 Kalamazoo fact finder

Preventive maintenance system

This also divides the preventive work into on-line routines—carried out without special planning—and off-line jobs that do need such planning.

The specification for each off-line job (there might be a number of these for each unit) is entered on a blank punched-edge card, as shown in Figure 7.31(a). Included on the card is a list of spares and references to manuals and drawings required. On the reverse side of the card (see Figure 7.31(b)) is the unit's description, identification number, location details, etc., and job information such as frequency, priority and trades and time required. Each job is scheduled into an appropriate week (with the help of a twelve-month bar chart) and the card is punched at that week number. Other selection information is then punched on the card edges and might include identification number, trade, job type, priority, etc.

The *on-line work* is classified into area, trade and periodicity. For each area, a card is made out for every routine, with periodicity, scheduled week or month, and other details punched on the appropriate edge indexes.

The planning office can extract the weekly off-line load for each area and trade by loading the cards into the Kalamazoo Factfinder, setting the selector bars to the required week and switching on the vibrator, which causes all the cards for that week to drop; these are then further divided by area and trade. The cards for the on-line routines can be similarly sorted.

Information on irregularly recurring jobs is also held on Factfinder cards, those for a particular unit being extracted when corrective work on that unit is needed. The advantage is that the job methods and drawings are listed ready.

In general, photocopy of each card (or of part thereof) is taken and acts as a Work Order. By placing the relevant cards in visible record format, as shown in Figure 7.32, the weekly (or shutdown) summary can likewise be produced. The planning office sends this summary, with the Work Orders, to the Area Supervisor who allocates the work. The operation is completed by the execution of the work and feedback of information.

WORK ORDER

G. 121 — BUILDING ZONE REF. NO.

PLANT DESCRIPTION: **Wulff Plant**

PLANT ITEM NO.: **4281**

MAINTENANCE: **PREVENTIVE**

PRIORITY: **A**

TRADE: **Mech.**

TIME ALLOCATED: **$2\frac{3}{4}$ hrs.**

AVAILABLE

ELECTRICAL INSPECTION 216
Blg. No. G. 121 UNIT No. 4281
Process   Wulff Plant
Item Starter-Sec. Stripper Btms Pump No. 2
Mech.   Item and No.
Matce Routine   Cost Code 5334
NATURE OF WORK - STARTER INSPECTIONS

		Item No.	Std. Time Per Man Hrs.	Std. Time Per Man Mins.	TIME TAKEN ON Hrs.	TIME TAKEN ON Mins.	TIME TAKEN OFF Hrs.	TIME TAKEN OFF Mins.	TOTAL HRS.	TOTAL MINS.
1	Isolate unit in accordance with regulations	1	-	25						
2	Check condition of the main and auxiliary contacts and that the spring pressures are satisfactory	2	-	15						
3	Ensure that all connections are electrically and mechanically sound	3		10						
4	Check level and appearance of the switch tank oil, and oil of the immersed potential transformers. If oil is discoloured, or if black deposit is detected on mechanism, contacts or arc suppression devices, change oil	4	1	5						
5	Check that operating mechanism works smoothly and positively and that contacts close in correct sequence	5		15						
6	Check that phase barriers are clean and undamaged	6		10						
7	For contactor operated starters, check that air gap between closing magnet poles is within specified limits	7		5						
8	Ensure that shading rings and pull off springs, where provided, are in order	8		5						
9	Check for looseness of contactor coils and rectify	9		15						

STANDARD MANNING	(NO. OF TASK CARDS TO BE ISSUED)	TOTAL	

THIS SHEET MUST BE RETURNED TO THE ISSUING OFFICE WITHIN _____ DAYS OF ISSUE
DETAILS OF REPAIRS UNDERTAKEN OR REQUIRED SHOULD BE ENTERED ➤

REASON FOR DIVERGENCE FROM STD. TIME & REPAIRS UNDERTAKEN OR REQUIRED

SPECIAL TOOLS REQUIRED

SPECIAL SPARES REQUIRED	DRAWINGS AND MANUAL REFERENCES

OPERATIVE'S NAME	CLOCK NO.	PAYMENT CODE	JOB CARD SERIAL NO.

Figure 7.31(a) Job specification (front)—acts as work order when photocopied

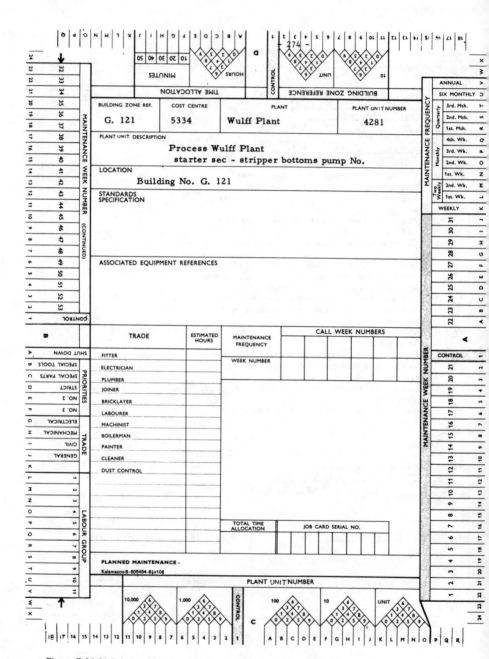

Figure 7.31(b) Job specification (back)—technical and planning data

TO ....ISSUE DATE ....MAINTENANCE NOTIFICATION SCHEDULE   WEEK No.........

The following maintenance work falls due for the week commencing Monday, the ....of ....19.....
Please arrange when the work may be started, and enter the day and time agreed in the appropriate space in the
schedule. Indicate also whether plant labour is available for the work, or whether additional labour is required.
Please return the completed schedule to the Planning Department.

Signed ....

Planning Engineer

Building zone ref. no.	Plant description	Plant item no.	Maintenance	Priority	Trade	Time allocated	Available
G.121	Wulff Plant	21703	Prev. M		Elect.	45 mins.	
G.121	Wulff Plant	4281	Prev. M		Mech.	2¼ hours	
G.121	Wulff Plant	16251	Prev. M		Elect.	1¼ hours	
G.121*	Wulff Plant	26957	Major PM		Mech.	1¾ hours	
G.121	Wulff Plant	10267	Prev. M		Mech.	30 mins.	
G.121	Wulff Plant	29576	Prev. M		Mech.	2 hours	
G.121	Wulff Plant	19243	Prev. M.		Elect.	30 mins.	
G.121	Wulff Plant	24139	Prev. M		Mech.	45 mins.	
G.121	Wulff Plant	20259	Prev. M		Elect.	20 mins.	

Figure 7.32 Weekly summary of preventive maintenance

Comments

Up to 3000 record cards can be sorted in as little as 45 minutes. The 'job catalogue' method, used in conjunction with the Factfinder, cuts down the clerical effort involved in operating a documentation system for providing detailed information about each job.

Although the Factfinder can store specifications of irregularly occurring jobs, it cannot be used for scheduling such work and this must be done with the help of conventional planning boards.

History Records could also be entered on punched-edged cards to facilitate sorting of failure and cost data. The Factfinder offers a low-cost method of handling preventive maintenance documentation, combined with some of the advantages of computerisation.

References

1. Corder, A.S. *Maintenance Management Techniques*, McGraw Hill, 1975.
2. Idhammar Konsult A.B., Viksansvagen 10, 5-151-57, Sodertalje, Sweden.
3. Mainwork Ltd., 24 West Street, Porchester, Hants. PO16 942, U.K.
4. Kalamazoo Business Systems, Northfield, Birmingham B31 2KW, U.K.

Chapter 8

Some computerised documentation systems

Computer technology has developed extremely rapidly over the last ten years and a wide variety of computerised documentation systems have become available. Early applications in the field of maintenance were based on expensive and powerful main-frame machines. These were shared with other departments and data was processed in batches, often at night or at weekends if the maintenance function was considered to be of low priority. This limited maintenance usage to the more straightforward tasks, such as the scheduling of preventive routines. However such tasks form only a part of a full planning and control operation. In order to have an effective computerised maintenance system, that carries out all the functions of Figure 6.1, it is essential that the computer is available on demand for interactive work (on-line processing).

The development of on-line maintenance systems has been rendered possible by the introduction of improved data-handling techniques for storing and retrieving data (database techniques—a method of storing data on disc that facilitates on-line output and input via VDU). Such techniques allow time-sharing, i.e. the on-line use of the computer by a number of users. In addition the advent of less expensive but relatively powerful machines has meant that computers can be dedicated solely to the maintenance function.

Maintenance systems currently in operation fall into the following categories.

(i) Those which use a main-frame, jointly with other departments or sites, on a time-sharing basis. Such systems are restricted to large organisations that can justify the possession of a main frame computer. The maintenance system is multi-user i.e. several terminals (VDUs) are connected to the computer, but often has low priority of usage and although the computer is on-line the response times might be slow.

(ii) Those which use a dedicated mini-computer backed up by a time-shared main-frame computer (distributed processing). The maintenance system is multi-user and, to facilitate immediate access, the main functions are on the mini. Such systems are expensive but permit adoption of the full software package required by a large plant.

(iii) Those which use a dedicated mini-computer only. These systems are mostly multi-user and can provide on-line processing of the totality of documentation required by medium size and small plant. Such systems are less expensive than those of (ii) above and the majority of computerised maintenance packages in current use fall into this category.

(iv) Those which use a micro-computer. These are relatively cheap. However, they are only single-user, small core-storage, and their mainstorage is on floppy disks. The processing capacity of a computer is indicated by the size of its core storage. Typically a micro has 32 Kbytes core-storage, a main-frame 8000 Kbytes (1000 Kbytes = 1 Mbyte = 200 pages A4). The main data storage of a computer is held on disk, usually on hard disk connected permanently to the computer. A floppy disk can hold only 500 Kbytes of storage, which is much less than can be held on hard disk. Floppy disks are stored and loaded into a disk drive as required. Micro-computers are therefore slow in operation and only allow full documentation in the case of a small plant. If, however, their use is limited to one aspect of documentation, e.g. compilation of a history record, this can be tackled on a considerable scale.

Micro-computers of increased power are beginning to appear on the market. These allow hard-disk storage and may be connected to a small number of terminals. Such machines are cheaper than those of (iii) and will compete in the same market. Another development is the network connection of a number of micro-computers (distributed processing) to form a multi-user system.

Examples of categories (ii) and (iv) will be outlined and discussed in terms of the general model of Figure 6.1

A mainframe-based system

This[1] is in operation at one of the largest ironmaking works in Europe, part of the British Steel Corporation (BSC). The works is made up of some 7600 units of plant, covers an area of approximately 13 km^2, and has a capital value of about £600 million. The maintenance force is about 600 strong and completes about 6000 discrete jobs each week.

It was decided during the plant design that handling of the vast amount of maintenance information that would be generated would have to be computerised. Mainframe dedication to this purpose would have been far too expensive. Mainframe sharing, with batch processing, would have been insufficiently flexible and too costly in clerical effort. It was therefore decided to install a distributed processing system—a dedicated mini-computer backed up by a shared mainframe computer (see Figure 8.1 and Table 8.1). The hardware cost (much less than that of a dedicated mainframe) is mainly that of the mini-computer and associated terminals. The advantage of the system is that it gives considerable flexibility in the method of data storage and processing.

The quantity of data held on the mini-computer is limited to the capacity of the disk drive (192 megabytes), but the data can be updated, interrogated or extracted as desired, on-line. A much greater quantity can be held

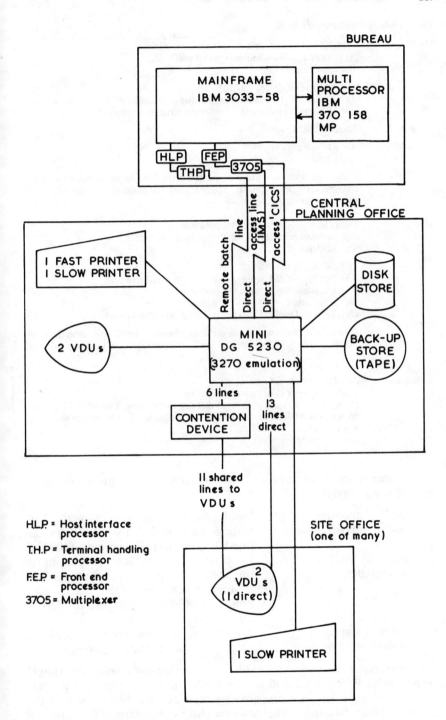

Figure 8.1 Hardware system

TABLE 8.1. System hardware details

Mainframe:	IBM 3033-58 backed by a 370/158 multiprocessor Approximate cost £4.5 million over 5 years The IBM 3033-58 has

  (i) 8 Mbyte core store (RAM)
  (ii) 10,200 Mbyte disk storage (34 disk drive units at 300 Mbyte each)
  (iii) the capacity to handle 2.5 million instructions per sec (2.5 mlps)

The 370/158 MP has

  (i) 8 Mbyte core store
  (ii) 1.7 mlps

(Note: the multiprocessor is connected to the 3033-58 and allows it to carry out operations more quickly. The processor can perform a number of processes simultaneously).

Mini: Data General 5230 with 32 70 emulation
Approximate cost £200,000 with terminals and cables
The 5230 has

  (i) 384 Kbyte core store
  (ii) 192 Mbyte disk storage and a single disk drive unit
       (magnetic tape is used as a backup)
  (iii) a fast printer (600 lines per minute)
  (iv) 2 Visual Display Units (VDU) used as control consoles

(Note: 32 70 emulation allows the data general terminal to speak to the IBM machine. The 3270 Emulator translates the messages into IBM terminal protocol).

Terminals: 24 VDUs by Data General
12 slow printers (180 characters per sec)
(Note: 13 VDUs are connected directly to the mini. The other 11 VDUs have to share 6 lines controlled by a contention device which gives access on a first come first served basis).

---

on the main frame and can be updated, interrogated or extracted in any of the following ways:

(i) On line updating
    on-line interrogation

Needs database storage (a method of storing data on disk that facilitates on-line VDU output). Expensive—£1000/hr.

(ii) Batch updating,
     batch output

Information for storage or updating is prepared on tape or punched card to facilitate batch input. Cost of computer time low—£300/hr—but cost of clerical effort high.

(iii) Batch updating
      on-line interrogation

An economic compromise but files are only up-to-date to the last input.

On-line input and output are via VDU keyboard and display (or printer) respectively. Batch input and output are via magnetic tape and printer. The system programs are prepared on tape and batch-entered into the mini-computer disk store. The mini-computer then operates the system in response to on-line receipt of instructions; it can use data from its own store or can interrogate the mainframe database.

Planning structure

As indicated in Figure 8.1, maintenance planning is carried out at a number of levels.

The *Central Planning Office* is next to the main workshops and its main function is assisting the efforts of the site planning offices. It does this in three principal ways—

(i)   establishment of work programmes and co-ordination of resources required,
(ii) provision of a 24-hour maintenance information service,
(iii) provision of a management reporting service.

In order to do this the office can make use of the maintenance management systems listed in Figure 8.2 and indicated in Figure 8.3. The majority of these systems are held on the computer and can be accessed via two VDUs (one direct, one shared) and output via two printers (one fast, one slow). The Work Order Management programs (WEPAC and CEWSS) are held on the mini-computer and can be obtained via the menu listed in Table 8.2. Plant and Equipment Management programs and

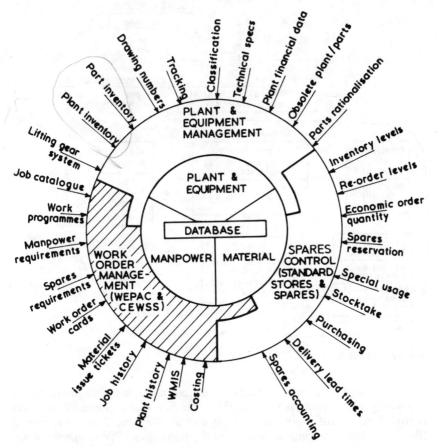

Figure 8.2 Maintenance management systems

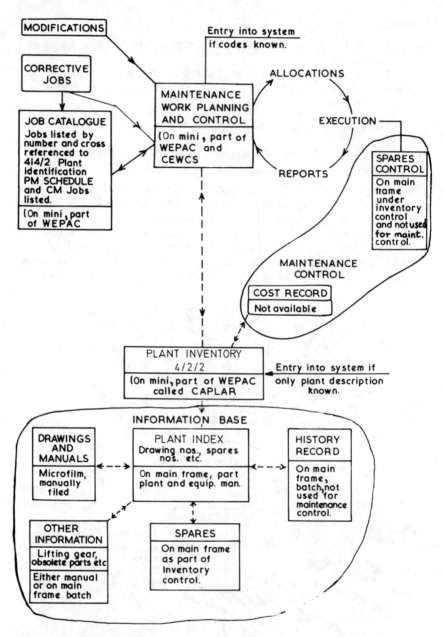

Figure 8.3 The BSC System

Spares Control programs are held on the mainframe, separate menus being accessed via key numbers (24 and 25) on the first menu. Some information is stored on microfilm or on manuals and drawings held in conventional files. Such information is accessed via the plant inventory number obtainable from the computer by using a plant description.

The Maintenance Management Systems are updated from the Central Planning Office. This reduces the administrative effort, and staff required, in the Site Planning Offices. Communication with site office, stores and personnel can be via telephone, VDU or two-way radio. The latter is particularly useful for direct communication with foremen and engineers on plant during a maintenance emergency.

TABLE 8.2. Engineering planning system menu

Key No.	Program
1	WORK PROGRAM INTERROGATION
2	JOB CATALOGUE INDEX
3	JOB CATALOGUE INTERROGATION
4	RANDOM FEEBACK
5	SIMPLE JOB FEEDBACK
6	FEEDBACK AGAINST WORK PROGRAM
7	INPUTS TO BATCH SYSTEM
8	CAPLAR INTERROGATION
9	WORK PROGRAM CALL-OFF
10	JOB CATALOGUE CREATION (RTS)
11	JOB CATALOGUE AMENDMENT
12	RTS JOB CATALOGUE KEY CREATE
13	WORK ORDER CARD SET-UP
14	TO BE DEVELOPED
15	JOB DELETION RTS AND BUREAU FILES
16	GROUP ITEM DELETIONS OFF RTS FILES
17	WORK PROGRAM SPARES LIST
18	WORK PROGRAM MANNING LIST
19	MAJOR STOP WORK PROGRAM
20	BLOCK CANCELLATION
21	PRELIMINARY PROGRAM
22	WORK PROGRAM LIST
23	CATALOGUE INDEX INTERROGATION
24	SPARES INTERROGATION
25	PLANT INDEX

The *Site Planning Offices* are located at the plant and at the area workshop. At each, a small number of planners work in conjunction with site engineers and Central Planning Office to prepare the work programmes and co-ordinate resource movement. There is a continual transfer of information between these groups of people via the VDUs, telephones and two-way radio. Each site office has two VDUs (one direct) and a slow printer.

Software

The relationship between the different parts of the Maintenance Management System is shown in Figure 8.3. The key to this system is the 4/2/2 plant number (see Figure 8.4) which accesses WEPAC and also the Plant Information Base. If the plant description is known, the number can be found from one of the WEPAC programs—CAPLAR—Computer Assisted Plant Registration (see Example 8.1). The CAPLAR program is held on the mini-computer and can be used on-line.

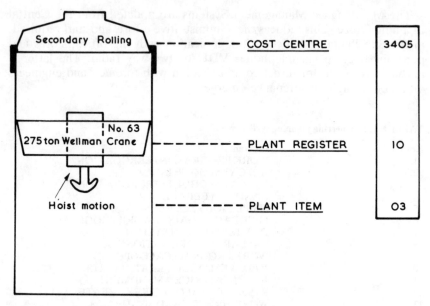

Figure 8.4 Example of a 4/2/2 plant identification number

The plant and equipment management system

This is the plant information base (see Figure 8.2). The programs most used are—

(i) The Plant Index: stored in data-base form on the mainframe and accessible on-line through the 4/2/2 plant number. It itemizes down to component level (see Figure 8.5) and gives stores codes and brief technical data for components and for 'exchangeable units' (see Example 8.2).

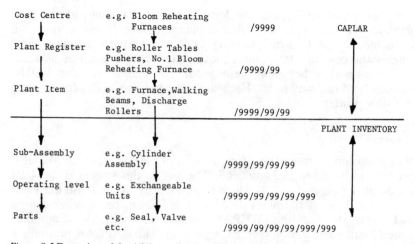

Figure 8.5 Extension of the 4/2/2 number for plant inventory purposes

TABLE 8.3. Printout of drawings listed against suppliers number

Program No. ORO 4   SUPPLIER/MANUFACTURER DRAWING NUMBER INDEX   Date 28/09/79   Time 14.28

SUPP/MAN — 3 ASHMORE SUPPLIER/ MANUFACTURER DRAWING NUMBER	BSC DRAWING NUMBER	ENG. FUNC CODES	DRAWING DESCRIPTION	CAPLAR REF.
2951/1973/122/521B	RBF 1560A	06 00 00 00 00	Dtls of ferrous bins sloping sides fbs 6 and 7	043/1508/23/09
2951/1973/122/526C	RBF 1561A	06 00 00 00 00	Dtls of ferrous bins sloping sides fbs 4 and 13	043/1508/23/25
2951/1973/122/5288	RBF 1562	06 00 00 00 00	Dtls of ferrous bins sloping sides for 1 and 2	043/1508/23/01
2951/1973/129/16	RBF 4638	01 06 00 00 00	Arrgi and dtls of wearing plates for fe weigh hopper	043/1508/23/05
2951/1973/235/55	RBF 110604	01 00 00 00 00	Lubrication system for clay gun 180 deg type	043/1508/45/13
2951/1973/350/26G	RBF 4090B	07 00 00 00 00	Dtls of clean gas main 1 of 4	043/1516/22/01
2951/1973/350/28M	RBF 2526D	07 00 00 00 00	Dtls of clean gas main sheet 3	043/1516/22/11
2951/1973/387/20	RBF 10497A	01 00 00 00 00	Stoves mcc sheet 2 of 2	043/1510/32/11
2951/1973/387/22	RBF 10498A	01 00 00 00 00	Stockhouse de dust coke side	043/1504/26/39
2951/1973/842/214A	RBF 557F	01 07 00 00 00	Shelved staves and stove valves cooling system flowsheet	043/1508/40/11
2951/1973/847/12R	RBF 559F	07 00 00 00 00	Effluent treatment flowsheet	043/1515/30/01
2951/1973/847/458	RBF 7877	01 04 00 00 00	Line no 11-450 egc-504 area 5 gas cleaning	043/1515/28/01
2951/1973/852/11W	RBF 561G	01 07 00 00 00	Nitrogen flowsheet—sheet 1	043/1516/85/01
2951/1973/853/11 2 of 2	RBF 5898B	07 00 00 00 00	Compressed air flowsheet	043/1520/30/01
2951/1973/853/11A	RBF 563E	07 00 00 00 00	Compressed air flowsheet sheet 1 of 2	043/1520/28/01
2951/1973/853/11R	RBF 563E	01 07 00 00 00	Compressed air flowsheet	043/1520/22/11

(ii) Spares Information : stored and accessed as above and is constructed from, and linked into, Stores Inventory Control. The inventory is updated every 48 hours.

(iii) Drawing Records and Amendment : a mixture of batch access mainframe storage and manual documentation. The batch output can be sorted in a number of ways. e.g. drawing number against the 4/2/2 code, Company number against Suppliers Number (see Table 8.3), or any combination of the above within function code i.e. civil, electrical, mechanical.

(iv) Lifting Gear : a separate batch-access mainframe-stored program producing three forms (recall note; examination report; safe order note) some three weeks before a statutory inspection. The forms are used to plan and control the inspection and after completion of the inspection are manually filed for scrutiny by the Factories Inspectorate (A UK government regulatory agency).

Work planning and maintenance control

These functions make use of those systems listed in Figure 8.2 under Work Order Management (WEPAC and CEWSS) and of information on parts usage provided by Inventory Control.

The basis of work planning is a computerised job specification catalogue. Each job has its own number and its specification includes the following information:

The 4/2/2 number of the plant to which the job refers,
The job class,
Responsibility (mechanical, electrical, etc)
Schedule (week and day) when last carried out,
Manning requirements and allowed time,
Spares requirements and stock number,
Spares delivery instructions,
Special tools required,
Mobile plant required,
Job procedure reference (filed separately at Site Office)—

This catalogue is built up by the Central Planning Office and the Site Office planners from known preventive work and from new jobs (e.g. emergency work) as and when they arise. A job is interrogated, entered, amended, or deleted from the catalogue by calling up the appropriate program on the WEPAC Menu (Table 8.2). Regularly occurring jobs are part of the on-going work program; irregularly occurring jobs lie dormant until included by request on a work program.

Once the Job Catalogue has been created the central and site planners can be provided with several useful programs, some automatic and some on-request, such as

Job catalogue index : (No. 2, Table 8.2) : an index of the jobs appearing in the catalogue against job number or against 4/2/2 plant number. Other basic information is also included.

Work program interrogation : (No. 1, Table 8.2) : a means of establishing for any week, or day, the work scheduled for a particular responsibility, cost centre or plant item.

Preliminary work program : (No. 21, Table 8.2) : provides on request, the work scheduled for a particular day up to 52 weeks ahead.

Provisional work program : a program of the work scheduled for the next two weeks is produced automatically each week.

Final work program : when the Plant Engineer is satisfied that the work on the Provisional Program is feasible and the list complete, a Final Program is requested using *work program call off* (No. 9, Table 8.2). This causes the Work Orders and Spares requisitions to be printed. Planners can also ask for the *spares list* (No. 17) and *Manning requirement* (No. 16) for any programs scheduled. A weekly *backlog report*, with a preliminary program for its clearance and an estimate of resources required, is produced automatically. Jobs on the backlog are those where work orders have been printed but no feedback about completion or delay received. *Feedback programs* (Nos 4, 5 and 6) allow information (causes of failure, resource hours used, etc.) on completed work to be fed in for updating programs and history records.

Maintenance control printouts can be requested. These contain, for example, the spares usage recorded against each plant number.

Planning a job into the current work program using WEPAC is illustrated in Example 8.3.

Comments

The computer is being used as an electronic filing cabinet. Visible-edge binders and drop-leaf files are replaced by computer storage, with programs for manipulating the data contained therein. The advantages of computerisation are exemplified by its use as a history record. If well programmed it can rapidly analyse large and complex files of information, providing a powerful control facility at minimal clerical cost.

The cost of setting up such a system, hardware plus software, is considerable. In addition considerable clerical effort has to go into providing the necessary operating data. The information base of this example needed some fifty man-years for its accumulation and the cost of this has to be weighed against potential future savings. In general, higher management would need to be assured of these savings, by a well thought out and quantified case, before commiting themselves to such large expenditure.

The most impressive part of the BSC system is the Information Base. This part of the system is considered invaluable by all the staff, especially the foremen and engineers. The Central Planning Office guarantees to respond to any emergency request in less than thirty minutes, such response to include delivery of drawings and spares (if in stores). This would not be possible at such a large plant without the on-line use of a computer.

Although extensively used, the WEPAC system has not proved so successful. It is particularly useful for scheduling preventive work, but not so for scheduling high-priority known jobs and emergency work. This latter relies heavily upon the discipline of the site planners and engineers. Work is often carried out without the necessary Work Order, thus by-passing the system and limiting the build up of the job catalogue.

In practice, the BSC system lacks maintenance control. This stems from poor Work Order discipline, cards not being handed back, or being scantily completed. Cost control is therefore ineffective and history recording patchy. Spare parts control, on the other hand, *is* effective because spares cannot be drawn from stores without a Stores Requisition.

To sum up, the BSC system is strong on work planning, weak on plant condition control and very weak indeed on cost and availability control.

EXAMPLE 8.1 Finding the 4/2/2 number for a gearbox of the No.35 Michigan 273 loading shovel

The planner uses the WEPAC system on the mini-computer and accesses CAPLAR INTERROGATION (No. 8 WEPAC menu). This gives him the following screen.

```
BSC–WORKS ENGINEERING PLANNING
                  CAPLAR DESCRIPTIONS
  1 LIST OF COST CENTRE DESCRIPTIONS
  2 LIST OF PLANT REGISTERS FOR SELECTED COST CENTRE
  3 LIST OF PLANT ITEMS FOR SELECTED COST CENTRE/PLANT REG.

    ENTER YOUR SELECTION HERE –
```

The planner selects 1, followed by 0, to obtain:

```
BSC–WORKS ENGINEERING PLANNING
                  COST CENTRE LIST FOR WORKS
Cost centre 1429 No 3 Stacker Reclaimer
            1431 Administration
            1435 No. 5 Boomstacker (Ore Blend)
            1436 No. 6 Boomstacker (Ore Blend)
            1437 No. 7 Boomstacker (Ore Blend)
            1439 No. 9 Barrel Reclaimer (Ore Blend)
            1440 No. 10 Barrel Reclaimer (Ore Blend)
            1443 No. 13 Boomstacker (Misc Stock)
            1444 No. 16 Stacker/Reclaimer (Coal Stock)
            1445 No. 17 Stacker/Reclaimer
            1446 No. 19 Boomstacker (Coal Blend)
            1447 No Caplar Record for this C.C.
            1448 No. 21 Barrel Reclaimer (Coal Blend)
            1451 Loading Shovel – Michigan 55(1) ROS
            1453 Loading Shovels – Michigan 275 ROS
            1454 Loading Shovel – Thomas (1) ROS
            1455 Dump Trucks Heathfields
            1456 Articulated Dozer-Michigan (1) ROS
            1457 Loading Shovels Michigan 275 Misc Stock

  ENTER COST CENTRE SELECTION ELSE ENTER ZEROES
    Enter 1 for Next Page    Enter 2 for End of Transaction
```

The planner selects 1457 to obtain:

BSC–WORKS ENGINEERING PLANNING
PLANT REGISTER LIST FOR A SELECTED
COST CENTRE
Cost centre 1457 Loading Shovels Michigan 275 Misc Stock
06 No. 33 Michigan 275 (S88)
07 No. 35 Michigan 275 (S18)
08 No. 38 Michigan 275 (S18)
00 Plant Register does not exist
.. ..
.. ..
.. ..
.. ..

ENTER PLANT REGISTER SELECTION ELSE ENTER ZEROES
Enter 1 for Next Page   Enter 2 for End of Transaction

The planner selects 07 and obtains:

BSC–WORKS ENGINEERING PLANNING
PLANT ITEM LISTED FOR SELECTION COST CENTRE/PLANT REG.

COST CENTRE 1457 Loading Shovels Michigan 275 Misc Stock
PLANT REG 07 No. 35 Michigan 275 (S10)
00
01 Engine (Cummins NTA 853 & 380)
03 Cooling System
05 Transmission wheels and axles
07
09
10 etc
12
13

XXX If Cat Index Required   XXX Resp .. Plant then
Enter 1 for Next Page   Enter 2 for End of Transaction

The planner enters 2

The plant 4/2/2 number is 1457-07-05

He is now able to access the other computer systems as necessary.

EXAMPLE 8.2. Using the Plant and Equipment Management Programs to provide information on drawings, spares, etc., for an emergency job

No. 3 unloading grab crane (located in the wharf) failed because of a seized bearing on the Trod-wheel axle of the long-travel drive-bogie. The repair was of top priority.

The planner accesses the plant inventory system using the 4/2/2 number to provide the following screen.

```
1D10
                  PLANT INVENTORY ENQUIRY              WK/AR
C/CENTRE   1327   NO 3 UNLOADING GRAB CRANE-WHARF   043
PL/REG      23    LONG TRAVEL
PL/ITEM     02    LANDSIDE 6 7 8 9 10
                      SUB-ASSEMBLY SELECTION LIST   STOCK REFERENCE RESP
            04    HIGH SPEED COUPLING
            05    SPEED REDUCER
            06    DRIVING TRODWHEEL   No 6
            07    TRAILING TRODWHEEL  No 6
            08    SWIVEL UNIT BETWEEN DRIVING BOGIE No 6
            10    PRIME MOVER NO 7
                                                     TECHNICAL-SPEC
LIST MORE S/ASBLY                             REMARKS    SUB/ASBLY SEL 06
```

Selecting 06 as the required operating level (sub-assembly) of plant provides the next screen, part of the stores technical specification, including part numbers.

```
                  PLANT INVENTORY ENQUIRY  WK/AR  C/CT  PR  P1
S/ASSBY  06       DRIVING TRODWHEEL   NO 6  043    1327  23  02
                  OPERATING LEVEL (EXCHANGE UNITS) STOCK REF. RESP
         900      DRIVING BOGIE  COMPLETE EXCLUDING 816131103
                  MOTOR AND BRAKE  R/HAND
         902      TRODWHEEL & AXLE C/W BEARINGS        816131059
                  TYRE TYPE SINGLE FIG O/ALL DIA
                  O/ALL WIDTH 216MM TREAD DIA 900MM
                  TREAD WIDTH 150MM AXLE O/L 1905MM
                  DIA 260MM  JNL DIA 200MM
         905      TRODWHEELS  TYRE TYPE SINGLE FLG  816131134
                  O/ALL DIA  O/ALL WIDTH 216MM
                  TREAD DIA 900MM  TREAD WIDTH 150MM
LIST MORE OPER-LEVELS                REMARKS  TECHNICAL-SPEC  Y
                                             OPER LVL SEL  900
```

Knowing the Stores Number (816 13 1103), the parts inventory can be entered, providing the following information

```
STO2  ACC01-ACCEPTED, ENTER ANOTHER ITEM NO.  DATE 21/08/81
                             STORES  ITEM  STATUS
ITEM NO.  816 13 1103
                                            .           STORES HEAD 16

DESCRIPTION    BOGIE      ASSY     (DRIVING)   RH (EXCLUDING MOTOR AND BRAKE)
       UOM     EA         UCC      NOT CODED   RESP CODE 216

$-STD PRICE    $-STOCK VAL  LAST-YR-ISS  LAST-YR-REC  YRLY-ISS-RATE  CALC EXCESS
32062.02       0.00         0            1            4              0

LOC CURRENT MONTHLY MONTHLY ANNUAL  ANNUAL  M OPEN  YR OPEN  DATE      DATE
NO  BALANCE ISSUES  RCPTS   ISSUES  RCPTS   BAL     BAL      LAST ISS  LAST REC
16    1     0       0       1       0       0       1        7/781     19/05/00
```

Thus, through the 4/2/2 number the planner can supply technical specification, drawing number, stores number and location. Drawings and parts can be with the tradesman in less than 30 minutes.

Another way of providing this information would be to use the 4/2/2 number to access WEPAC JOB INDEX CATALOGUE to establish whether the job is on file and, if so, to find the job number (see Example 8.3).

EXAMPLE 8.3 Using WEPAC to programme a corrective job

A site planner asks the central planner to schedule the replacing of the gear-box seals of the No. 35 Michigan 275 Loading Shovel into the current work programme. Using the 4/2/2 number and the responsibility code (in this case M, for mechanical) he accesses JOB CATALOGUE INDEX (No. 2, WEPAC Menu). This gives the following screen

---

BSC–WORKS ENGINEERING PLANNING

                JOB CATALOGUE INDEX

Responsibility AWM
Cost Centre 1457 LOADING SHOVELS MICHIGAN 275 MISC STORES
Plant Register 07   NO 35 MICHIGAN 275 (S10)
Plant Item   05   TRANSMISSION WHEELS AXLES & STEERING

Key Name	Job Class	Job Title	Job Number
G/Box	57	Replacement of Oil Seals	(JP 123) 333
		Regd week ... Day	Date last done
			25/3/79

        etc ....
        Enter 1 for next page   Enter 2 for end of transaction

---

He establishes that the job (No. 333, Procedure JP 123) is held on file and was last carried out on 25/3/79. He now accesses JOB CATALOGUE INTERROGATION (No. 3, WEPAC Menu) using the code M-1457-07-05-333 and obtains the following screen.

BSC–WORKS ENGINEERING PLANNING
           JOB CATALOGUE INTERROGATION

Responsibility   AWM   Plant Req
Cost Centre   1457   LOADING SHOVELS MICHIGAN 275 MISC STOCK
Plant Register   87   NO 35 MICHIGAN 275 (S10)   S
Plant Item   85   TRANSMISSION WHEELS AXLES & STEERING
Job No C/B   Key Name   G/BOX/BROWN BUB788   Job Class 57
333   1   Job Title   REPLACEMENT OF OIL SEALS   JP123
Job Description   Prior Job   Routine

CLEAN & DRAIN THE UNIT

FOLLOW JOB PROCEDURE JP123 ATTACHED TO   Safety Procedures
THIS WORK ORDER CARD   11234   H1234
TEST JLC   Nos WOC   Job Burn
                                        81   83 00

	Maj	Plant		Frequency Details		
	Stop	Hist	Code	Cycle	Base 1	Base 2
	0	0	0	00	0 00 0	0 00 0

Enter 1 for Next Page   Enter 2 for End of Transaction

This gives him access to full details of resources and job methods, held in manual files. The S at the top right-hand corner indicates the level at which the plant must be stopped for the work to be carried out*. Additional information on spares, drawings etc., can be found as in Example 8.2.

In order to schedule the job for a particular day the planner checks the situation for that day on WORK PROGRAM INTERROGATION (No.1, WEPAC Menu)

WEPAC – WORK PROGRAM INTERROGATION

Responsibility: M Week Number : 28 Day : 8

Cost Centre: 1429   M83 STACKER RECLAIMER
Plant Reg: 22   MAIN MOTIONS
Plant Item: 10   LONG. TRAVEL (SOUTH) 1-2-3-4

Job No:	Burn.	CO	FB	C	Freq.	Key Name/Job Title
003	1.28	1	0	0	04	LONG TRAVEL
						B INSPECTION (FITTER 4WO)
004	1.00	1	0	0	01	LONG TRAVEL
						A INSPECTION (FITTER 1WO)
011	0.50	1	0	0	04	PULSE GENERATOR
						B INSPECTION (FITTER 4WO)
013	1.20	1	0	0	04	LONG TRAVEL
						B INSPECTION (FITTER 4WO)
014	1.00	1	0	0	01	LONG TRAVEL
						A INSPECTION (FITTER 1WO)

IF YOU REQUIRE ANY MORE RECORDS REPLY 1 ELSE REPLY 2

If resources are available the planner can schedule Job 333 for week 28 day 1 by accessing JOB CATALOGUE INDEX (see 1st screen) and entering week 28, day 1 against Job 333.

If the planner wishes to call off the job he accesses WORK PROGRAM CALL-OFF (No. 9, WEPAC menu)

BSC–WORKS ENGINEERING PLANNING
CALL OFF SELECTION 3
Responsibility AWM

Week	Day	Cost Centre	Plant Reg.
28	1	1457	87
—	—	—	—
—	—	—	—
—	—	—	—
—	—	—	—

ENTER 1 FOR NEXT PAGE, ENTER 2 FOR END OF TRANSACTION.

---

and enters the necessary details. This will cause the Work Order Card shown in Figure 8.6 to be printed.

In addition the stores requisition is printed and an entry created in FEEDBACK AGAINST WORK PROGRAM (No 6 WEPAC menu) to await job completion and update.

WORK ORDER CARD

No. | Request No. | Start Time | Day: 1 | Week: 48 | Job Reference: 1457 07 05 333 1

Plant Req.: S

Location and Identity:
LOADING SHOVELS MICHIGAN 275 MISC STOCK
NO 34 MICHIGAN 275 (SO 9)
TRANSMISSION WHEELS AXLES & STEERING
X GEARBOX

Grade | Std. Man Hrs. | Tot. Std. Hours

Job Title: OIL SEALS DEMO PURPOSES ONLY JLC

Job Description:
CLEAN & DRAIN THE UNIT.
FOLLOW MAKERS RECOMMENDATIONS AS SET OUT
IN JOB PROCEDURE AWM753
REFILL WITH OIL
RETURN GEARBOX TO STORES

Special Tools: DRG NO BSC1234

Locn.: 10

Mobile Plant

Safety Procedures: H35124 112345 SP1234 SP1234

Routine No.

STOCK NO.	Quantity	SPARES DESCRIPTION	Unit Code	Location
123456789	0003	MACOMA 72	64	01
234567891	0001	OIL SEAL FOR 1ST RDTN WORMSHFT	01	11
345678912	0001	OIL SEAL FOR 2ND RDTN WORMSHFT	01	11
456789123	0001	OIL SEAL FOR 2ND RDTN WHEELSFT	01	11

Prior Job

Planned by

Issued by

REF. C/275/62 Roneo Vickers Business Forms Ltd. 07 85010

Figure 8.6(a) Work order card (front)

204

NAME	CLOCK No.	GROUP CODE	TIME ON JOB (HOURS)	Additional Work
				Excess Work
				Inspected by	Approved by	Elapsed Time

Figure 8.6(b) Work order card (back)

A micro-computer-based system

COMAC (COmputer MAintenance Control)[2] is a software package designed for use on the Commodore range of micro-computers.

The necessary hardware is outlined in Figure 8.7. It can be seen that COMAC is a single terminal system, of limited storage capacity, suitable for centralised planning and control of a small organisation's maintenance

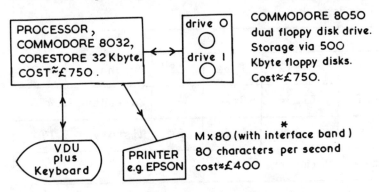

* Gives the printer compatibility with the Commodore hardware.

Figure 8.7 Hardware system for Commodore microcomputer

function, or for independent planning and control of *part* of a large organisation's maintenance. The system shown is not linked in any way to the spare parts system or to any other computerised planning system.

The total cost (hardware and software) is about £5000. The package is being used by a number of companies, including Redland Brick Ltd and Heinz Limited in the U.K.

System operation

This consists of five modules : Asset Register, Maintenance Plan, Work Order System, Plant History and Manpower Analysis. The system operating program, and the operating programs for each of these modules are contained on a master floppy disk. Additional information (see Figure 8.8) is stored on separate disks for each module. There is no limit to the number of disks that can be used to store this additional information.

When the master disk is loaded the system can be operated from the keyboard. Instructions from the keyboard allow programming information to transfer between master disk and the core store of the processor and cause the processor to become COMAC—a menu-driven user-friendly maintenance system.

The user can ask COMAC for the menu (see Figure 8.9). The main menu is given on the top line (displayed first) and the subsidiary menus underneath. Entering the number 1, followed by 2, accesses the search Register program. The screen commands the user to load the Asset Register disk. This done, the material of Table 8.4 is displayed. The left-hand column indicates the search fields available and the two columns

COMAC   ASSET   REGISTER   WEEK NO. 25

| Area 00 3 | Unit | PR0127 | Priority | 2 |

Main Plant Room
Pressure Vessel

Model No	P12	Type	12	Purchase	4578
User Ref	B1234	Size	45	Warranty	4583
Cost New	4.00	Life	30	History	UT
Comment	Permit Required				

Please Enter Command

Figure 8.8 Asset description, screen display

TABLE 8.4. Searching the Asset Register, a typical search field selection

Search field	Upper limit	Lower limit
0. Unit Code	AF 01	FF 99 All units from AF 01 to FF99 inclusive
1. Priority	2	2 Priority 2
2. Model No.	—	—
3. Equip. Type		
4. Purchase Date	2970	2981 Purchase date 2970 to 2981
5. Warranty date	—	—
6. User Ref.		
7. Size		
8. Cost (100's)		200 cost from £300 to £20,000
9. History Group	TD	To History Group TD only

to the right the lower and upper limits of the search. Once the search fields have been completed the user initiates the asset search, producing a result as shown in Table 8.5.

Similar procedures are used for the other programs. Thus the system operates through the interaction of the user keyboard inputs, the operating programs (held on the master disk and transferred as necessary to the processor) and the additional plant information held on separate disks.

System details

In most respects this (see Figure 8.10) is a computer version of the manual system described in Section 7.2. Information base and preventive maintenance plan are operated in terms of the plant unit.

COMAC

Asset Register Programs (1)	Maintenance Plan Programs (2)	Work Order Programs (3)	Plant History Programs (4)	Manpower Analysis Programs (5)
11 Edit Register	21 Edit Plan	31 Edit Work Orders	41 Edit History	51 Edit Man Record
12 Search Register	22 Search Plan	32 Search Work Orders	42 Update History	52 Summarise Orders
13 Asset Valuation	23 Update Plan	33 Cost Summary	43 Search History	53 Reconcile Orders
	24 Project Workload	34 Print Work Orders	44 Incident Analysis	54 Cost Orders
	25 Edit Schedule	35 Condense File		55 Print Controls

Figure 8.9 Comac program menu

TABLE 8.5. Search print out

60

ASSET REGISTER   COMAC II DEMONSTRATION

AREA	UNIT	PRIORITY	MODEL	TYPE	BOUGHT	REF.	SIZE	WARRANTY	COST	LIFE	HG
001	AF01	2	AF2	25	2970	A2345	8	2975	15000	20	TD
ADDITIVE FEEDER COMPLETE					SAME AS AF02						
001	BF0101	2	451	SD	2980	A2345	10	2982	20000	20	TD
BOX FEEDER NO 1 COMPLETE											
001	CV0301	2	ASD	KK	2970	A2345	PL	3075	2100	20	TD
BELT CONVEYOR NO 1					REPLACES CV0101						
001	CV0302	2	ASD	K1	2970	A2345	PR	2975	3500	20	TD
BELT CONVEYOR.NO 2					ACCESS POOR						
001	CV0601	2	TH1	45	2970	A2345	1	2973	300	20	TD
FEEDER SLAT CONVEYOR											

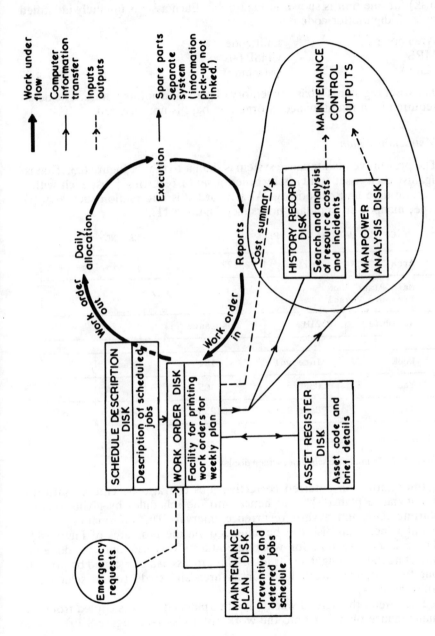

Figure 8.10 The COMAC system

Asset register

An example of the information held on disk (about 5000 asset entries per disk) for one unit is shown in Figure 8.8. Each asset is uniquely identified by a 12 digit/letter code e.g.

Area code   Unit code
MRS   CHSP 001
(Line)   (Machine)

The asset register is a basic inventory of plant and nothing more. The detail required by a maintenance information base is not included.

Maintenance plan

The preventive maintenance system is similar to that of Figure 6.3. That is, against each asset (unit) is recorded a *set* of recurring jobs, each with a starting date and periodicity. Also recorded is information such as work type, manpower, standard hours (see Figure 8.11).

```
       COMAC  MAINTENANCE  PLAN                    WEEK NO. 25
```

Area	003	Unit	PRo127		Priority	2
Main Plant Room Pressure Vessel						
Schedule	P521M		Insurance Test			

Week	27	Interval	104	Trade	2
Year	81	Contract	M5	No. Men	1
Type	1	User Ref	B123D	Hours	1.00

```
Please Enter Command
```

Figure 8.11 Maintenance schedule, screen display

Information on deferred corrective jobs can also be entered into the maintenance plan disk (and hence into the schedule) by giving them a starting date and a zero recurrence interval. The information on the maintenance plan disk can be amended via the programs of Figure 8.9. There is no program for work-smoothing. This can only be done by adjusting the starting date for jobs. This process can be assisted by printing out the projected work load for an area and trade (menu selection 2 followed by 4).

Each week the agreed weekly load of planned work is copied from the maintenance plan disk onto the work order disk (see Figure 8.10).

Work order system

All preventive jobs, and some deferred jobs, have job specifications held on disk. The specifications for the jobs in a week's schedule are copied

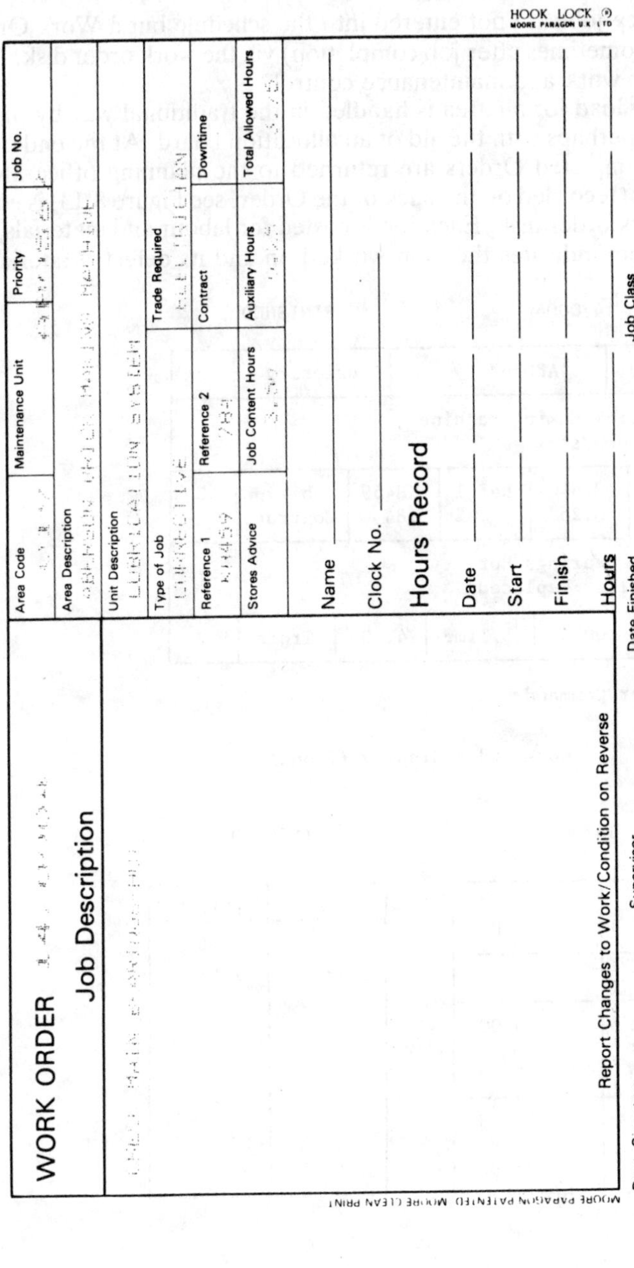

Figure 8.12 Work order (COMAC)

from the job specification disk on to the work order disk (see Figure 8.10). (A maximum of 9 discs is allowed with approximately 650 Work Orders per disc). The Work Orders required are then printed and are classified by area and trade (see Figure 8.12).

Emergency jobs are not entered into the schedule but a Work Order is produced (sometimes after job completion) via the work order disk. This is essential for work and maintenance control.

The work load for an area is handled in the traditional way by the area supervisor, perhaps with the aid of an allocation board. At the end of each week the completed Orders are returned to the planning office and job information (recorded on the back of the Order, see Figure 8.13) is entered into the work order disk. Each job is costed for labour and materials and a coding system indicates the item worked on and its defect. Materials are

```
ORDER NO.  14/0004                    FINISHED
```

Area	019	AB0567		Priority	2
Aberson Brick Making Machine Lubrication System					
Job Hrs. Aux Hrs	3.50 0.25	Ref 1 2	KH459 784	Job Type Contract	2
Check Main Bearings Hot Blocked Filter Replaced					
Job No.	0004	D/Time	4.00	Trade	2

```
Please Enter Command
```

Work order display (front)

```
ORDER NO.  14/0004                    FINISHED
```

Job Class History	2 HG
Clock No	1
H R S	Current F/Weeks Premium	4.00 0.50
Labour Materials Advice No.	28.18 5.87 25894

ITEM	DEFECT
20	46
12	87

```
Please Enter Command
```

Work order display (back)

Figure 8.13 Work order display with completed job entered

TABLE 8.6. Print out of cost summary (£)

```
60

COMAC II DEMONSTRATION

ORDERS SORTED BY AREA CODE
```

ORDER	JOB	ACT	AREA	UNIT CODE	DOWNTIME	PLANNED	ACTUAL	LABOUR	MATERIAL
ADDITIVE FEEDER COMPLETE									
36/0007	0007	4	001	AF01	8.50	7.00	8.00	25.60	85.50
SCHEDULE AF123 QUARTERLY OVERHAUL									
BOX FEEDER NO 1 COMPLETE									
36/0008	0008	4	001	BF0101	9.50	10.00	8.00	26.00	
SCHEDULE BF245 STATUTORY CHECK									
BELT CONVEYOR NO 1									
36/0012	0012	4	001	CV0301	1.50	1.00	1.00	3.25	
SCHEDULE EB01M WEEKLY LUBRICATION									
FEEDER SLAT CONVEYOR									
36/0023	0023	4	001	CV0601	7.50	3.50	7.00	22.75	
SCHEDULE C5698 WEEKLY LUBRICATION									
FEEDER SLAT CONVEYOR									
36/0032	0032	4	001	CV0601	3.50	5.50	3.00	9.75	15.50
SHEDULE CV13M QUARTERLY OVERHAUL									
ADDITIVE FEEDER COMPLETE									
36/0036	0036	4	001	AF01	18.00	13.00	16.50	53.62	550.80
REPLACE NO 2 ROLLER BEARING									
SUB TOTAL FOR AREA CODE 001					48.50	40.00	43.50	140.97	651.80
PRESSURE VESSEL									
36/0002	0002	4	003	PR0127	8.00	1.50	1.25	4.37	7.50
SCHEDULE P521M INSURANCE TEST									
CALORIFIER SHOWER SUPPLY									
36/0018	0018	4	003	CA021216	9.00	7.00	8.00	26.00	
SCHEDULE C1236 ASBESTOS LAGGING									
PRESSURE VESSEL									
36/0039	0001	4	003	PR0127	22.00		14.50	47.13	
SCHEDULE BP11M ANNUAL OVERHAUL									
SUB TOTAL FOR AREA CODE 003					39.00	8.50	23.75	77.50	7.50
GRAND TOTALS					87.50	48.50	67.25	218.47	659.30

costed by linking the Stores Requisition number with Work Order and by directing the costed requisition back to COMAC. The work order system can provide a cost summary for each week's completed Work Orders (see Table 8.6).

Work Orders not printed in their scheduled week, or printed but not started, are automatically carried over as a backlog. COMAC has no facilities, however, for automatically rescheduling to allow for the backlog.

Maintenance control

Information on the completed Work Orders can be transferred from the work order disk to the history record disk and stored under the asset code

TABLE 8.7. Summary of plant history (extract)

UNIT: 3231   CARRUTHERS 10 TON E.O.T. CRANE   AREA: 150

WEEK	YEAR	JOB	TYPE	CLASS	REF 1	REF 2	TRADE	CT	DOWNTIME	ACT.HRS	LABOUR	MATERIAL
46	81	78	2	2			2			2	16	

FIT CAPACITOR ON LIGHT FITTING
NEW CAPACITOR & CABLE FITTED
FOUND CAP U/S & CABLE DAMAGED

WEEK	YEAR	JOB	TYPE	CLASS	REF 1	REF 2	TRADE	CT	DOWNTIME	ACT.HRS	LABOUR	MATERIAL
46	81	43	2	2			2			3	24	

CAB HEATER NOT WORKING ON CRANE
TERMINAL BOX. MADE GOOD
HEATER WIRING ADRIFT IN

WEEK	YEAR	JOB	TYPE	CLASS	REF 1	REF 2	TRADE	CT	DOWNTIME	ACT.HRS	LABOUR	MATERIAL
46	81	43	8				2			3	24	

'WORK WITH' RECORD

WEEK	YEAR	JOB	TYPE	CLASS	REF 1	REF 2	TRADE	CT	DOWNTIME	ACT.HRS	LABOUR	MATERIAL
48	81	121	1	8			2			1	8	

CHECK LT OP/OP SEEMS OK. NEEDS TWO
HEATER. TO BE FOLLOWED   UP
PEOPLE TO OPERATE CRANE & CHECK

WEEK	YEAR	JOB	TYPE	CLASS	REF 1	REF 2	TRADE	CT	DOWNTIME	ACT.HRS	LABOUR	MATERIAL
49	81	150	1	2			1		1	1	8	

ROPE OFF PULLEY
REFIT ROPE AS REQUIRED

WEEK	YEAR	JOB	TYPE	CLASS	REF 1	REF 2	TRADE	CT	DOWNTIME	ACT.HRS	LABOUR	MATERIAL
49	81	150	8				1			1	8	

'WORK WITH' RECORD

WEEK	YEAR	JOB	TYPE	CLASS	REF 1	REF 2	TRADE	CT	DOWNTIME	ACT.HRS	LABOUR	MATERIAL
49	81	150	8				1			1	8	

'WORK WITH' RECORD

WEEK	YEAR	JOB	TYPE	CLASS	REF 1	REF 2	TRADE	CT	DOWNTIME	ACT.HRS	LABOUR	MATERIAL
49	81	8	1	6			1		1	1	8	

RENEW CROSS TRAVEL BUFFER STOP
2 BUFFER STOPS RENEWED AS REQD

WEEK	YEAR	JOB	TYPE	CLASS	REF 1	REF 2	TRADE	CT	DOWNTIME	ACT.HRS	LABOUR	MATERIAL
49	81	8	8				1			1	8	

'WORK WITH' RECORD

WEEK	YEAR	JOB	TYPE	CLASS	REF 1	REF 2	TRADE	CT	DOWNTIME	ACT.HRS	LABOUR	MATERIAL
49	81	8	8				1			1	8	

'WORK WITH' RECORD

WEEK	YEAR	JOB	TYPE	CLASS	REF 1	REF 2	TRADE	CT	DOWNTIME	ACT.HRS	LABOUR	MATERIAL
49	81	13	3	2			2		2	2	16	

MAGNET CABLE REPAIRS REQD/NEW PLUG
-ENED. FUSES REPAIRED
FITTED ON CABLE. TERMINALS TIGHT

WEEK	YEAR	JOB	TYPE	CLASS	REF 1	REF 2	TRADE	CT	DOWNTIME	ACT.HRS	LABOUR	MATERIAL
49	81	13	8				2			2	16	

'WORK WITH' RECORD

(the history record disk can hold approximately 8000 such entries.) It can be seen from Figure 8.9 that several programs are available for interrogating the history record. For example, the record can be searched (Menu No. 4 followed by 3) for the history recorded against a specified range of asset codes, job types, job classes, weeks, years etc. (see Table 8.7).

The record can also provide a summary of jobs, occurring within specified search limits, according to work type, e.g. preventive or corrective (see Table 8.8).

An additional control is provided by the manpower analysis program. This is a record of hours worked, with rates, by each man. The information is derived direct from the completed Work Orders and checked by reconciliation program against the information on clock cards and work cards.

Comments

The main advantage of COMAC is its cheapness and ease of use. Even the smallest of maintenance departments could buy it and become familiar with the benefits of computerisation. Compared with the other systems discussed its information base is limited, being confined to the brief entry in the asset register. However, there seems to be no reason why this could not be supplemented by a further module with information for each asset on spares, manuals and drawings. The work planning system is adequate

TABLE 8.8. Plant history (incident analysis)

```
INCIDENT ANALYSIS  -  For Last 24 Weeks
```

UNIT - AF01/15   ADDITIVE FEEDER COMPLETE   AREA - 001

TYPE/CLASS OF INCIDENT	ORDER INTERVAL (WEEKS)	AVERAGE MANHOURS			AVERAGE MATERIAL COST		
		PER ORDER	PER WEEK	PERCENT	PER ORDER	PER WEEK	PERCENT
PLANNED MAINTENANCE							
INSPECTION	8.0	1.1	.1	7.9	.0	.0	.0
ADJUSTMENT	8.0	.6	.1	4.2	.5	.1	.9
OVERHAUL	24.0	17.0	.7	41.2	98.5	4.1	58.2
TOTAL	3.4	3.1	.9	53.3	14.3	4.2	59.0
BREAKDOWNS							
ADJUSTMENT	24.0	1.5	.1	3.6	18.5	.8	10.9
ACCIDENT	24.0	15.5	.6	37.6	35.8	1.5	21.1
TOTAL	12.0	1.1	.1	5.5	7.5	.6	8.9
REQUISITIONS							
ADJUSTMENT	24.0	1.5	.1	3.6	2.6	.1	1.5
REPLACEMENT	24.0	.8	.0	1.8	12.5	.5	7.4
TOTAL	12.0	1.1	.1	5.5	7.5	.6	8.9
TOTAL OF ALL INCIDENTS							
INSPECTION	8.0	1.1	.1	7.9	.0	.0	.0
ADJUSTMENT	4.8	1.0	.2	11.5	4.5	.9	13.3
REPLACEMENT	24.0	.8	.0	1.8	12.5	.5	7.4
OVERHAUL	24.0	17.0	.7	41.2	98.5	4.1	58.2
ACCIDENT	24.0	15.5	.6	37.6	35.8	1.5	21.1
TOTAL	2.2	3.8	1.7	100.0	15.4	7.1	100.0

but lacks facilities for work smoothing or backlog re-scheduling. The floppy discs are not suitable for site offices in a dirty environment—they need to be handled and stored with care.

COMAC is a single terminal system with no linkage to other planning offices or to the stores system. This, with its limited storage capacity, renders it suitable only as a central planning aid for a small company. In addition, being designed in terms of the identifiable unit it is more suitable for manufacturing than process plant. However the rapid advances being made in the technology of micro-computers should not be forgotten. It is clear that in the near future* these will have the capabilities of today's minicomputers—multi-terminal operation, megabytes of core store and multi-megabytes of hard disk storage (possibly using laser techniques)— but at micro computer costs.

A mini-computer-based system

TEREMA[3] (TErotechnology, REliability, MAintenance) is a complete maintenance system developed by Idhammar Konsult AB of Sweden. It is designed on a software module basis and can be installed in a number of ways:

(i) The user buys one or more modules but not the hardware, the processing being carried out by a computer service bureau (the most popular option).
(ii) The user buys the software, and backup documentation for one or more modules, for installation on an existing computer. However the software needs to be modified to become compatible with other computers and this can be expensive.
(iii) The user buys the complete system including the hardware (an option chosen by several companies).

A typical hardware configuration is shown in Figure 8.14. In this form it is an on-line multi-terminal system, with up to 64 terminals. The storage capacity of its Nord mini-computer matches the needs of a complete maintenance documentation system for a medium-sized company. For larger companies the mini-computer can be connected up to a mainframe as described in the first example. The complete software package costs from £7,000 to £35,000 and the hardware from £10,000 to £100,000 depending on the arrangement.

System details

The component modules are as follows : Information Base, Preventive Maintenance, Work Planning and Technical Analysis. Stores inventory control can also be integrated. The principles of operation follow closely those outlined in Chapter 6 and illustrated in Figure 6.1. There are also many similarities to the BSC system. The description will therefore focus on the Preventive Maintenance and Technical Analysis Modules.

Preventive maintenance module

This is based on the ideas of the Idhammar manual system discussed in section 7.3. The plant inventory itemises plant down to unit level. Each unit is identified by a number which is the key to the appropriate

---

*COMAC III has now been developed to operate on a Sirius computer with hard disk storage. This system includes an information base and a condition monitoring package.

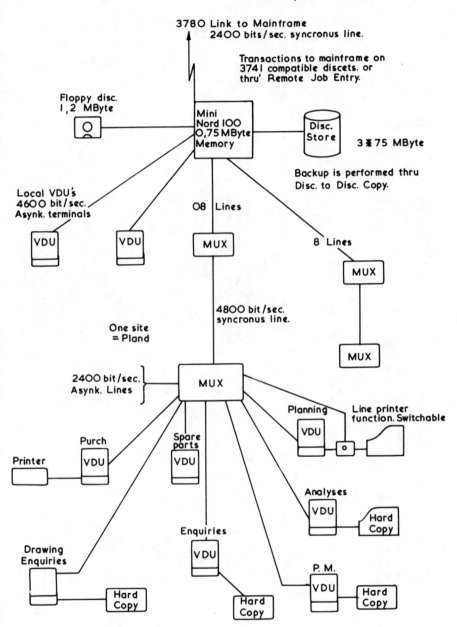

Figure 8.14 Idhammer hardware layout

computerised information on technical records, drawing and manual numbers and, above all, spare parts.

The Idhammar preventive maintenance philosophy is to base the maintenance plan as far as possible on condition-based-maintenance (see the Paper Machine of Section 4.3). Therefore the plan is made up mainly of periodic inspections followed up by the identified corrective work. The

PM CO. (05)	MAIN SCHEDULE FOREST INDUSTRY LTD.	PRINTOUT: 1981-01-09 FACTORY: (02) PULP MILL 1		CLASSIFICATION: POSITION NUMBER AREA: (02) DRIER, LINE 4 PAGE.			
POS. NO. OWN I.D.NO. INSP. NO.	MACHINE NAME 1 MACHINE NAME 2 MACHINE PART NAME	INTERVAL STOP/OPER.F	CATEGORY DATE	INSTRUCTIONS, WORK, ETC.	NOTES NO. VOLUME COST ACCOUNT	JOB SPEC.	S-CODE
74-31-7701	White water pump	4	Mech	Bearing temperatures max 75 C, abnormal noise, vibrations, leakage, seal cooling water, shaft glands, mountings			70
74-31-7701 549	White water pump 1st press Electric motor	4	Mech 8123	Motor temperature, abnormal noise, vibration,mountings,moisture, cleaning requirements			001D 44
74-31-7701 M3062 550	White water pump 1st press Electric Motor	26	Elect 8125	Clean and check motor, damaged cables Seals and cable clamps. Check disconnector and starter. Bearing noise			500D 500
74-31-7701 551	White water pump 1st press Coupling	4	Mech 8123	Look for run-out and vibrations. Rubber marks on inside of guard indicate misaligned coupling			22
74-31-7701 552	White water pump 1st press Coupling	52	SP 81101	Inspect coupling rubber element. Measure distance between scribe marks, Max. 8 mm			032S 21
74-31-7701 74-72-0060 553	White water pump 1st press Water Separator	12	M 8123	External inspection of insulation, support devices, pipe connections. Check for leaks or damage			102
74-32-5200	Condensate pump	4	M 8112	Bearing temperatures Max 75 C, abnormal noise, vibrations, leakage, seal cooling water, shaft glands, mountings			110D 70
74-32-5200 12	Condensate pump	520	SM 8101	Pump and motor bearings, spm measurement every three months, see spm system			
74-32-5200 M9412 532	Condensate pump Electric Motor	4	M 8112	Motor temperature, abnormal noise, vibration, mountings, moisture, cleaning requirements			001D 44

Figure 8.15 Main list

PM ROUTINE XI (05)	INSPECTION LIST FOREST INDUSTRY LTD.	PRINTOUT: WEEK 11, 1981 FACTORY: (02) PULP MILL 1	CLASSIFICATION: POSITION NUMBER AREA: (02) DRIER, LINE 4 PAGE 18	
POS. NO. OWN I.D.NO. INSP. NO.	MACHINE NAME 1 MACHINE NAME 2 MACHINE PART NAME	MAINT. INSTR. STD CODE INTERVAL	INSTRUCTIONS, WORK, ETC.	NOTES NO. VOLUME COST ACCOUNT
74-35-0010 476	Reject Pump	110D	Bearing temperature max 75 C. abnormal noise, vibration, seal Cooling water, shaft glands, mounting	
74-35-0010 477	Reject Pump Electric Motor	1D 44 4	Motor temperature, abnormal noise, vibration, mountings, moisture, cleaning	
74-83-4430 480	Bird Strainer	255 4	General inspection for damage, cracks, loose bolts, leakage etc.	
74-83-4430 481	Bird Strainer Electric Motor	1D 44 4	Motor temperature, abnormal noise, vibration, mountings, moisture, cleaning	
74-83-4430 483	Bird Strainer Vee-belt drive	13D 116 4	Noise, whipping, oil, belt guard, belt tension, bolts	
74-31-7701 548	White water pump 1st press	70 4	Bearing temperature Max 75C, Abnormal noise, vibration, seal cooling water, shaft glands, mounting	
74-31-7701 549	White water pump 1st press Electric motor	001D 44 4	Motor temperature, abnormal noise, vibration, mountings, moisture, cleaning	

Figure 8.16 Routine inspection list

plan for the plant is held in the computer in the form of a list of maintenance procedures—the Main List (see Fig. 8.15). Thus the white water pump of Figure 8.15 has seven procedures listed against it, and in each case an indication of

(a) whether it is on-line maintenance (work that can be performed without special planning) or off-line (work that requires special planning),
(b) trade,
(c) periodicity,
(d) work to be performed,
(e) job specification code.

The work is planned in a way similar to that of the Idhammer system of Chapter 7. That is, inspection lists (see Figure 8.16) are drawn up for each area and preventive maintenance cards for each unit (or line) trade and frequency (see Figure 8.17). Programs smooth the work load and arrange it

```
PM CARD    PLANT 02    AREA 02    TM LINE 4      WEEK 4      YEAR 1981

                                                MAINTENANCE INSTRUCTION 013S

71-31-0412      Exhaust Gas Fan  4              INTERVAL              26

MD 113                                          S-CODE                117


ACTION:

CHECK VEE-BELTS

MEASURE BELT TENSION WITH TENSIOMETER



WORK CODE:

WORK PERFORMED:  .................................................................

       ..................................................................
```

Figure 8.17 Preventive maintenance card

into weekly loads. Thus, the computer can print out, on request or automatically, the weekly preventive work load. Where the tradesman wants detailed instructions he can use the Job Specification Code and refer to the Specification Manual (see Figure 6.4). Operation of the system is outlined in Figure 8.18.

Technical analysis module

In its most sophisticated form this uses inputs from the work orders, preventive maintenance inspection lists and cards, stores requisitions and downtime records to build up the history record, which has menu-driven user-friendly on-line search facilities. The principal output from the history

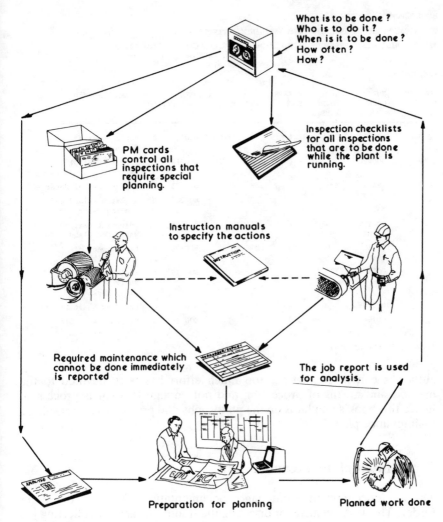

Figure 8.18 System operation

record is the Main Report (see Figure 8.19). In addition three 'Top Ten' lists are printed each month (see Tables 8.20 a, b, and c).

Comments

TEREMA has been designed by engineers with the help of computer analysts and not vice versa. In particular great emphasis is put on the preventive maintenance component which relies on condition-monitoring, carefully thought-out maintenance procedures, and well-documented job specifications. The strength of the system lies in the experience of the consultants and a large library of job specifications that they have built up over many years. A maintenance documentation system can only be as good as the information it processes. Having investigated many systems the

MAIN REPORT

TECHNICAL/ECONOMIC ANALYSIS OF MAINTENANCE ACTIVITIES

PERIOD: 8101-8120 PRINTOUT DATE: 81-06-10   SEQUENCE: POSITION NO.,
                                              NO, CATEGORY, WORK ORDER

(ACCOUNT NO.)

POSITION NUMBER OWN I.D.	WORK ORDER	SHUT-DOWN TIME	REPAIR CODE	COSTS LAB.	COSTS MATL.	DATE	CATEGORY	WORK PERFORMED
72-088 4619	600419		4	90	140	800112	E	Replacement of Brushes
4619	000420		4	250	420	800312	E	Fitting Control Switch
4619	99421	189	3	279	2900	800601	E	Replacement of Motor
	Prev. Maint.		1			800302	M	Adjusting Gland and Sealing Water
	Prev. Maint.		1			800405	M	Adjusting Sealing Water and Gland
	000107	40	3	120	50	800106	M	Replacement of Gland Packing
	000108	120	3	360	120	800119	M	Replacement of Shaft Sleeve and Gland Packing
	000109		4	80		800326	M	Grinding Shaft Sleeve
	00114		2	80	170	800519	S	Oil Change in Gear Box, 55 Litre

Figure 8.19 Main report

author is convinced that far too much effort has been devoted to the method and means of processing and not enough to what is processed, hence this book's emphasis on the philosophy and practice of establishing a maintenance plan.

Direct input of maintenance data

The key document in maintenance documentation systems is the Work Order. This is the vehicle for directing the tradeforce and for collecting job information for maintenance control. The BSC example, in particular, showed that in practice there is considerable difficulty in ensuring that emergency work (especially on shift) is covered by Work Orders. In addition, difficulty is experienced in ensuring their return, and proper completion. Without a high-percentage return of Work Orders, maintenance control becomes impossible. One company[4] has developed a computerised maintenance system that can overcome this difficulty. It also provides an alternative method of planning shift maintenance work.

The hardware consists of a dedicated minicomputer and a number of terminals situated in the production areas and in the maintenance repair shop. The system is aimed at the shift maintenance work, which has short repair times, random incidence and usually involves only one trade (and never more than two). When such work occurs the plant operators input the following information on the nearest VDU : Plant code, Priority (1 to 5, from a clearly defined classification), Trade (electrical, mechanical,

TOP TEN NO. 1

MACHINES WHICH, IN RELATION TO THEIR VALUE, HAVE HAD THE HIGHEST MAINTENANCE COSTS DURING THE PERIOD 8101-8121.

MACHINE NO.	PERCENTAGE MAINTENANCE COST	COSTS MATERIALS	LABOUR	VALUE
72-088	68%	244.020	399.260	946.000
16-042	67%	40.090	35.620	113.000
19-146	59%	242.540	236.540	812.000
14-019	55%	215.430	196.520	749.000
15-073	51%	96.480	139.650	463.000
28-463	51%	1.100	1.960	6.000
22-012	40%	204.900	412.300	1.543.000
39-073	30%	251.000	263.200	1.714.000
54-114	30%	1.920	1.680	12.000
63-212	29%	457.840	396.500	2.946.000
TOTAL		1.755.320	2.083.230	9.304.000

Percentage of total maintenance costs during same period = 20.2%
Actual Maintenance cost during same period   (Swedish kroner) 18.980.000

TOP TEN LIST NO. 2

MACHINES WHICH HAVE HAD THE GREATEST NUMBER OF FAULTS DURING THE PERIOD FROM 8001 TO 8021

MACHINE NO.	PERCENTAGE OF NO. OF FAULTS	NUMBER OF FAULTS
14-046	1.03	146
72-018	0.79	112
68-193	0.79	112
19-146	0.78	111
14.136	0.78	110
15-002	0.78	110
15-019	0.66	93
26-419	0.64	91
28-416	0.58	82
39-073	0.58	82
TOTAL	1.049	

Total Number of Faults: 14.163

TOP TEN NO. 3

MACHINES WITH THE GREATEST TOTAL OF SHUTDOWN TIMES DURING THE PERIOD FROM 8101 TO 8120

OBJECT NO.	MINUTES SHUTDOWN TIME	NUMBER OF SHUTDOWNS
19-146	632	26
21-001	612	21
01-006	401	20
27-013	309	20
71-072	112	19
69-006	90	19
54-006	88	19
32-416	80	12
76-312	12	8
19-192	6	7

2342 Min=45.3% of total   171=33.4% of total

Total Number of Operation Interruptions   512
Total Stop Time   5173 Min

Figure 8.20 Top ten reports

steam or refrigeration), Comment (one line of free comment), Time recorded.

The job thus enters automatically onto the work backlog which is listed according to job priority and time. The backlog can be consulted via the VDUs by the repair shop tradesmen and the plant and production management (major jobs are put on hard copy and planned, before acceptance by a tradesman). The shift tradesmen themselves decide (taking priorities into consideration) the order in which the work is performed. Before starting a job a fitter inputs his initials and the starting time against the selected job (foremen do not plan work, instead they act as advisors, providing craft and technical input). On completion of the job the tradesman inputs (at a VDU) the following information :

Reasons—(selected from a menu)

Actions—(selected from a menu, 3 selections allowed and must enter at least 1)

Comments—(adds to the originator's comments, up to a total of 2 lines)

Time completed

Shift

The job will not leave the backlog display until this information has been entered. The job will then automatically pass into the history file for future analysis. This method of operation provides the following advantages :

(i)   Paperwork and supervision is minimised

(ii) Work Order feedback is encouraged by the attraction of using the terminals

(iii) Communication between tradesmen and plant operators is improved.

This is unquestionably a move in the right direction, although difficulties could be foreseen in some industries (steelmaking for example) in siting VDUs in production areas.

Commercially available computer packages

A survey[5] of these is given in Table 8.9 and the variation in their cost in Figure 8.21. The cost does not include the cost of the resources required for setting up the maintenance plan, information base etc. This latter is the most important part of implementation and its cost (especially if it is carried out by consultants) can exceed that of the computer package itself. A more detailed survey, carried out by Smit[6] is given in Table 8.10, the suppliers addresses being listed at the end of the chapter. This survey was restricted to packages which can be used on mini and micro-computers. Probably the most complete and up-to-date survey has been carried out by Parkes[7].

The selection of the most appropriate computerised system for a given industrial plant is not a straightforward process. Computer requirements—for hardware and software—must be matched to the requirements of the maintenance system and such matching must be carried out in an ordered

TABLE 8.9. Survey of computerised maintenance packages (based on the questionnaire of Appendix 6)

NAME	WIMS	COMPASS	COMAC	SAMSON	SAMSON	I.B.M.	MMS	PAMIS	TEROMAN	CAMS	SCOMAGG	ICL	MPMS
SUPPLIER	ABS	Bonner & Moore	Comac	Davy	Davy	I.B.M.	MMS	P.A.Consultants	Scicon	Vosper Thorneycroft	Scomagg	ICL	Microtech
MICRO/MINI	Mini	Mini	Micro	Micro	Mini	Mini	Micro	Micro	Mini	Mini	Mini	Mini	Micro
COMPUTER	ABS MX	Data General	Commodore Pet	Any	HP1000	8100	Any CP/M	Any CP/M	HP3000	Mini PDP/Vax	PDP11	2903,ME29	Any
HARDWARE COST	£18,000+	£200,000	£2,000	£10,000	£70,000+	£70,000	£5,000+	£7,000	£80,000	£15,000	£20,000+	£30,000	£3,000
SOFTWARE COST	£5,000	£100,000	£3,000	£15,000	£50,000+	£30,000	£8,000+	£15,000	£70,000	£25,000	£12,000	£11,000	£500
PACKAGE COST	£23,000+	£300,000	£5,000	£25,000	£120,000	£100,000	£13,000+	£22,000	£150,000	£40,000	£32,000+	£41,000	£3,500
INVENTORY	Y	Y	Y	Y	Y	Y	Y	Y	Y	Y	Y	Y	Y
TECHNICAL	N	Y	N	Y	Y	Y	Y	N	Y	Y	Y	Y	Y
INFORMATION DRAWINGS AND MANUALS REF	N	Y	N	Y	Y	Y	Y	N	Y	Y	N	N	Y
ON-LINE LINK TO SPARES	Y	Y	N	Y	Y	Y	Y	N	Y	Y	Y	Y	Y
INFORMATION ON REPAIRABLE ITEMS	Y	Y	N	Y	Y	Y	Y	N	Y	N	N	Y	N
JOB CATALOGUE OR UNIT SCHEDULES	J.C	J.C.	U.S.	J.C.	J.C.	No PM	U.S.	J.C	J.C.	J.C.	J.C	J.C.	U.S
WORK SMOOTHING FACILITY	N	N	N	N	N	N	N	N	N	Y	N	N	N
MINIMUM WORKING PERIOD	Week	Day	Week	Day	Day	Day	Day	Week	Day	Day	Day	Day	Day
FACILITY FOR WORK ORDER PRINTING	Y	Y	Y	Y	Y	Y	Y	Y	Y	Y	Y	Y	Y
FACILITY FOR PRINTING EMERGENCY WORK ORDERS	N	Y	Y	Y	Y	N	Y	Y	Y	Y	Y	N	N
BACKLOG REPROGRAMMING FACILITY	N	N	N	Y	Y	N	Y	N	N	Y	Y	Y	N
ANALYSIS OF WEEKLY WORK ORDERS	Y	Y	N	Y	Y	N	Y	Y	Y	Y	Y	Y	Y
HISTORY RECORD	Y	Y	Y	Y	Y	N	Y	Y	Y	Y	Y	Y	Y
ONLINE SEARCH AND ANALYSIS	Y	Y	N	Y	Y	N	Y	Y	Y	N	Y	Y	Y
TOP-TEN	N	Y	N	Y	Y	N	Y	N	N	N	Y	Y	N
COST CONTROL	Y	Y	N	Y	Y	N	Y	N	N	Y	Y	Y	Y

TABLE 8.10. Evaluation of software packages (Smit)

No. Supplier	Program	(1) Devl Stage	(2) Type of Suppl.	(3) Work Plan	Func. Spares Contr.	Character Maint. Contr.	Info. Base
1 ABS COMPUTERS	WIMS	E	C+S	3	2	3	2
2 AKZO SYSTEMS	BISTRO	E	S+O	3	2	2	0
3 COMAC SYSTEMS	COMAC	L	M	?	0	?	0
4 DAVY	SAMSON	E	C+S	1	0	0	3
5 IBM	DPM	E	C+O	3	2	2	2
	OPMS	F	C+O	0	2	0	3
6 ICL	PMS	E	C	1	4	1	3
7 IDHAMMAR	TEREMA	L	M+S	1	4	3	4
8 IMO	CMMS	L	M	4	3	1	2
9 MAYNARD	MANCOM	L	M	?	0	0	?
10 MOM OFFSHORE	MYRIAD	E	M	?	±	0	?
11 QUARTO		L	M+S	3	3	2	4
12 RIVA	ROMEO	E	S	2	4	2	3
13 SCICON	TEROMAN	L	S+O	4	0	0	3
14 SCOMAGG		E	C	?	0	?	?
15 TRANSCON	COMPASS	F	S	3	4	3	4

Key: 1) F = Fully Developed
    L = Largely Developed
    E = Limited

2) M = Maintenance Consultant
   S = Software House
   C = Computer Manufacturer
   O = Operating Company

3) 4 75%
  3 50% 75%
  2 25% 50%
  1 25%
  0 nothing
  ? size unknown

and rational way. Several procedures have been outlined[8,9], in the literature, the principal steps being as follows—

(1) Define the current maintenance system and construct an outline specification for the desired system, taking into consideration such factors as—
  the number of plant units,
  the extent of the information base,
  the type of preventive maintenance system required,
  the number of preventive jobs,
  the number of work orders issued per week,
  the extent of feedback required,
  the difficulty in achieving feedback,
  the sophistication of the data analysis required,
  the extent of on-line history required.

(2) Decide whether the specification outlined in (1) will be best achieved via a manual system or via a computerised system. Remember that a computer facilitates storing and accessing data, printing work orders, and allows multi-user access to centralised files. On the other hand, the cost of setting up an information base and the effort required to get

Computer	Operating System	Program Language	Data Mgt. System	Hardware Cost £	Software Cost £
ABS-MX	RTXE	SIMPLE	FMS/SRG	35,000	40,000
DEC PDP 11/34	RSTS/E	BASIC	—	35,000	25,000
COMMODORE	—	—	—	3,000	3,000+
HP-1000	RTE IV B	FORTRAN	IMAGE 1000	50,000	50,000
IBM81xx	DPPX	COBOL	DTMS/DPS	60,000	(7,500*)
IBM370/303/x/ 43xx	DOS/VS(E)	COBOL	DLI/CICS		(11,500*)
ICL ME 29	TME	COBOL	RPG/IDMS	65,000	10,000
NORD 100	SINTRAN III/VS	FORTRAN	SIBAS	75,000	40,000
IBM 34/38	SSP-7	RPG 11	ISAM/	40,000	50,000
IBM 34		RPG			10,000
HP 1000	RTE PLUS	HIGH LEVEL	ARTEMIS		
DEC LSLLL/23	RT-11	COBOL	TSX-PLUS	25,000	30,000
HP 1000	RTE IV	FORTRAN	IMAGE 1000	50,000	140,000
HP 3000	MPE IV	COBOL	IMAGE 3000	62,000	80,000
DEC VAX			TOTAL		
DEC PDP 11/24	RSX 11 M	HIGH LEVEL	WFDS		
DG ECLIPSE	AOS/VS	COBOL	INFOS 11	98,000	53,000
IBM 43xx	DOS/VSE	COBOL	VSAM/CICS		53,000
IBM 81xx	DPPX	COBOL	DTMS/DMS		53,000

*Yearly Rental Cost

sensible feedback, via work orders, for the history record are both considerable.

(3) If the decision is to go for a computerised system, it must be specified in the light of the hardware currently available within the company. Assess the availability of spare processing and storage capacity. Determine the hardware characteristics; the programming language, the data management system, operating systems, etc.

(4) Survey the available software packages to determine which most closely match the specification outlined in (1). An important property in this respect is the degree to which a package can be modified (*flexibility*) to suit a specification. Most of the packages currently on the market are not flexible. It is the author's opinion that many more 'flexible' packages will become available in the next few years and it is likely that most users will then be able to find a good match. It is therefore often worthwhile considering modifying the maintenance system specification in order to match the software, since the cost of software modification is often greater than the cost of the software itself. The cost of developing tailor-made software is orders of magnitude greater than that of acquiring package software. Thus the development of bespoke software should be left to those large organisations which carry their own computer staff. See Figure 8.22. When software packages are bought the user must, at the contract stage, clearly state his requirements, for software maintenance and future modifications.

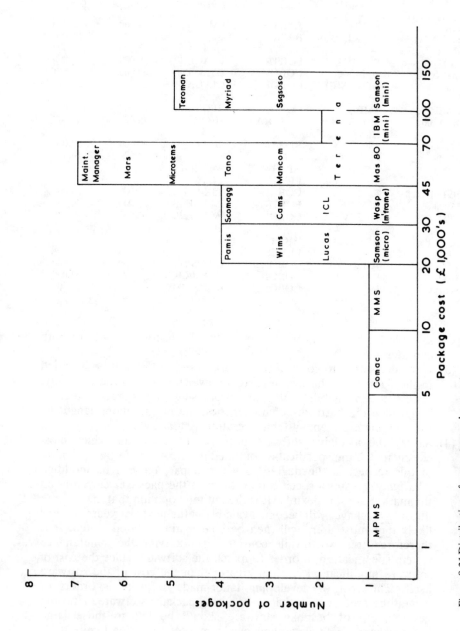

Figure 8.21 Distribution of computer-package costs

(5) Select the hardware system to suit software and maintenance system requirements. The majority of maintenance software packages have been designed to operate on specific computer hardware, often of a particular model type. Such packages are often not transferable without considerable, and very expensive, software modifications and it is then cheaper and simpler to buy the hardware that matches the

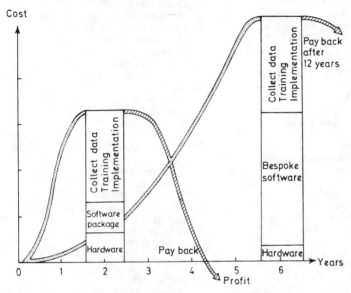

Figure 8.22 Cost comparison of software packages and bespoke software

software, (see Tables 8.9 and 8.10). It may be possible to utilise the storage capacity of existing hardware by providing suitable interfacing between it and the new hardware. This is an area where the maintenance systems engineer must consult the computer specialist. The portability of software packages is likely to improve during the next few years.

References

1. Macleod, R.A., Flegg, P.A., Prout, R. *'Minimising the cost of maintenance in a large integrated steelworks'*, The Metals Society, Book 271, 1980.
2. Comac Ltd., Poyle Rd, Colnbrook, Bucks, U.K.
3. Idhammar Konsult AB, Viksangswagen 10, S-151-57, Sodertalje, Sweden.
4. Mars Bars Ltd., Slough, Bucks. U.K.
5. Bamford M. and Kelly, A. Ph.D. project, University of Manchester, Manchester, U.K.
6. Smit, K. National Maintenance Congress, Café Royal, London. Nov. 1982.
7. *Software Survey*, 4th National Conference on Computers for Maintenance Managers, 9–10th March 1982, Café Royal, London.
8. Hopson, G., *A suggested approach* National Maintenance Congress, November 1982, Café Royal, London.
9. Slavin, M., *Horses for courses* National Maintenance Congress, November 1982, Café Royal, London.

List of addresses of software suppliers

(numbers refer to corresponding numbers of Table 8.10)

1 ABS Computers Limited
Multibus House
Station Approach, Woking
Surrey GU11 7UZ
tel: 048 62 70516

2 AKZO Systems Nederland B.V.
Postbus 930
6800 AX Arnhem
The Netherlands
tel: 085-664433

3 Comac Systems
Spaceregal House
Coln Estate
Old Bath Road, Colnbrook
Slough, Berkshire
tel: 028 12-2248

4 Davy Plant Management Limited
Powergas House
8 Baker Street
London W1A 4RD
tel: 01-486 3654

5 IBM (United Kingdom) Limited
389 Chiswick High Road
London W4
tel: 01-995 1441

6 International Computers Limited
Planned Maintenance Project Team
1 Derry Street
London W8 5EF
tel: 01-937 8133

7 Idhammar Konsult AB
Viksängsväg 10
S-151-57 Södertälje
Sweden
tel: 0753-31045

8 International Maintenance Organisation
Fluor House
PO Box 309
London NW1 2DJ
tel: 01-388 4222

9 H.B. Maynard & Co. Ltd.
Berkeley Square House
Berkeley Square
London W1X 5PB
tel: 01-491 3575

10 MOM (Offshore) Limited
41 Windmill Street
Gravesend
Kent DA12 1BA
tel: 0474 57746

11 MPA
Raamweg 38
2596 HN Den Haag
The Netherlands
tel: 070-469242

12 RIVA Turnkey Computer Systems Ltd.
Adam House
66 Chorley Street
Bolton BL1 4AL
tel: 0204 391423

13 Scicon Consultancy International Ltd.
Sanderson House
49 Berners Street
London W1P 4AQ
tel: 01-580 5599

14 Scomagg Limited
100 Park Street
Motherwell ML1 1PF
Scotland
tel: 0698 51421

15 Transcon Offshore Services Ltd.
11 Bingham Place
London W1M 3FH
tel: 01-486 9527

Chapter 9

Planning and scheduling of plant shutdowns

Annual overhauls and major plant shutdowns pose planning problems that are quite different from those of the ongoing workload. Shutdowns consist of a multiplicity of inter-related activities, all of which have to be co-ordinated if the work is to be completed in the desired time. Over-running the shutdown time can result in extremely high unavailability costs. Such work is therefore often treated as a separate planning entity calling for barchart control and/or network analysis. The individual tasks (normally undertaken by a combination of resident tradeforce and contract labour) being controlled via the customary documentation (WO s etc.).

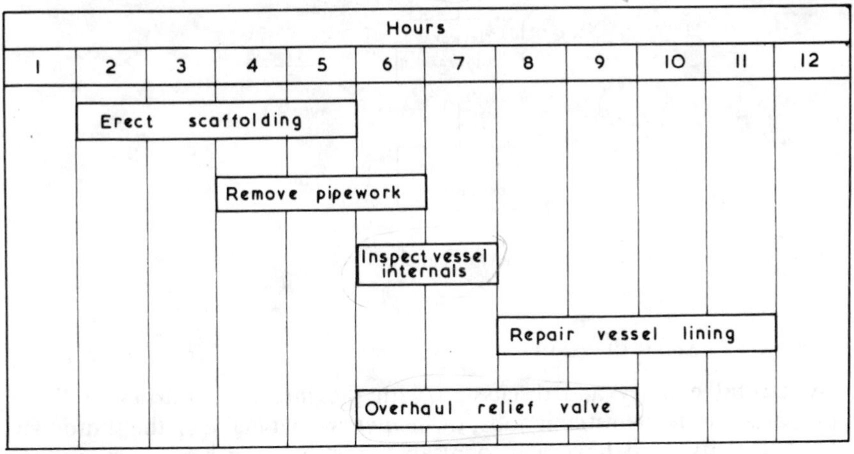

Hours											
1	2	3	4	5	6	7	8	9	10	11	12

Erect scaffolding

Remove pipework

Inspect vessel internals

Repair vessel lining

Overhaul relief valve

Figure 9.1 Barchart

A wall-mounted barchart (see Figure 9.1) is an adequate vehicle for planning a shutdown (e.g. a boiler overhaul) with no more than, say, 300 tasks; major shutdowns, however, may involve upwards of 3000 tasks. Many tens of tasks may then be simultaneous and logistic analysis demands some form of network method. For smaller shutdowns such analysis can be manual, with extraction on to barcharts to facilitate control. For larger projects network planning, and the associated scheduling and control, must be computerised. Computer packages are available which can produce barcharts and analyse resource needs from the input of basic information on each task. The main advantage of computerised network planning is its facility for rapid updating of the shutdown schedule in the light of alterations to planning constraints, either before or during the shutdown.

The basics of network planning

The procedure for establishing a network for a maintenance shutdown is shown in Figure 9.2. The various stages will be explained by reference to an illustrative example, viz: the repair of a chemical reactor.

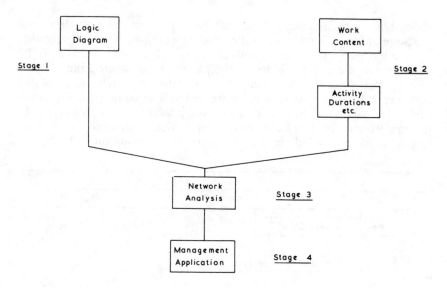

Figure 9.2 System of planning using network analysis

Stage 1—The logic diagram

By careful enquiry and discussion with the interested parties, a list is prepared of the identifiable jobs, the *activities*, that make up the shutdown. Each activity must have a recognisable start and finish. An activity can consume time only (e.g. waiting for paint to dry) or time and resources (e.g. building a wall). In the logic diagram each activity is represented by a Node with a number and description (see Figure 9.3). The next step is to identify the relationships between activities (see Table 9.1).

The activity nodes are now linked, by time-directional Arrows indicative of the relationships, into a Logic diagram or network. For example, 'open up vessel and inspect' cannot be started until 'preparatory work' has been completed (see Figure 9.4). On the other hand, 'repair damaged agitator', 'overhaul run-off valve' and 'fit new V-belt to drive' are independent of

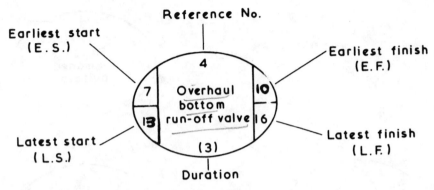

Figure 9.3 Diagrammatic representation of an activity

TABLE 9.1. A list of activities with their inter-relationship

No.	Description of activity	Inter-relationships	Activity duration (hrs)
1	Preparatory work	Independent of all other activities	1
2	Open up vessel and inspect	Depends upon 1	6
3	Repair damaged agitator	Depends upon 2	10
4	Overhaul bottom run-off valve	Depends upon 2	3
5	Fit new V-belts to drum	Depends upon 2	2
6	Re-fit bottom run-off valve	Depends upon 4	1
7	Box up vessel and sign off	Depends upon 3, 5 and 6	4

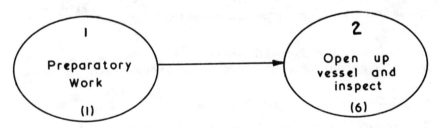

Figure 9.4 Diagrammatic representation of dependence

each other and are dependent on Activity 2 (see Figure 9.5). When drawing such a network the following rules must be obeyed :

(i) all activities must be connected to the start and finish activities,
(ii) no activity can start until all the activities leading into it have been completed.

The diagram is started by drawing the first activity (that which is independent of all others) and then the activity, or activities, which depend upon it (see Figure 9.4). For example, the next activity would be 'repair damaged agitator' which depends upon Activity 2 (see Figure 9.5). In the same way Activities 4 and 5 can be drawn. Activity 6 (dependent upon Activity 4) is drawn next and finally Activity 7 (dependent upon 3, 5

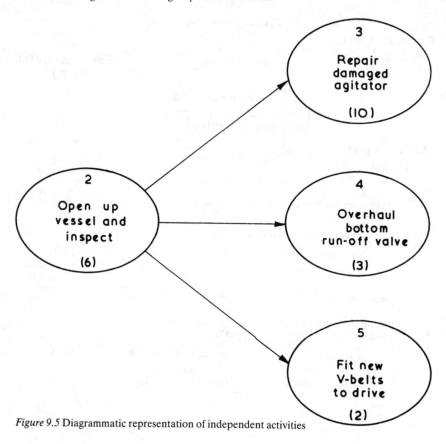

Figure 9.5 Diagrammatic representation of independent activities

and 6). The completed network (see Figure 9.6) is a graphical representation of the activities necessary for achieving the objectives of the project.

Stage 2—work content and activity duration

The time required for the individual activities and for the whole project must now be established. The time required to complete an activity is termed the *duration of the activity*. It can be estimated by careful discussion with Supervisors and Engineers or from the type of work measurement described in Appendix 4. In addition, a resource loading must also be established.

Stage 3—network analysis

This involves adding the activity durations to the logic diagram and calculating the shutdown duration and the degrees of criticality of the various activities. Each activity has assigned to it an earliest start (ES) and latest start (LS) time and an earliest finish (EF) and latest finish (LF), (see Figure 9.3). The degree of criticality of any particular activity is indicated by its *total float* = LS-ES. If this is zero the activity is critical.

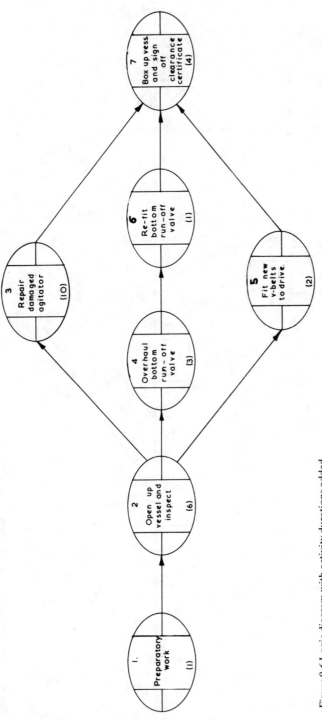

Figure 9.6 Logic diagram with activity durations added

236

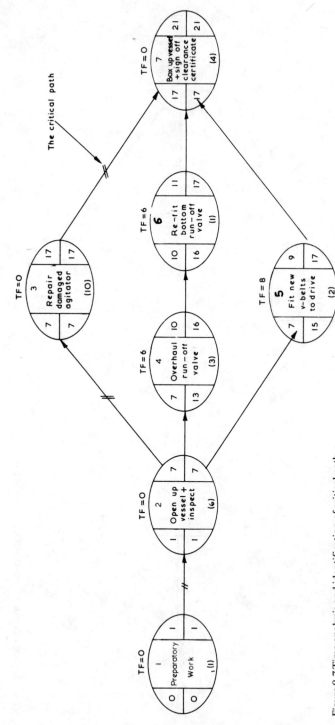

Figure 9.7 Time analysis and identification of critical path

The earliest and latest times for the activities of a project can be calculated from the estimated durations and the diagram logic. The earliest times are calculated from a forward pass through the diagram from the start activity to the end activity (see Figure 9.7). For an example, the ES for Activity 1 is zero. The duration is 1 time unit and therefore the EF is time unit 1. There is only one path between Activity 1 and Activity 2 therefore the ES for Activity 2 is time unit 1 (the same time as the EF for Activity 1). Since the duration of Activity 2 is 6 time units, its EF is time unit 7. The same procedure is followed for Activities 3, 4, 5 and 6. When considering the ES for Activity 7 the presence of three paths into it has to be taken into consideration. The ES for Activity 7 is time unit 17, which is the EF of the longest path to Activity 7. The EF for Activity 7 is time unit 21 which is also the project time.

The latest times are calculated from a backward pass through the diagram from the end activity to the start activity. For an example, the LF for Activity 7 is time unit 21 and the LS time unit 17. The LF for Activity 6 is time unit 17 (only one path back) and the LS is time unit 16 because the duration of Activity 6 is 1 time unit. Activities 5, 4 and 3 are dealt with in the same way. When considering Activity 2, the existence of three paths back to this activity has to be taken into consideration. The LF for Activity 2 is time unit 7, which is the LS of the shortest path back to Activity 2.

For each activity the total float should be shown. The critical path through the network is defined as that chain of activities which has the least total float, (i.e. for the example, Activities 1, 2, 3, 7). The first step in reducing the shutdown duration is to shorten the critical path activities. Opportunities for resource smoothing are revealed by an examination of the non-critical activities. In the example Activities 4, 5 and 6 each have a total float greater than zero.

This means that the start of Activity 4 can be delayed by up to 6 days and that of Activity 5 by up to 8 days without extending the shutdown duration.

Stage 4—Management applications

Two examples illustrate the various ways in which the network can be used to aid maintenance management.

Case A—unlimited resources/limited time

This normally applies to shutdowns of short duration. Control of duration is accomplished via control of the critical path and of the total float on the non-critical activities. The activities on the critical path must be started and finished at the earliest times. In the example of Figure 9.7 the correct procedure is to distribute the manpower in order of criticality, i.e. man up on Activity 3 before 4 and 6.

The network has obvious advantages for planning and analysis but lacks the barchart's capacity for displaying the progress of the shutdown. In order to control progress it is therefore necessary to extract a barchart presentation (see Figure 9.8). The time scale is plotted along the top of the chart and the activity numbers down the left-hand side. The critical activities are listed first, in order of execution, and then the non-critical

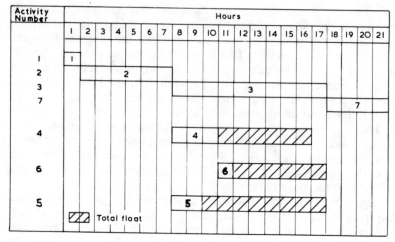

Figure 9.8 Barchart showing total float

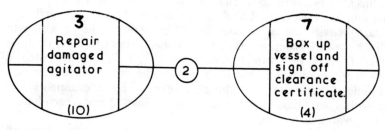

Figure 9.9 Overlapping activities

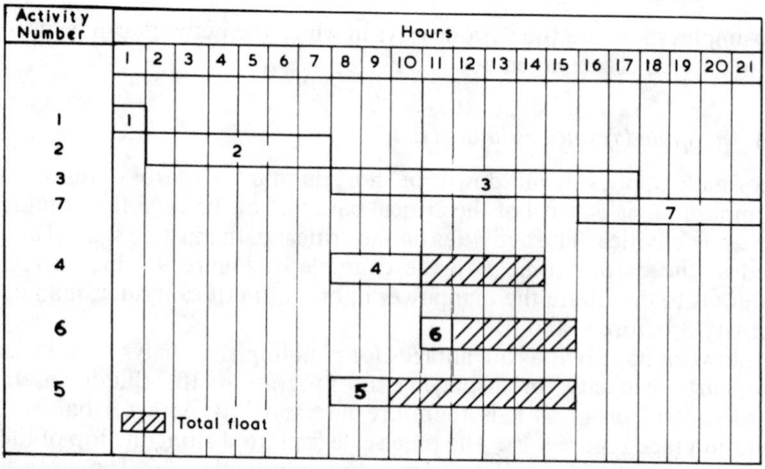

Figure 9.10 Barchart showing total float and overlap

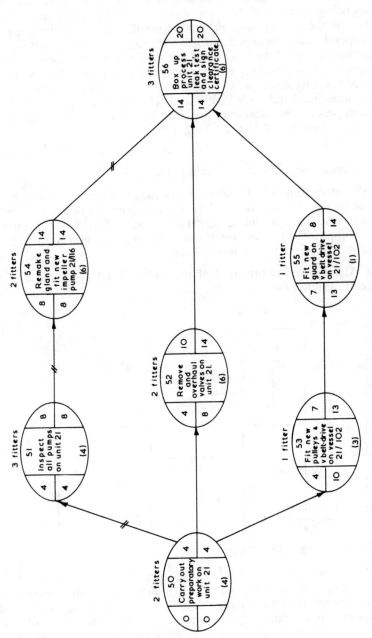

Figure 9.11 Network showing activity durations and associated resource loading

activities. It can be seen that the critical activities are like the links in a chain, with no overlap.

The shutdown time can be reduced in a number of ways, the most obvious being to concentrate extra resources (or better job methods) on activities on the critical path, although this will only be worthwhile if the extra expenditure is recouped through the profits of earlier plant startup. An alternative way of reducing shutdown time is to use overlaps on critical activities. In the example it might have been possible to start Activity 7 before completing Activity 3. This is shown in network form in Figure 9.9 and as a modified barchart in Figure 9.10. The overall effect of introducing the overlap would be to shorten the critical path by 2 days and to reduce the float on Activities 4, 5 and 6 by 2 days.

Case B—limited resources and/or limited time

The main attraction of using network planning of large shutdowns is that once the time calculation is complete the total float can be used to control the use of resources. Resource allocation on large shutdowns (see later) is usually computerised. However, the standard hand approach is illustrated in Figures 9.11 to 9.15. The method is as follows:

Step 1 A histogram is prepared of the earliest start aggregation of the resource utilisation (see Figure 9.12).

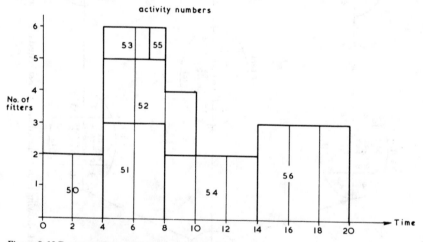

Figure 9.12 Resource aggregation by earliest start

Step 2 An assessment is made of the approximate minimum level of manning required to carry out the shutdown without extending the duration beyond the critical path completion time. In the case illustrated it would appear probable that the trough between the earliest finish of 51 and the earliest start of 56 can be filled by using the float on Activities 52, 53 and 55 with a maximum level of four men.

Step 3 The exact availability of the resource is established and activities identified which can be split between different shifts (see Figure 9.13).

① extra resources
and better job methods.

② use overlaps on critical
activities.

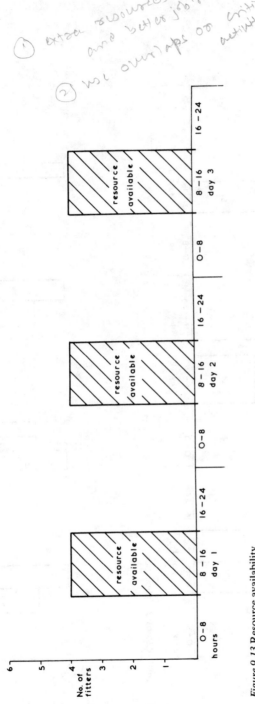

Figure 9.13 Resource availability

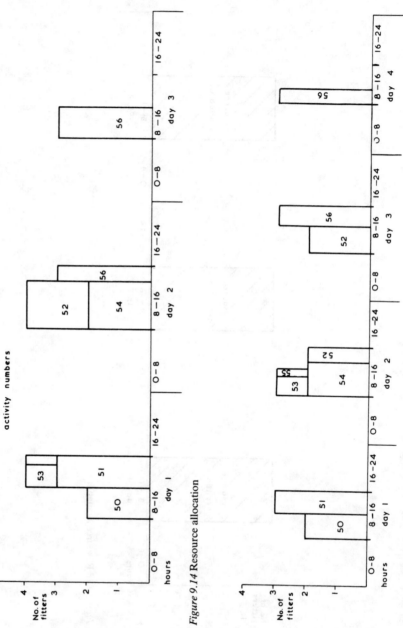

Figure 9.14 Resource allocation

Figure 9.15 Resource allocation—resource limited

Step 4 The resource allocation is shown in Figure 9.14. The first stage is to show the activities forming the critical path, i.e. 50, 51, 54 and 56 and the assumption is made that Activity 56 can be split between two shifts.

The whole period is divided, for the purpose of the analysis, into units of four hours. At time unit 3 Activity 51 requires three men which leaves one man in the pool of labour. Activity 53 can be started and the start of Activity 52 delayed. Similarly, at the completion of Activity 53, Activity 55 should begin with a further delay to Activity 52. Finally, Activity 56 is begun and is finished by time unit 15, i.e. within the available float.

One of the main objectives of this step is to obtain, for each resource, a smooth build-up to the peak working level and to hold this peak for as long as possible before starting a smooth run-down.

Step 5 It may be that after the initial resource calculation several activities are left with float. In this instance the resource allocation should be carried out by reducing the manning availability. Figure 9.15 shows the effect of reducing the manning level from four to three men, i.e. an extension of the shutdown by six time units.

Step 6 The histogram showing resource allocation should finally be translated into barchart form so that monitoring and control can be carried out during the shutdown.

The case for computer-aided network analysis

As stated, it is normal practice to computerise network planning of large shutdowns. Experience shows that the use of a computer is justified if, broadly speaking, one of the following conditions is met :

1. If the shutdown is purely time limited (i.e. ample resources are available), and there are more than 250 activities in the network.
2. If the shutdown has no time restraint but has limitations on the availability of resources, and there are more than 150 activities in the network.

Advantages of computerised network planning

(i) *Speed and accuracy* : A time-calculation of a 3000 activity network can be done manually in four to five days. However, the probability of errors is high. The same calculation using a computer can be carried out initially in two days, thereafter in anything from 3 to 24 hours depending upon the degree of priority.
(ii) *Prior investigation of work programme* : The logic diagrams are normally prepared by professional planning engineers who may not be fully aware of the possibilities of revising the overall work schedule to shorten the shutdown. Consultations between planning engineers and supervisors can highlight areas where the work sequence could be profitably altered and this can readily be checked. Furthermore, it is possible to investigate the introduction to the programme of decision logic in order to streamline the use of resources. For example, if the

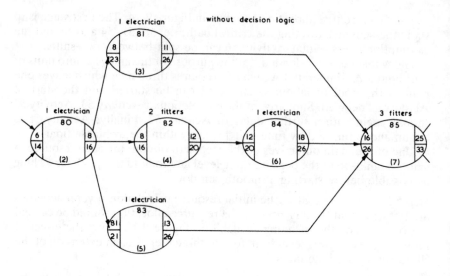

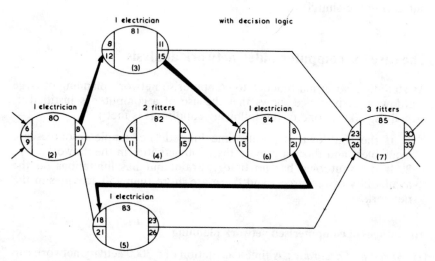

Figure 9.16 The application of decision logic to smooth resource working

initial resource-allocation runs showed that the electricians were not a
limiting resource it might then be possible to optimise their work
sequence so that, when isolating electric drives, they work along one
floor of the plant then along the next floor, etc. Figure 9.16 illustrates
the application of decision logic to a typical network.

(iii) *Identification of criticality* : Clearly, the appropriate personnel should
be fully aware of the truly critical activities and resource loadings. In
the initial calculations activity durations and resource loadings are
based on standard times, etc., achieved in previous shutdowns. Key

activities can therefore be shortened by, for example, adding more resources. When several shutdowns are planned for a particular plant computer output should be standardised as far as possible. This assists communication and can lead to greater control over critical areas of the shutdowns.

(iv) *Optimisation of resource utilisation* : The main benefit of network analysis of shutdowns is in facilitating the control of large resources. This is particularly so where contract labour is being used and forecasted requirements must match actual numbers used. On large shutdowns, up to 200 contract men can be employed and the planning should be in such detail that, for example, when a fitter has to open a pump for inspection, before he receives the work order the necessary prior activities (disconnection of electrics, issue of protective clothing, provision of essential spares, etc.) should be known to be complete.

(v) *Issue of useful computer output* : One of the advantages of the recent developments in computer language is that it is relatively easy to convert standard computer output into any required format. In addition, the output can be sub-divided in detail so that fewer sheets of information have to be issued to cover any one particular case (say, activities involving one class of tradesman on one type of process unit in one area of the plant). Before detailed shutdown planning goes beyond the logic diagram stage the output required by each level of staff should be established.

(vi) *Updating during shutdown* : Any planning system must be capable of coping with changes as and when they occur so that planning is always done on the basis of the most up-to-date information on the situation. Experience has shown that the initial stages (production run-down, cleaning out process lines, etc.) of a two to three week shutdown usually go more-or-less according to programme. The first major review of progress should take place after this first phase and the additional work arising due to unforeseen circumstances should also be examined. If a decision is made to update the computing program then the revised print-outs should be available within 5–7 hours i.e. within a normal working shift. During the period when the new print-outs are awaited, the shutdown should be controlled on the basis of the existing program, as far as possible, the additional work being 'manually' planned on barcharts.

The establishment of a shutdown programme

Before establishing a formal system for planning individual shutdowns it is essential for management to accept that it must prepare, and regularly review, a 12-monthly plan showing the basic timing for each of the major shutdowns. Figure 9.17 shows the procedure for producing a detailed programme. This is based on controlling the sequence of activities starting

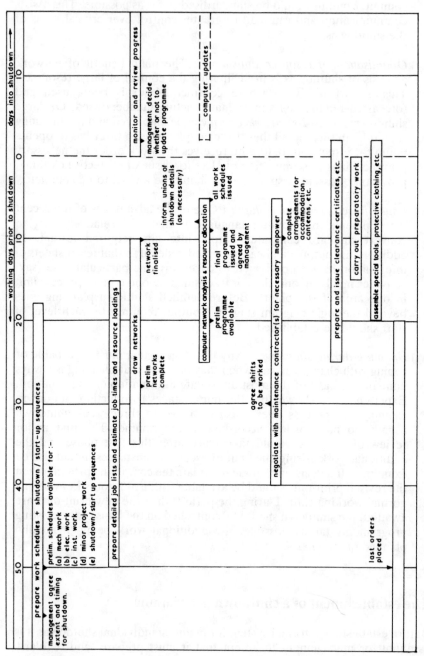

Figure 9.17 Sequence of work required to be carried out to produce realistic shut-down programme

10 weeks (i.e. 50 working days) before the shutdown is due to start. The most important features of the 50-day programme are as follows :

1. Management meets on a formal basis to agree the extent of the shutdown.
2. A good data retrieval system, for estimating job times and resource loadings for standard repetitive activities, is in operation.
3. The planning engineers actively encourage the personnel responsible for implementing the shutdown programme to comment on the logic diagram for their particular areas of work.
4. The computer service is available as and when required.
5. Adequate arrangements are made for issuing work schedules and monitoring progress.
6. Preparatory work is properly planned and controlled.

Control during shutdown
The three basic activities necessary to ensure that the detailed programme is being fully implemented are

(i) monitoring progress,
(ii) issuing job instructions, and
(iii) reviewing and updating.

Monitoring progress : large shutdowns are normally planned in one hour time units. Ideally, progress reports should be made every two hours. They should be delivered to the Central Planning Office and should include the following information :

(a) the estimated completion time of all 'live' activities,
(b) the actual completion time of activities,
(c) a review of impending activities,
(d) excesses or shortfalls on resources,
(e) additional work arisen or arising.

The reports should be vetted by the planning engineers and their content registered on the computer/manual barcharts. Any additional work should be analysed into elements having standard times, and durations and resource requirements estimated.

Job allocation : when a progress report is made the reporter receives detailed instructions of the next work. Work orders are normally issued and appended to them are such items as clearance certificates, instructions regarding access to special tools, etc.

Reviewing and updating the programme : as reports are received the planning engineer monitors progress on various barcharts. Clearly, there will be deviations from the programme but provided they can be corrected there is no need for major updating. If, however, a major unforeseen item arises this should be quickly analysed into 'standard' activities. It may be that the additional work can be planned by manually superimposing the activities on the computer print-outs. The difficult problem will probably involve the use of resources—in all such cases reference should be made to the original float on the computer program and men transferred from those jobs with most float. The maintenance contractor will have to be asked to provide additional manpower if the shutdown has still to be completed on the target date.

If major deviations from the logic diagram and large extensions to the work content arise then the computer program will require updating. The central planning engineer should automatically list completed activities on a computer input form as the progress reports are received. When the decision to update is reached immediate arrangements should be made to prepare input cards and to access the computer. The planning engineer will have to complete input forms for revised logic, modified durations and modified resource loadings. With tight control over these tasks turnaround times of between four and seven hours can be achieved.

Chapter 10

Maintenance planning and control at a large chemical process factory

A work planning and work control system, used for a large multi-trade labour force in a chemical process factory, is outlined. It illustrates in particular the application of the ideas and techniques of Chapters 5 and 6. The factory in question was that of Lever Bros. Ltd., Port Sunlight, U.K., whose own maintenance terminology is used throughout.

Basic requirements

The typical process factory is called upon to produce many diverse products at differing production rates and times and using a variety of machines. In order to meet the engineering demands, the planning function should be flexible and have the ability to adjust the sequence in which it carries out work, at short notice. If these requirements are to be fulfilled the flow of plannable work must be controlled. Hence the over-riding need to organise and maintain economic control over both the size and effectiveness of the labour force.

Engineering work is often complex and expensive. It therefore needs to be controlled in the light of a clear and overriding objective. In the present case the objective was 'to provide production with a service enabling the factory to produce finished products of an acceptable quality at a rate sufficient to meet marketing and sales requirements, at optimum engineering cost'. Also, it was felt that whatever method of planning and control was introduced it ought not to compound the problem by complicating the system of control itself. Many planning operations fail through being over elaborate and not clearly defining responsibility.

In essence a successful planning function should ensure that wherever practical, plannable man hours are directed on to work which has previously had its content estimated and its priority, relative to the factory needs, established.

In relating priorities the question constantly asked is 'who decides?'. The answer is that most experienced maintenance engineers and planning functions can, and do, set priorities intuitively. Nevertheless, in the present case, it was decided that a more disciplined approach would be to set priorities according to the guidelines of Table 10.1. Although it is

TABLE 10.1. Maintenance Job Priority List

Class	Title	Description
Class 1	Breakdowns & 'Real safety'	
Class 2	Preventive maintenance	Work aimed at preventing breakdowns or repair work.
Class 3	Production service	Necessary work performed during operating periods.
Class 4	Spares corrective maintenance	Work on spare parts or units when no additional spares are available.
Class 5	Shutdown work	Necessary shutdown work including safety work that can only be done during a shutdown period, but not critical enough to require an immediate shutdown.
Class 6	Routine work & normal safety maintenance	Work on spare parts or unit, normal maintenance, including repairs to tools and equipment and routine safety work.
Class 7	Special jobs & modifications	Work of a non-repair nature which is to improve the quality or quantity of product. Good housekeeping.

necessary, from time to time, to amend the rules by which maintenance expenditure, and hence the setting of priorities, is justified, the majority of maintenance, construction and repair jobs fall under the headings shown, with the work that is most important to production falling in the highest class.

Management information—labour costs

Any planning system must indicate where labour costs are being incurred.

Cost coding

The work to be done is sorted into three main cost centres, the cost number being made up as follows.

(i) *Factory departments and products* : These are given specific location numbers which are generally initiated by the accounts department and are often referred to as 'accounting numbers'. An example of this could be a departmental packing room. All costs which are incurred within that particular location are recorded against this number.

TABLE 10.2. Coding for engineering sections

Section/trade group	Reference number
Electrical	1
Installation fitters	2
Area fitters (Packing Room 1)	3
Area fitters (Packing Room 2)	4
Area fitters (Packing Room 3)	5
Joiners	6
Bricklayers/labourers	7
Painters	8
Fabrication shop	9
Machine	10

(ii) *Engineering sections* : Each of these has its number (see Table 10.2) which is allocated by the engineering department. It is important to ensure that all jobs for a given section can be fed to the supervisor/foreman who controls the labour within that section.

(iii) *Categories of engineering work* : A number or letter reference is used for this. The engineering department establishes the categories of work which need to be costed, e.g. it might have to be decided whether it is important to know the cost of the machine changeovers which normally occur when changing from one product to another. The need could be established on the basis of the frequency and duration of this operation.

Categories can be added or deleted as necessary, care being taken to ensure that all parties who are responsible for operating it are fully conversant with category definitions (see Table 10.3 for some examples of these). Agreed understanding of these is essential if the resultant cost analyses are to be accurate.

An example of the construction of a cost coding is given in Table 10.4. Such a coding may be further particularised (and hence the cost analysis made more detailed) by introducing building, plant, or even machine numbers (see Table 10.5).

Where work other than maintenance is carried out, e.g. capital work, a capital proposal number or project number would take the place of the department or product number (as shown in Table 10.6).

TABLE 10.3. Classes of work, titles and definitions

M.S.	Major Services All major service work, including de-installation and re-installation before and after Major Service and test running time following the Major Service but not including modifications or additions which are authorised on a works order, or capital and repairs to work.
B.	Breakdowns All breakdowns repairs to plant of an emergency nature, which have to be done immediately to maintain production.
R.M.	Running Maintenance Any work carried out as a result of inspections or lubrications, together with small simple jobs for which no EWR is issued, but not including Major Services, Breakdowns, Inspections and Lubrication Routines, Line Assigned Duty, Special Jobs or Capital.
L.A.	Line Assigned Duty Location of men to a specific production area with responsibility for maintaining the production lines within that area.
A.D.	Administration Engineering operating, i.e. storekeepers, equipment assistants, meter reading and battery charging.
P.R.	Preventive Routines
L.R.	Lubrication Routines
S.J.	Special Jobs Work other than Major Services, Breakdowns, Inspection and Lubrication Routines, Line Assigned Duty, Running Maintenance and Capital, which the engineering department is requested to carry out for other departments.
C	Capital Cost of installing new plant, and work on new building covered by Approved Capital Finance.
T	Training
A.C.	Associated and Allied Companies

TABLE 10.4. Construction of cost number

	Dept.	Engineering Section	Class of work
(a) Factory department (packing room 1)	30050		
(b) Engineering Section (electrical)		1	
(c) Class of work (major service)			MS
Cost number	30050	1	MS

TABLE 10.5. Extension of cost number

	Dept.	Engineering Section	Class of work	Plant Blg. No.
Factory department (packing area 1)	30050			
Engineering section (electrical)		1		
Class of work (major service)			MS	
Item of plant (wrapping machine)				26840
Cost number	30050	1	MS	26840

TABLE 10.6. A capital work cost number

	Capital Proposal No.	Eng. Sect.	Class of work
Capital Proposal No.	01506		
Engineering section (electrical)		1	
Class of work (capital)			C
Cost number	01506	1	C

Labour summary from weekly work sheet

This (see Figure 10.1) is produced for both the engineering department and each of its sections. The example shows the weekly man hour returns under their appropriate work headings. These are extracted from the men's weekly work sheets (see Figure 10.2) it being a straightforward clerical procedure to gather all the work sheets under their respective section references, collating the man hours spent against the respective class of work.

The weekly labour summary can be used to examine high cost areas, for budget estimating and control, or for setting departmental targets.

Computer-based management information system

The original simple manual information system outlined on page 250 has been developed into an on-line mini-computer-based system. Much clerical effort was required to operate the manual system and lead times for making information available to management were considerable.

The prime sources of input are the 'man's weekly work sheet' and Engineering Work Requests (EWRs), that is the work order of Chapter 6. The EWR information is inserted into the computer file via a VDU. Each man has a unique work sheet indicating EWRs worked on together with the time spent on each job. The work sheets are processed weekly by the

Classes of Engineering Work

Total Clocked Hours

1981 QTR. NO. 3rd

WEEKLY LABOUR SUMMARY

DEPARTMENT ENGINEERING | SECTION ELECTRICAL | SECTION REF. 1

WEEK ENDING	MAINT. TOTALS	MAJOR SERVICE MS	PREV. ROUTINES PR	LB	RUNNING MAINT. RM	BREAK DOWNS	LINE ASSOC DUTY LA	CHANGE OVERS CO	ADMIN. AM	TRAINING T	SPECIAL JOBS SJ	ASSOC. ALL'D CO. AC	CAPITAL C	CLOCK HOURS	OVERTIME 1½	OVERTIME 2
7.7.81	1,823		159		1183	402	79		402		34	63	846	3168	336	41
14.7.81	1,891	13	176		1278	348	76		399		16	33	784	3123	442	32
21.7.81	1,936		167		1316	383	70		340		173	71	711	3231	303	163
26.7.81	1,947	13	175		1250	443	66		398		77	31	499	2952	362	40
4.8.81	1,642	8	129		1030	413	62		378		83	30	433	2566	455	8
11.8.81	1,849	37	98		1288	320	106		301		16	103	541	2810	456	212
18.8.81	1,720		137		1128	365	90		278		355	93	387	2833	454	133
25.8.81	1,532		149		993	288	102		262		418	50	216	2478	272	145
1.9.81	1,236		139		810	209	78		218		259	27	361	2104	338	–
8.9.81	1,255		175		1008	467	73		264	51	159	14	426	2669	324	24
15.9.81	2,041	8	166		1325	477	65		350	24	62	87	463	3032	471	80
22.9.81	2,013	15	134		1377	465	22		348		8	147	395	2911	297	152
29.9.81	1,798	2	185		1123	406	82	32	330	25	136	61	469	2819	447	73
QTR. TOTALS	23,183	96	1989		15109	4986	971	32	4268	100	1796	810	6539	36696	4957	1103
AV. WEEK	1,783	7	153		1162	384	75	2	328	8	138	62	503	2822	381	85
QTLY. TARGETS																
LAST YEAR COMP. QTR.	2,099	77	204		1122	694	2		356	23	112	32	901	3523	590	114

13 weeks

Weekly Averages

Weekly Averages Previous Comparable Quarter

Figure 10.1 Typical weekly labour summary

254

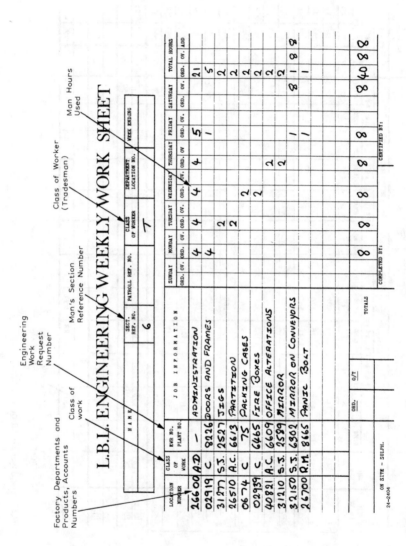

Figure 10.2 Typical weekly work sheet

mini-computer which checks each EWR against the input files and indicates any incorrect entries on the work sheet (e.g. if it does not recognise an EWR number it rejects it and requests clarification). From this basic input the following output reports can be called up:

Manhour distribution
Weekly labour summary
Weekly overtime
Repairs and maintenance: class of work costs
Repairs and maintenance: paid hours
Repairs and maintenance: labour materials costs
Engineering work request progress
Capital project progress

Repairs and maintenance costs can be analysed by:

Engineering division,
Engineering group,
Engineering section,
Individual production cost centre.

The 'capital-work-in-progress' recording system is capable of producing summaries of all expenditure, incurred or committed. The expenditure for each project is automatically transferred to the Engineering Labour Control System and a request can then be made for a comparison of *actual* expenditure, on labour and on materials, with the *estimated* expenditure for individual projects. The following output reports can be produced—

Detail of purchase orders,
Summary of purchases,
Summary of all recorded purchases.

Work planning and work control

It has been recognised that many planning systems fail simply because they attempt to *overplan*. They try to organise and co-ordinate multi-trade activities to the extent of selecting the men and the precise times of the

TABLE 10.7. Allocation of responsibilities and roles

Responsibility	Time scale
Management/planner	
The selection of jobs and the order in which they are done	One week to one year
Forecasting, both short and long range	
Allocation of the number of men involved	
Overall control	
Supervisor/foreman	
Man/men for job	One minute and
Emergency job work	one to three weeks
Agreed routine work i.e. lubrication and preventive routines	
Small single trade jobs of under 2 hours duration	

This Copy to be Retained by the Originator

ENGINEERING WORK REQUEST

No 17703

1ST ISSUE

PERMIT TO WORK REQUIRED   YES [ ]   NO [ ]

Subwork Request Issued

Requesting Dept:	Requested by:	Extn. No.:	Date Issued:	Date Required:

Location No.:	Class of Work	Eng. Sect. Ref.	Plant No.	Planning Dates Required	Plan Week No.

From: To:

Instructions:

MULTI TRADES INVOLVED

Section	Man Hr. Slot	Section	Man Hr. Slot
Constr. Workers		Electrical	
Plumbers		Instr. Elect.	
Fitting Shop		Instr. Physical	
Laggers		Blocklayers	
Machine Shop		Bricklayers	
Engraving		Glaziers	
Sheetmetal		Joiners	
Boiler Shop		Navvies	
Welding Shop		Painters	
Dept. Fitters		Scaffolders	
Sprinklers		Rigg & Sail	
Installn. Fitters		Heavy Gang	

CO-ORDINATING SUPERVISOR

Authorised by:	Date Completed:	EXT. No.	Comp. Sign. Super.:

Figure 10.3 A typical engineering work request

work. These duties are clearly the responsibility of the supervisor/foreman, who will not only resent, quite rightly, any interference in this field, but is furthermore the only person who is in a position to deal effectively with a sudden emergency or breakdown and offset its possible effect upon the planned work programme. In the light of these observations the responsibilities and role of the planning management and supervisors were defined as shown in Table 10.7.

The engineering work request

An example is shown in Figure 10.3. Five copies are produced for each job and used by the following :

Originator (top copy)
Planning department (second copy)
Supervisor/foreman (third copy)
Estimating (fourth copy—may not be required)
Accounts (fifth copy—may not be required)

Each copy is a different colour but they are otherwise identical.

In the example of Figure 10.4 it can be seen that there were four trades involved, i.e.

Section	Section Reference Numbers (see Table 10.2)
Electrical	1
Installation Fitters	2
Fabrication Shop	9
Machine Shop	10

The EWR is addressed to the installation fitters. Their section reference number therefore appears in the appropriate box. Since there are three other sections involved it will be necessary for engineering planning to make out an additional EWR for each one. These are raised on special 'sub' EWR forms which have been printed with a blank space where the EWR identification number is normally printed. In this is inserted the number on the original EWR thus ensuring that all parties are referring to

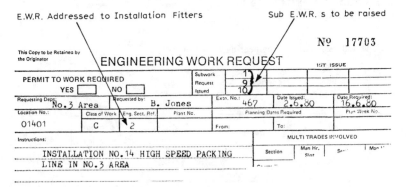

Figure 10.4 An example of an addressed engineering work request

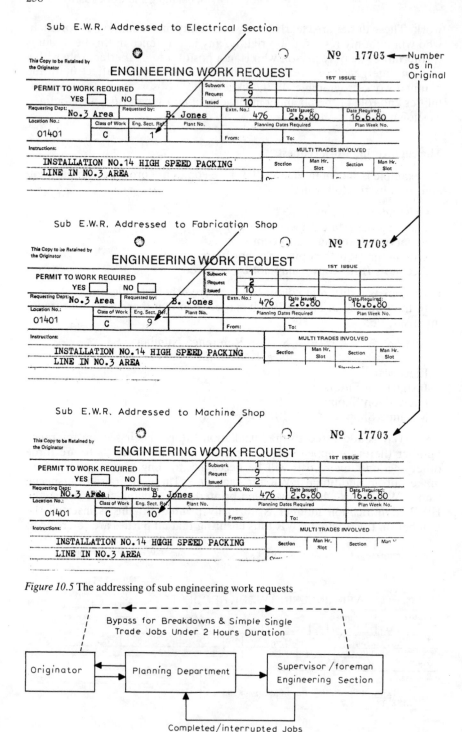

Figure 10.5 The addressing of sub engineering work requests

Figure 10.6 Engineering work request flowchart

the same EWR when discussing the work. The addressing of each sub-EWR is illustrated in Figure 10.5.

The flow of EWR, is shown in Figure 10.6. All requests for engineering work are raised on EWRs and forwarded to planning. There should be no bypassing of the engineering planning department with requests for work made directly to the supervisor/foreman. This does not mean that discussions do not take place between originators and supervisors in deciding upon possible work methods and improvements to design. This is necessary, of course, and is encouraged, but in the final analysis planning decides the order in which work is done. The exceptions to this rule are breakdowns, emergencies or simple single-trade jobs of under 2 hours duration. It was clear that a bypass for this type of work was needed since it would have been nonsensical to have breakdowns waiting until EWRs were raised.

The originator requesting the emergency or simple job contacts supervisor/foreman directly, quoting an EWR number and an accounts cost location number. This is all the supervisor/foreman requires in order to allocate men's time to weekly time-sheets. The completed EWR can follow later. In this way a check can be kept upon the number of emergency requests and control exercised over any abuse of the bypass system.

Example to illustrate manpower resource planning

Consider a section called, say, the installation fitting group and consisting of 15 men (10 skilled + 5 semi-skilled).

15 men × 40 hour working week × 52 = 31,200 man hours per year
Less 7% Sickness (variable, but approximately the UK average)
Less 3 weeks holiday per man per year
Less 6 days statutory holidays per man per year
Total reductions = 4,704 man hours per year
Total man hours available per year = 31,200 − 4,704 = 26,496
Average man hours available per week = 510.

Resources can now be allocated. This is done by simply listing the chosen classes of work on to a 13 week or quarterly allocation as in Figure 10.7.

On examining the classes of work it is found that there are those that require estimation (average weekly assessments AWA) and those that can be calculated (calculated weekly commitments—CWC).

Breakdowns/emergencies and running maintenance require AWA and a system of apportioning man-hours per week and inserting these estimates into the appropriate estimating column, is adopted. In the example it is estimated that 80 and 40 man-hours per week will be spent, on average on running maintenance and breakdowns respectively. It is not imperative that these initial estimates should prove accurate. After a while the original estimates can be adjusted in the light of actual returns taken from the work sheets. A check would be made on the accuracy of estimates approximately every 4 weeks.

Estimated Average Weekly Assessments

Actual Man Hour Returns from mens weekly work sheets

Installation Fitters

WEEKLY ALLOCATION SCHEDULE   SECTION REF. NO:-   QUARTERLY PERIOD WEEKS

	Week No. 1			Week No. 2			Week No. 3			Week No. 13			TOTALS			AV. ACT.
	Est.	Act.	Var.	Est.	Act.	Var.	Est.	Act.	Var.	Est.	Act.	Var.	Est.	Act.	Var.	
TOTAL AVAILABLE WEEKLY HOURS →	510	520	+10	510	515	+5	510	505	-5							
Major Service	-	-	-	-	-	-	140	148	-8							
Preventive Routines	20	16	4	20	24	4	20	20	-							
Lubrication Routines	-	-	-	-	-	-	-	-	-							
Running Maintenance	80	60	20	80	55	25	80	65	15							
Breakdowns	40	25	15	40	15	25	40	20	20							
Line Attendance	80	82	2	80	78	2	80	80	-							
Changeovers	-	-	-	-	-	-	-	-	-							
TOTAL MAINTENANCE:-	220	183	-31	220	173	-48	360	333	-27							
Plant Operating (Admin.)	40	40	-	40	41	1	40	39	1							
Training	10	8	2	10	9	1	10	13	3							
TOTAL OVERHEADS:-	50	48	-2	50	50	-	50	52	+2							
Special Jobs	160	179	19	140	168	28										
Associated Companies	-	-	-	-	-	-	-	-	-							
Capital	80	110	30	100	125	25	100	120	20							
TOTAL CAPITAL:-	240	298	-49	240	293	+53	100	120	+20							
No. of E.W.R.s issued																
No. of E.W.R.s returned																

Calculated Weekly Commitments

Figure 10.7 Quarterly allocation schedule

Routines, line attendance, administration, training (see Table 10.3) come into the category of CWC. In the example of Figure 10.7 the values calculated for these classes are

Routines—20 hours
Line attendance—80 hours
Administration—40 hours
Training—10 hours

Giving a total CWC of 150 hours. So, for the Installation Fitting Group—

$$\begin{pmatrix} \text{Average man} \\ \text{hours available} \\ \text{per week} \end{pmatrix} \text{ minus (AWA) minus (CWC)} = \begin{pmatrix} \text{Weekly balance} \\ \text{available for} \\ \text{planned jobs} \end{pmatrix}$$

i.e. $510 - 120 - 150 = 240$

A similar calculation is made for each section.

The planned jobs are scheduled for each section and a *set* of 52 week planning schedules, one for each class of work (see Figures 10.8, 10.9, and 10.10) is drawn up. The jobs are listed in pencil down the left hand side. If the job is multi-trade then it will appear on the relevant schedule of several sections.

SECTION: INSTALLATION FITTERS

52 WEEK/WORK SCHEDULE

Major Services

Sheet No. 1

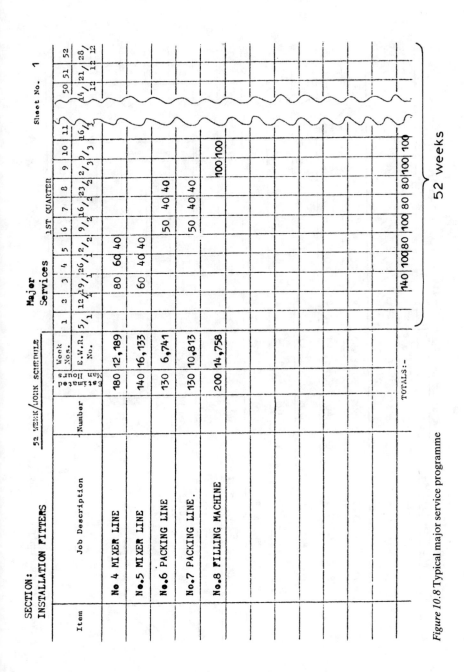

Item	Job Description	Number	Estimated Man Hours	Work Nos. E.W.R. No.	1 — 5/1	2 — 12/1	3 — 19/1	4 — 26/1	5 — 2/2	6 — 9/2	7 — 16/2	8 — 23/2	9 — 2/3	10 — 9/3	11 — 16/3	50 — 14/12	51 — 21/12	52 — 28/12
	No 4 MIXER LINE	180	12,189			80	60	40										
	No.5 MIXER LINE	140	16,133			60	40	40										
	No.6 PACKING LINE	130	6,741						50	40	40							
	No.7 PACKING LINE.	130	10,813						50	40	40							
	No.8 FILLING MACHINE	200	14,758									100	100				
	TOTALS:-					140	100	80	100	80	100	80	100	100				

52 weeks

Figure 10.8 Typical major service programme

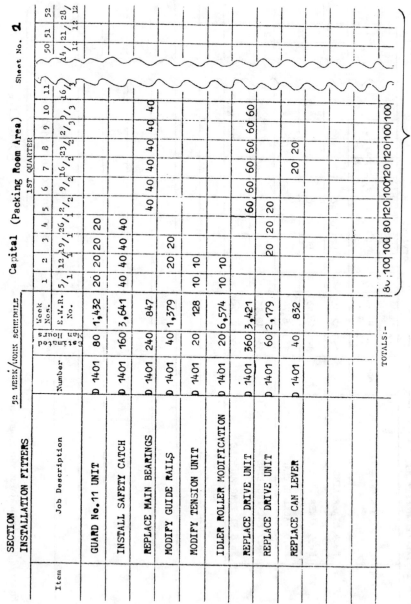

Figure 10.9 Capital and new work listing

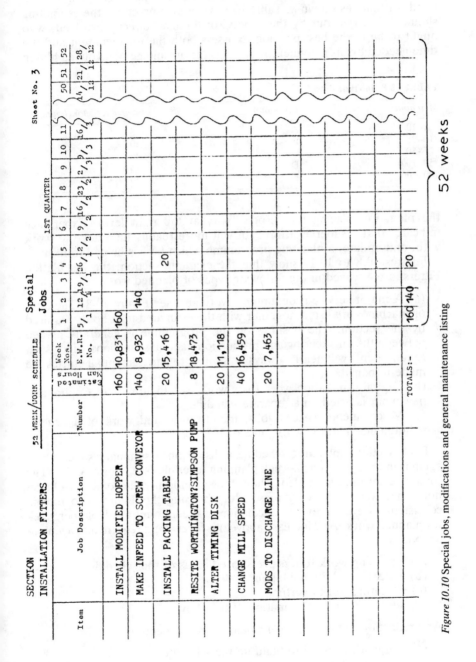

Figure 10.10 Special jobs, modifications and general maintenance listing

The man hour content of each job is estimated by trade. A useful method of doing this is to use a slotting method, jobs being placed into bands of time, as shown in Table 10.8. Wherever practical, the estimating should be carried out by the supervisor/foreman directly involved, who ought to be in the best position to assess both the work content and the time needed by his man/men. It also has the advantage of involving him in

TABLE 10.8. Job time slots

Man hours	Est. group	Plannable factor (hours)
1–10	A	8
10–25	B	20
25–50	C	40
50–100	D	75
100–200	E	150

the plan, i.e. placing the responsibility at the right level. Experience indicates that a supervisor/foreman will more readily undertake to work with, and update, a planning programme which he has helped to form.

Figures 10.8 to 10.10 show that the example section, the Installation Fitters, are engaged in the following types of planned work:

(a) A major service programme (overhauls, see Figure 10.8) The lines or machines are listed, together with the estimated man-hours required by the section. The position on the programme is generally agreed between the engineering and production planning functions. Since such requirements will nearly always be subject to amendment all entries are made in pencil.

(b) Capital installation work (new work, see Figure 10.9). Capital and new work is listed on a separate schedule.

(c) Miscellaneous special jobs, modification and work of a general maintenance nature (see Figure 10.10).

Each section's planning schedule is listed on a summary sheet which again is in the form of a 52-week planning schedule (see Figure 10.11). The totals are set out and added. They show a smooth work load of 240 man hours per week. The only reason for choosing this figure is to remain consistent with the previous calculation of the amount available per week for planned work. Any increase above this level could require management action, i.e.

(a) rephasing work to less pressurised areas of the schedule,
(b) allocating additional labour,
(c) allocating work overtime,
(d) adopting some combination of the above.

Any reduction below this level would suggest a need to—

(a) pull work forward to build up the schedule,
(b) divert or reduce labour levels,
(c) reduce overtime levels,
(d) carry out some combination of the above.

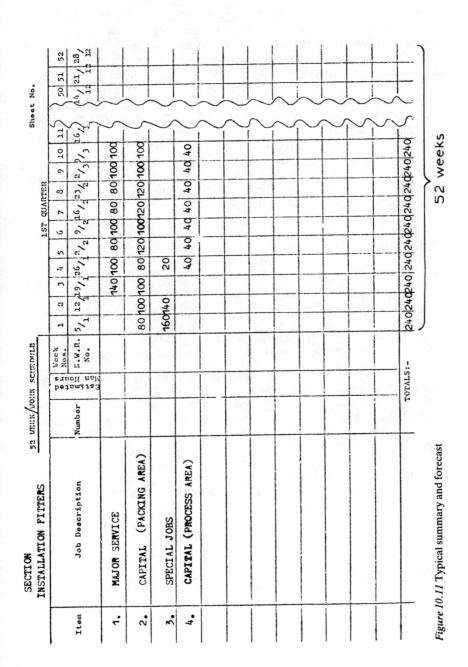

Figure 10.11 Typical summary and forecast

If the programme includes all the known work a comprehensive picture, for a 12 month period for each section, can be built up.

At the end of each week the supervisor/foreman responsible for the section updates the plant with the engineering planning department. Any jobs which have not been completed are assessed in order to ascertain how many man-hours remain outstanding and these hours are moved forward into the following week/weeks. Jobs which have been completed can be deleted from the schedules to make way for further entries.

The importance of the update meeting between supervision and planning cannot be over-stressed. It familiarises both parties with the current situation, and allows for adjustments to be made, on a weekly basis, to both the short- and long-term plan.

In general, it has been found that the ideal time for such meetings is on Thursdays, thus allowing the forthcoming weekly work to be issued in advance and enabling prior discussion to take place between supervisors, particularly with regard to multi-trade work.

Basic rules for success

(1) Keep the whole system as simple as possible.
(2) Make all entries on schedules in pencil.
(3) Hold weekly update sessions between planning and supervisor/foreman.
(4) Feed only sufficient work per week per section.
(5) Supervisors should estimate the work content (man-hours).

On multi-trade work it is essential that planning ensures that each section has the resources available before issuing the work. If, at the update session, a section involved does not have the resources, then arrangements have to be made either to provide the resources by rephasing work or, should this not be desirable, to re-schedule the job to another period in the forward work programme, thus ensuring that each section involved has its appropriate schedule altered. It has also been found an advantage, on complex multi-trade work, to appoint a co-ordinating supervisor responsible for seeing that trades arrive at a time most suitable to expedite the work.

Chapter 11

Failure statistics

The importance of the collection, storage and analysis of failure data as a means of highlighting maintenance problem areas has been discussed in the previous chapter. This chapter will show how such data can be used in the diagnosis of recurrent failures and in the establishment of a maintenance procedure.

In Chapter 2 a large and complex industrial plant was viewed as a hierarchy of parts ranked according to their function and replaceability (see Figure 2.4). Every item of plant has to perform a function. When this performance becomes inadequate (as judged by some predetermined criterion) the item is said to have failed.

The time-to-failure of an item is a probabilistic variable. Analysis therefore demands an understanding of the basic elements, at least, of *failure statistics*, which I shall here take to be the application of statistical techniques to the description and analysis of the patterns of failure of plant or its separate units and items.

Basic statistical ideas

Graphical representation of failure data

Let us assume that one hundred filament lamps have been run continuously and the time-to-failure noted in each case. A table such as 11.1 can then be drawn up. Using the data in the fourth column a histogram of the relative frequency densities can be constructed (see Figure 11.1). By drawing the histogram this way the area of the block above each class interval equals the relative frequency of failure in that interval (even if unequal class intervals were to be used, which is sometimes more convenient).

The assumption might now be made that the pattern of failure of this particular sample of 100 lamps represents the probable failure pattern of the generality of such lamps, i.e. the *observed* relative frequencies truly reflect the *expected* probabilities of failure. The probability that a lamp of this kind will last longer than say, 700 hours is then given by the shaded area in the histogram, i.e. $0.19 + 0.08 + 0.01 = 0.28$.

TABLE 11.1. Lamp failure data

Class interval	Frequency	Relative frequency	Relative frequency density
Time to failure (hours)	No. of lamps	Fraction of total	Fraction per hour
300–400	2	0.02	0.0002
400–500	9	0.09	0.0009
500–	21	0.21	0.0021
600–	40	0.40	0.0040
700–	19	0.19	0.0019
800–	8	0.08	0.0008
900–	1	0.01	0.0001
	100	1.00	

NOTE: The figures in the fourth column are obtained by dividing those in the third by 100 h, the width of the class interval.

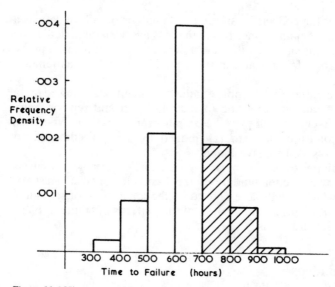

Figure 11.1 Histogram of data in Table 11.1

Mean, variance and standard deviation

Having displayed the general form of the variability in time-to-failure, some parameters are now required which can usefully characterise the various features of the variability :

1. For the typifying value, or *central tendency*, of the observed times-to-failure, we often use the arithmetic mean,

$$m = \Sigma f_r t_r$$

where

Σ = 'the sum of all such terms as .....'

f_r = relative frequency in the rth class interval

t_r = mid point of the rth class interval

Thus, for the sample of lamps,

$$m = (0.02 \times 350) + (0.09 \times 450) + (0.21 \times 550) + ... \text{ etc.}$$
$$= 642 \text{ h}$$

2. For the spread, or *dispersion*, of the times-to-failure we often use the variance

$$s^2 = \Sigma f_r(t_r - m)^2$$

So, for the lamps

$$s^2 = 0.02(350 - 642)^2 + 0.09(450 - 642)^2 + ... \text{ etc.}$$
$$= 13\,500 \text{ h}^2$$

A quantity that is measured in squared hours seems rather fanciful; however, it can be shown that if a given variability results from the combined effect of several separate sources of variability then the net variance is often a simple additive function of the separate variances. Such a simple relationship does not exist for more obvious measures of dispersion, such as the range (= greatest value minus least value). Nevertheless, when presenting information regarding dispersion it is clearly more meaningful to present it in the same dimensions as the quantity of interest and for this purpose we use the standard deviation, s, i.e. the square-root of the variance.

So, for the lamps

$$s = (13\,500)^{1/2} = 116 \text{ h}$$

Failure probability, survival probability

The time-to-failure information in Table 11.1 can be presented in other forms that may be more useful for the study of causes of failure.

Failure probability : a graph can be drawn (see Table 11.2 and Figure 11.2) of the rise in the total fraction, F(t), of the items that have failed by any given time t.

TABLE 11.2. Variation with time of total fraction failed (data of Table 11.1)

Time t	0	100	200	300	400	500	600	700	800	900	1000
Total fraction $F(t)$ failed	0	0	0	0	0.02	0.11	0.32	0.72	0.91	0.99	1.00

If the sampled 100 lamps are assumed to be representative then F(t) is the fraction of all such lamps which can be expected to fail by the running time, t, since new. That is, for any given lamp, F(t) = probability of failure before a running time t.

Survival probability : by contrast with the above the fraction, P(t), of items surviving at running time t could be tabulated and plotted (see Table 11.3 and Figure 11.3). Clearly, P(t) = 1 – F(t).

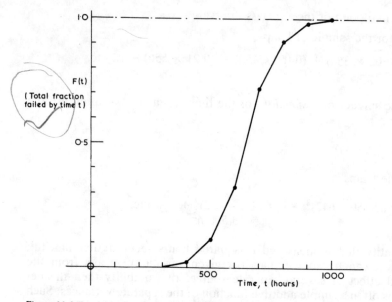

Figure 11.2 Total (or cumulative) fraction failed, as a function of time: data from Table 11.2

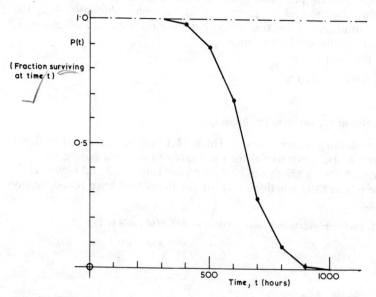

Figure 11.3 Fraction surviving, as a function of time: data from Table 11.3

TABLE 11.3. Variation of fraction surviving (data of Table 11.1)

Time	t	100	200	300	400	500	600	700	800	900	1000
Fraction	$P(t)$	1.0	1.0	1.0	0.98	0.89	0.68	0.28	0.09	0.01	0.00

Again, assuming that the 100 lamps are representative, P(*t*) is the survival probability, at time *t*, for any one lamp. In the literature on this subject P(*t*) is very commonly called the 'reliability', at time *t*, and the symbol R(*t*) is used. The term 'survival probability' is used here in order to distinguish this measure of reliability from that which is appropriate in the case of things like pressure release valves, temperature sensitive trip-mechanisms, and safety mechanisms generally, which are normally inoperative until called on. Expected fraction of demands meeting with the required response would then be a more relevant parameter of reliability.

Probability Density Functions—Cumulative Distribution Functions

If, instead of just 100 lamps, many thousands had been tested the width of the class intervals in Figure 11.1 could have been reduced to such a degree that the step nature of the histogram would have been virtually eliminated and a continuous probability density distribution obtained, as in Figure 11.4. Similarly, the stepped graph of cumulative fraction failed shown in Figure 11.3 would have become a smooth curve, as shown in Figure 11.5, where $F(t) = \int_0^t f(t) \, dt$.

Probability density distributions that can be described by mathematical functions are referred to as Probability Density Functions (PDF s) each of which has an associated Cumulative Distribution Function (CDF).

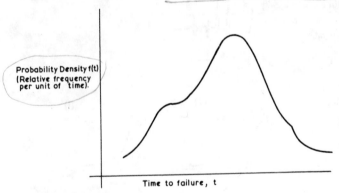

Probability Density f(t)
(Relative frequency per unit of time).

Time to failure, t

Figure 11.4 Continuous probability density distribution

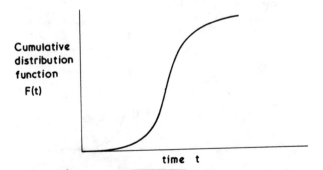

Cumulative distribution function F(t)

time t

Figure 11.5 Cumulative distribution function

Failure models

In Chapter 3 failures were classified as either predictable or unpredictable and were so classified in order to assist in the selection of the best maintenance procedure. It will be remembered that those items which failed totally unpredictably (time independent) were not suitable candidates for fixed-time-replacement. Obviously it would be of advantage if the failure pattern of an item of plant could be clearly described in terms of practically meaningful parameters.

Many failure-causing mechanisms give rise to measured distributions of times-to-failure which approximate quite closely to analytical probability density functions. Such functions therefore provide mathematical models of failure patterns which can be used to assist maintenance decision making.

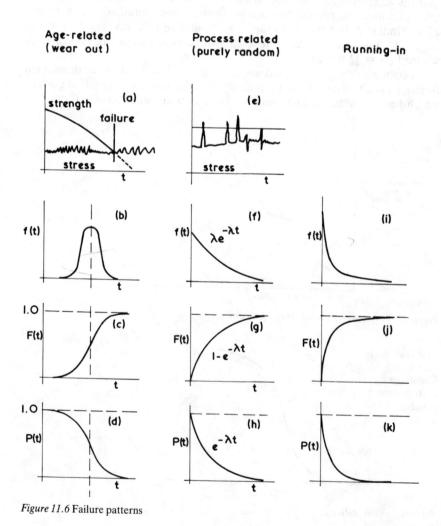

Figure 11.6 Failure patterns

mal operation
poor design.

Age-dependent failure—a predictable-failure model

A simplified model of an age-dependent failure process is shown in Figure 11.6(a). There is an increasing likelihood of failure as the component grows older and the times-to-failure of a large number of such components would therefore be distributed as in Figure 11.6(b) (where f(t) = probability of failing per unit time, at running time (t)). Figure 11.6(c) gives the fraction of items expected to have failed by some time t, i.e. the probability of failure F(t). Figure 11.6(d) gives the fraction of items surviving at running time t, i.e. the survival probability P(t).

A failure pattern of this type indicates that the failure is age-related and due to mechanisms such as abrasion, corrosion or fatigue. Often, the pattern approximates quite closely to the well known *Normal PDF* although analysts have shown that for certain specific mechanisms other functions, while broadly similar, may be more appropriate (e.g. for aircraft structural fatigue, the Birnbaum-Saunders[1] family of expressions).

Purely random failure—an unpredictable failure model

It is the experience with a very wide range of components and items that, under their normal operating conditions and during their normal operating life, they do not reach a point of wear-out failure at some likely time that could be called 'old-age'. On the contrary, a given item is as likely to fail in a given week shortly after installation as in a given week many months later. In short, the probability of failure is constant and independent of running time; the item is always effectively 'as good as new'. Very often, such behaviour indicates that the cause of failure is external to the item. For example, a fuse is always as good as new until a short circuit elsewhere in the system blows it. Whitaker[2] quotes a case in the chemical process industry where age-independent failure of pump seals was caused by gas locking and heat checking due to inappropriate design of other parts of the process flow path.

A simplified model of such a failure is indicated in Figures 11.6(e)–11.6(h). A failure pattern of this type indicates that the failure mechanism is process-related, e.g. maloperation and/or poor design.

Running-in failure—an early-failure model

With many types of equipment the probability of failure is found to be much higher during the period immediately following installation or maintenance than during its subsequent useful life. Such behaviour results in the *hyper-exponential PDF* of time-to-failure. This, by contrast with the negative exponential PDF which shows a single exponential fall-off, exhibits two phases—an initial rapid exponential fall and a later slower exponential fall. This is illustrated in Figures 11.6(i)–11.6(k). Some of the items are manufactured or installed with built-in defects which show up during the running-in stages. Those that survive this stage without failure were without such defects to begin with; they go on to exhibit the sort of time-dependent failure probability previously discussed. (The equipment is not improving with age! Some items merely start off with a better chance of survival than others).

A failure pattern of this type indicates that the failure mechanism is manufacture, assembly or recondition-related.

The Weibull PDF

Although the conventional PDF's discussed above can be used to describe failure patterns, the *Weibull PDF*[3] has been found particularly useful because it provides :

(a) a single PDF which can be made to represent any of the three types of PDF described earlier;
(b) meaningful parameters of the failure pattern, such as the probable minimum time-to-failure;
(c) simple graphical techniques for its practical application.

For this distribution

$$f(t) = \frac{\beta(t - t_0)^{\beta-1}}{\eta^\beta} \exp\left\{ - \left[\frac{t - t_0}{\eta} \right]^\beta \right\}$$

and

$$F(t) = 1 - \exp\left\{ - \left[\frac{t - t_0}{\eta} \right]^\beta \right\}$$

Each of the terms in the above expression has a practical meaning and significance.

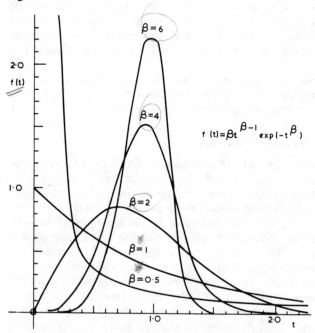

$$f(t) = \beta t^{\beta-1} \exp(-t^\beta)$$

Figure 11.7 Influence of shape factor β on Weibull distribution

The *threshold time-to-failure, or guaranteed life,* t_0. In many cases of wear-out the first failure does not appear until some significant running time t_0 has elapsed. In the Weibull expressions the time factor always occurs as the time interval $(t-t_0)$.

The *characteristic life,* η. When $(t-t_0) = \eta$, $P(t) = \exp(-1) = 0.37$, i.e. η is the interval between t_0 and the time at which it can be expected that 63 per cent of the items will have failed and 37 per cent survived.

The *shape factor,* β. Figure 11.7 shows how the various patterns of time-to-failure and of age-specific failure rate are characterised by the value of β. A 'running-in' or 'infant-mortality' failure process is characterised by a value significantly less than one, a purely random process by a value fairly close to one, wear-out by larger values, although if β is less than, say, three then a purely random factor is still significant.

Weibull probability paper

Given that data on times-to-failure have been obtained, how do we fit the Weibull PDF, i.e. how do we find the appropriate values of β, t_0 and η? One simple way is to use Weibull probability graph paper[4]. The Weibull cumulative distribution function is

$$F(t) = 1 - \exp - \left\{ \left[\frac{t - t_0}{\eta} \right]^{\beta} \right\}$$

Re-arranging and taking logarithms (twice) gives

$$\ln \ln \left[\frac{1}{1 - F(t)} \right] = \beta \ln(t - t_0) - \beta \ln(\eta)$$

A plot of the LHS function vs. $\ln (t-t_0)$ is a straight line of slope β. On Weibull probability paper the ordinate is $F(t)$, expressed in per cent, and the abscissa is $(t-t_0)$. The divisions are so arranged that a variable distributed according to the Weibull PDF will give a straight line when plotted on the paper. Its use is illustrated by the following two examples.

Weibull analysis of a large and complete sample of times-to-failure

One hundred identical pumps have been run continuously and their times-to-failure noted. A Weibull fit to the data is required.

1. The data is tabulated as in columns 1 and 2 of Table 11.4.
2. Successive addition of the figures in column 2 leads to column 3, the total percentages of pumps failed by the times, t that terminate each of the intervals in column 1.
3. Three or four possible values, thought likely to span the actual value, are assigned to t_0 (the threshold time-to-failure). The resultant values of $t-t_0$ are tabulated in columns 4, 5, 6 etc.
4. Weibull probability paper (in this case Chartwell Graph ref. 6572) is used to plot the column 3 figures against those in columns 4, 5 and 6 respectively. The result is shown in Figure 11.8 which also includes plots

TABLE 11.4. Pump failure data

(1) Time-to-failure (hours)	(2) Number of pumps	(3) Cumulative per cent failed, $F(t)$	(4) $t - t_0$ ($t_0 = 800$ h)	(5) $t - t_0$ ($t_0 = 900$ h)	(6) $t - t_0$ ($t_0 = 1000$ h)
1000–1100	2	2	300	200	100
1100–1200	6	8	400	300	200
1200–1300	16	24	500	400	300
1300–1400	14	38	600	500	400
1400–1500	26	64	700	600	500
1500–1600	22	86	800	700	600
1600–1700	7	93	900	800	700
1700–1800	6	99	1000	900	800
1800–1900	1	100	1100	1000	900

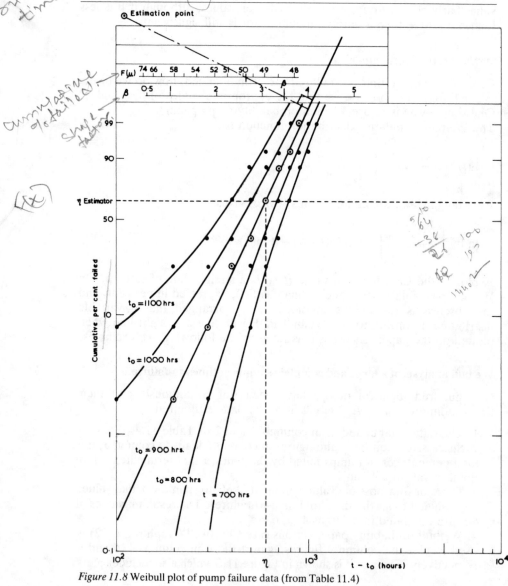

Figure 11.8 Weibull plot of pump failure data (from Table 11.4)

with $t_0 = 700$ h and $t_0 = 1100$ h. The value of t_0 finally adopted (in this case 900 h) is that which results in the straightest plot.

5. The characteristic life, η, is the value of $t-t_0$ (in this case 600 h) at which the line fitted to the straightest plot reaches the 63% failed level. (Note that $t-t_0 = 600$ h corresponds to a total actual running time of $t = 1500$ h, remembering that $t_0 = 900$ h.)

6. As shown, a perpendicular is dropped from the estimation point to the straight line fit. The point at which this intersects the special scale at the top of the graph gives the value of β (in this case 3.5 approximately). Note that the perpendicular also intersects another scale which indicates the value of the cumulative per cent failed, F, at the point $t-t_0$. In this case, F = 49.8%, which corresponds to $t-t_0 = 540$ h, or t(the mean pump life) = 1440 h.

To sum up, the observations fit a Weibull PDF of parameters

$t_0 = 900$ h

$\eta = 600$ h

and $\beta = 3.5$

We have also deduced that $t = 1440$ h

Weibull analysis of a small and incomplete sample

In the previous example sufficient data had been obtained to enable direct calculation of F for a range of values of t. The values calculated were also likely to be not too different from those which would have been obtained had enough time or money been available to have measured several thousand times-to-failure.

In practice, there may only have been opportunity to measure a handful of time-to-failure. Indeed, the items under examination might be large, expensive and of low failure rate, and as is likely in such a case, only a few might yet have been made. In addition, some of them might still be running, not having reached the failure point (i.e. 'suspended') or may have been withdrawn from the trial (i.e. 'censored') because, in their case, the test conditions were accidently altered. In this situation the results of any analysis will necessarily be subject to greater statistical uncertainty, but a Weibull analysis may be required, on the grounds, for example, that an approximate result at the end of a fortnight may be of more value than a precise one obtained by waiting for another three months. A technique using 'Median Ranks' as demonstrated in the following example, is then appropriate. The statistical reasoning underlying the method is fairly sophisticated and for a more full explanation, illustrated by practical examples, the reader should consult Reference 4.

TABLE 11.5. Spring failure data

Spring number	Cycles to failure	Spring number	Cycles to failure
1	9 100	6	(7200)*
2	8 000	7	4500
3	6 300	8	(5000)†
4	11 100	9	8400
5	3 300	10	5200

*Still running
†Test terminated, inadvertent overspeed

Ten oscillating springs are being tested to failure. The situation to date is as shown in Table 11.5. A Weibull fit to the data is required. The procedure is as below :

1. The failure points are ranked in ascending order (column 2 of Table 11.6) and classified as failed, f, or suspended (or censored), s, column 3.

TABLE 11.6. Spring-failure data ranked

(1) Spring number	(2) Cycles	(3) Class	(4) New Increment	(5) Order Number	(6) Median rank
5	3 300	f	1	1	0.067
7	4 500	f	1	2	0.163
8	5 000	s	—	—	—
10	5 200	f	1.125	3.125	0.272
3	6 300	f	1.125	4.250	0.380
6	7 200	s	—	—	—
2	8 000	f	1.350	5.600	0.510
9	8 400	f	1.350	6.950	0.639
1	9 100	f	1.350	8.300	0.770
4	11 100	f	1.350	9.650	0.898

2. For the first failed item the 'New Increment' is calculated from the formula

$$\text{New Increment} = \frac{N + 1 - (\text{Order Number of previous failed item})}{N + 1 - (\text{number of previous items})}$$

where N = total number of items in the sample (i.e. 10). Since this is the first failed item, the previous Order Number is zero. Also, in this case, the number of previous items is zero and therefore the calculated New Increment is 1 (column 4). Note that if the first failure had been preceded by some suspended items the New Increment would have been greater than 1, e.g. if the first two items had been suspended, the New Increment would have been $(10 + 1 - 0)/(10 + 1 - 2) = 1.22$.

3. The 'Order Number' of the first failed item is obtained from the expression

Order Number = New Increment + previous Order Number

i.e. in this case, Order Number = $1 + 0 = 1$ (column 5).

4. This procedure is repeated for all the remaining failed items, in succession, i.e.

Second failed item : New Increment $= \dfrac{10 + 1 - 1}{10 + 1 - 1} = 1$

Order Number $= 1 + 1 = 2$

Third failed item   : New Increment $= \dfrac{10 + 1 - 2}{10 + 1 - 3} = 1.125$

Order Number $= 1.125 + 2 = 3.125$

etc., etc.

The value of the New Increment obtained from the first failed item after a suspended item remains constant, and therefore need not be revised, until the next group of suspended items.

5. Having completed column 5, the corresponding 'Median Ranks' (column 6) are calculated from the formula

$$\text{Median Rank} = \frac{\text{Order Number} - 0.3}{N + 0.4}$$

e.g. for the fourth failed item

$$\text{Median Rank} = \frac{4.250 - 0.3}{10 + 0.4} = \frac{3.950}{10.4} = 0.380$$

6. The Median Ranks, expressed as percentages, are plotted against cycles (or time) to failure on Weibull graph paper, as in Figure 11.9 and values of η, β and μ (8200 cycles, 2.78 and 7400 cycles respectively) obtained, as in the previous example. In this case $t_0 = 0$, this giving a good straight line plot, but in the general case t_0 would be established by trial plots exactly as previously. (N.B. μ = mean number of cycles to failure.)

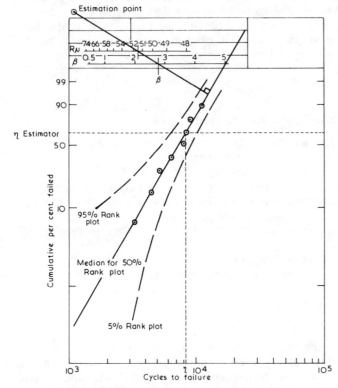

Figure 11.9 Weibull plot of spring failure median ranks (data from Table 11.5, 5% and 95% ranks also shown)

7. Johnson gives tables of 5% and 95% Ranks, for various sample sizes and Order Numbers. It is a simple matter to plot these, as well as the Median (or 50%) Ranks against the observed cycles (or times) to failure, thus obtaining (see Figure 11.9) the 90% confidence band for the data, i.e. the band within which it is 90% probable that the plot obtained from a very large number of items would lie.

In the absence of suspended items the procedure is simpler, in that the Order Numbers are simply 1, 2, 3, 4 ......N.

The application of failure statistics to maintenance management

Item replacement models

It was shown in Chapter 3 that when determining the maintenance for a plant the best procedure for each plant item (see Figure 3.10) has to be established. It was also pointed out that in the large majority of cases this can be determined without the use of failure statistics. However, in the case of items exhibiting the characteristics indicated by the heavy line in Figure 3.10—and where the cost of failure is high relative to the cost of fixed time-replacement—then fixed-time-replacement often is the best policy and failure statistics can be used to determine the optimum replacement period. This, of course, assumes that failure data are available.

Example : calculation of optimal replacement period

A certain type of pump being used in a continuous chemical process exhibits a wear-out pattern of failure as shown in Figure 11.10.

When one fails it is replaced promptly at a cost C_f of £300 (which includes unavailability cost and repair cost). At periodic intervals, of length t, all such components are replaced at a cost, C_s, of £100 per pump. The total number, N, of pumps in the plant is 100.

In any replacement interval of length t, the total cost of replacement will be $NC_s + E(t)C_f$
where $E(t)$ is the expected number of failure replacements during the interval t. The total replacement cost per unit time

$$C = \frac{NC_s + E(t)C_f}{t}$$

The objective is to find the replacement period which will minimise C. In order to do this it is necessary to establish the expected number of failure replacements $E(t)$ for each chosen replacement period, evaluate C, and then plot C against t to find the minimum value of C. The failure data obtained from Figure 11.10 is used to evaluate $E(t)$.

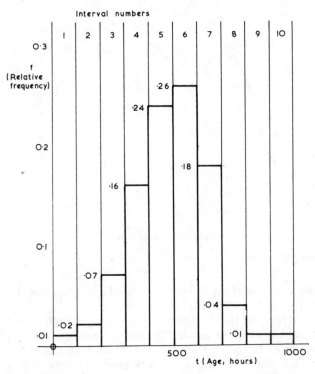

Figure 11.10 Pump failure pattern

For replacement period $t = 100$ hours

$$E(1) = Np(1)$$

where $p(1)$ = probability of failure of any one pump if re-placement occurs at the end of interval 1 i.e. 100 hours.

in this case, $p(1) = f(1) = 0.01$

so $E(1) = 100 \times 0.01 = 1$ pump

and $$C = \frac{(100 \times 100) + (1 \times 300)}{100} = £103/\text{hour}$$

For a replacement period $t = 200$ hours

$$E(2) = Np(2)$$

in this case, $p(2) = (1 + p(1)).f(1) + 1.f(2)^*$
$= (1.01 \times 0.01) + (1 \times 0.02) = 0.030$

so $E(2) = 100 \times 0.03 = 3$ pumps

and $$C = \frac{(100 \times 100) + (3 \times 300)}{200} = £545/\text{hour}$$

*It can be shown[5] that for the nth interval

$$p(n) = \sum_{j=n-1}^{j=0} (1 + p(j)).f(n-j)$$ which is a *recurrence formula*.

To evaluate it for a given n it must have been evaluated for all smaller values of n.

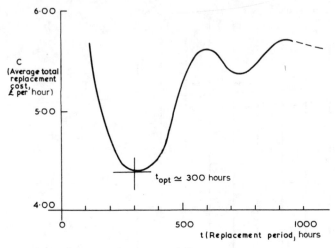

Figure 11.11 Cost vs. replacement period

The graph of C as a function of t is shown in Figure 11.11 and gives the optimum replacement period as 300 hours.

It will be appreciated that the failure pattern used in the example is not typical of industrial plant items in as much it is clearly wear-out with a t_0 value of zero. A much more likely wear-out failure pattern would be of the type given in Table 11.4 where the mean life was 1440 hours and the t_0 value about 900 hours. With the sort of cost values given in the last example it can be seen from the table (without the use of mathematics) that the best replacement period would be about 1300 hours.

Comparable models have been developed for other replacement procedures, e.g. optimum age replacement, group replacement, opportunistic replacement, etc.[6]

Failure diagnosis

One of the most important and difficult problems that will confront the maintenance engineer is the diagnosis of the cause of a recurring item-failure. Section 11.3 described how patterns of failure are an indication of the underlying cause of failure. This is summarised in terms of the Weibull shape parameter in Figure 11.12. Thus the analysis of times-to-failure can direct the engineer to the possible causes of failure.

An example of the diagnostic application of failure statistics was obtained by the author during an investigation into the low availability of diesel loaders in a large ore mine. Maintenance management were unsure of the cause of recurrent failures of universal couplings; poor reconditioning was suspected. Analysis of the data showed that the Weibull β parameter was close to 1.0, i.e. failures occurred quite randomly with respect to running time so that the possibility of a reconditioning-induced (running-in) failure mechanism, or of a wear-out mechanism, could be eliminated. Finally, the cause was found to be poor design of coupling bolts, which worked loose quite randomly with respect to time. Similar analysis of the failures of associated gearboxes gave a β of about 0.5, suggesting in their case, a reconditioning-induced problem.

What must be emphasised is that failure statistics is a diagnostic aid and should only be used where the cause of failure is difficult to establish. It should be an adjunct to *on-site emergency investigations* and/or *metallurgical analysis*. Failure statistics are not a substitute for good engineering investigation.

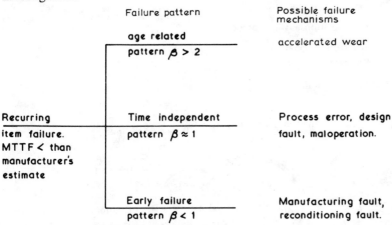

Figure 11.12 Relationship between β and cause of failure

Prescriptive action will depend on the cause of failure and can vary from design-out-maintenance to better eeconditioning procedures. Often, stop-gap measures need to be taken until the cause of failure is established, e.g. fixed time replacement in the case of a recurring 'wear-out' failure.

A case study of failure investigation

A local transport company operated a fleet of buses, 42 of which used a particular type of gearbox. It was the policy of the company to extend the use of this particular gearbox across the whole of its fleet since it was designed to the company's specifications.

An investigation of the vehicle history files and discussions with the garage maintenance staff revealed that the gearbox, both new and over-hauled, was one of the high cost areas in corrective maintenance.

The make of vehicle using this gearbox had been introduced in mid-1975 and, since only a small number of gearboxes had proceeded beyond the second overhaul, it was decided to classify them into two categories only. viz: (i) new and (ii) overhauled, which latter included all gearboxes that had been overhauled once or more.

Gearbox description

Figure 11.13 shows the gearbox transmitting power in 1st gear position. The gear trains are of basic epicycle design. Each gear position is engaged by clamping a brake around the relevant annulus to hold the annulus

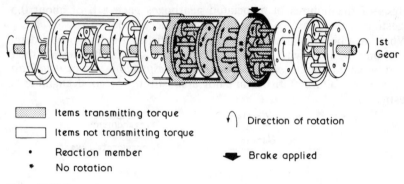

Items transmitting torque

Items not transmitting torque

• Reaction member

∗ No rotation

↱ Direction of rotation

➥ Brake applied

Figure 11.13 Power flow diagram

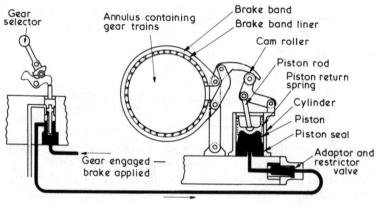

Figure 11.14 The air control diagram

stationary. The selection of the gear is via the electro-pneumatic selection mechanism shown in Figure 11.14. The gearbox employs the fully-charged fluid-coupling principle whereby oil is common to the fluid coupling, gearbox and angle drive. Thus five brake bands are used, including that for reverse gear. To allow for brake band liner wear, an automatic adjustment mechanism (not shown) is incorporated into the operating linkage. A multi-plate clutch is used for the fifth gear, consisting of phosphor bronze friction plates mating onto steel plates.

Data collection methods

The existing data collection system recorded a four-weekly mileage and cumulative mileage for each vehicle, gearbox and other major items. Unfortunately, mileage to failure was not recorded. A good estimation could be obtained, however, in the case of a gearbox, from the cumulative mileage and the failure data.

Gearbox failure data, cause of failure and components replaced during each overhaul were supposed to be recorded on an 'item change-over-card' and vehicle history file. However, the quality of the data collected was poor and, in some cases, non-existent. Little attention was given to data analysis. As a result of this, unnecessary time was spent extracting the failure mileage from the various files.

Since the causes of failure were not clearly recorded, it was necessary to observe the failed gearboxes being overhauled and to carry out detailed discussions with the workforce involved in order to understand the mechanisms, and, where possible, the causes of failure.

Failure analysis

Gearbox failures

The on-site work carried out by the author revealed that the gearboxes (new and reconditioned) could fail in one of six ways (see Figures 11.15 and 11.16) :

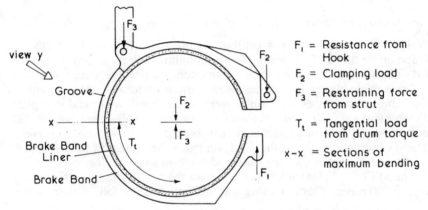

F_1 = Resistance from Hook

F_2 = Clamping load

F_3 = Restraining force from strut

T_t = Tangential load from drum torque

x–x = Sections of maximum bending

Figure 11.15 Schematic diagram of brake band showing forces applied

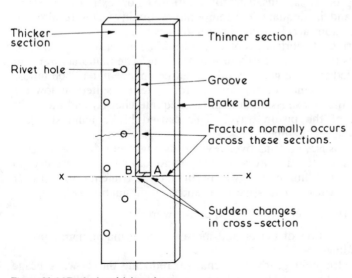

Figure 11.16 Brake band (view y)

(1) Brake Band Fracture—due to (a) the band being over-stressed because of incorrect band adjustment, inadequate pressure, malfunction and violent gearchange, (b) fatigue as the clamping and releasing of the band gave rise to alternating stresses, (c) stress concentration at sudden changes in section, sharp corners and rivet holes, (these could also initiate fatigue cracks), (d) material defects.

(2) Brake Band Liner Fracture—due to fatigue and stress concentration around the rivet holes.

(3) Brake Band Liner Wear—which includes three body abrasion.

(4) Top Gear Clutch Plates Wear and Seizure.

(5) Gear Train Failures—due to pitting fatigue caused by rolling and sliding actions.

(6) Other Mechanical Failures and Material Defects—such as broken shaft and casing, pump failure, etc.

Failure mode and causes of failure of new gearboxes

Weibull analysis of the new-gearbox failure data (Figure 11.17) gave a shape factor $\beta = 2.25$, indicating wear-out failure. The mean time to failure (MTTF) was 120,000 miles or approximately 3.1 years service.

The vehicle history records and observations on new gearboxes showed that the *main* causes of failure were brake-band wear and top-gear clutch-plate wear. Brake-band liner fracture was also observed, but this did not cause any gearbox failures. Brake band fracture was not observed. These observations, indicating that wear was the dominant failure mode, confirmed the validity of the observed Weibull shape factor.

The MTTF, 120,000 miles, was less than the manufacturer's claimed life of 200,000 miles. This low value was attributed to the following factors :

(1) The lubricant had poor oxidation resistance, no dispersant or detergent properties, unsatisfactory anti-wear or extreme pressure properties and inadequate low temperature fluidity. This resulted in sludge formation, accelerating three-body abrasion.

(2) The period of lubricant replacement had been set at 24 weeks, or 19,000 miles (approximately) and was too long. The manufacturer had recommended that the gearbox oil should be changed at 12,500 miles.

(3) Poor maintenance of the air control system resulted in low air pressure in the transmission system (inadequate checks) and incorrect adjustment of the piston travel. This caused brake band slip and excessive wear of the liners.

(4) Driver misuse, such as over-revving during rapid downward gear change. Full throttle upward gear change and idling in-gear also caused excessive wear. Idling in-gear was particularly detrimental to top gear clutch plates, causing excessive wear and heat dissipation.

The solutions recommended to the operator were :

(1) Implementation of better and more effective maintenance procedures including—

(i) More frequent gearbox oil change, reducing the 24-week usage period to 18 weeks. The correct periodicity could be determined by

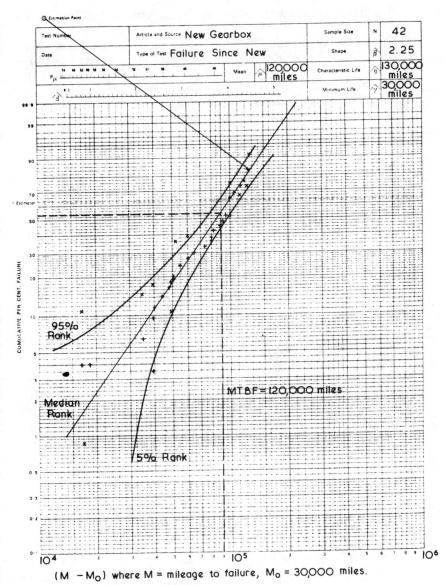

Figure 11.17 Weibull plot for new gearbox failure

lubricant analysis. The long-term solution would be to find a more suitable gearbox oil.

(ii) Checking and adjustment of all piston travel and brake band automatic adjusters every 18 weeks, when changing the gearbox oil.

(iii) Checking and rectifying air leaks in the transmission system every 6 weeks to ensure correct air pressure. Air leaks should be checked objectively (e.g. using a shock pulse meter with special probes so that even minor leaks would be detected) instead of the existing subjective, aural method.

(2) Training and education of drivers in the correct handling of the vehicle.

(3) Designing brake band liners that would be thicker and more wear resistant. Cox[7] showed that the life of another make of gearbox which used a thicker brake band liner (with the same frictional area and material) was double that of the gearbox studied.

(4) Reducing stress concentration by eliminating sudden changes in cross-section and sharp corners on brake bands (see Figures 11.16 and 11.20).

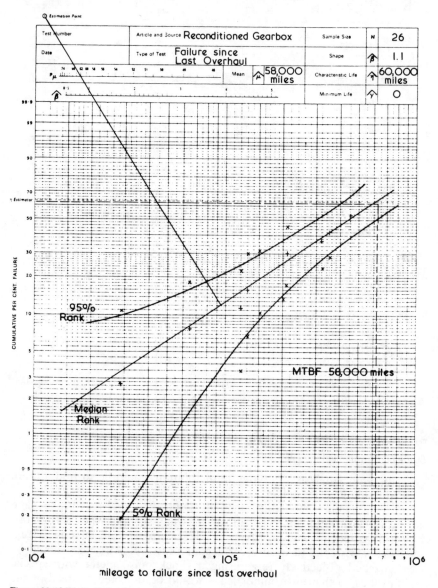

Figure 11.18 Weibull plot for reconditioned gearbox failure

Failure mode and causes of failure—reconditioned gearboxes

Weibull analysis of the failure data for the reconditioned gearboxes (Figure 11.18) gave a shape factor $\beta = 1.1$, indicating random failure. The MTTF from reconditioning was 58,000 miles, or approximately 1.5 years service. The life of the reconditioned gearboxes was therefore only half that of a new one.

The main causes of failure were brake band fractures (especially on the second gear) and top gear clutch plate seizure, the former being much more frequent. Pitting-fatigue of the gears, especially on the second gear, was observed but no tooth fracture occurred. there were no failures due to brake-band liner or top-gear clutch-plate wear.

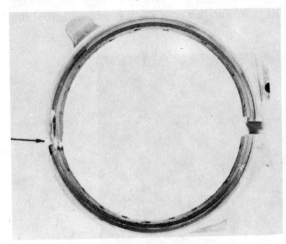

Figure 11.19 Brake band fracture at section of maximum bending

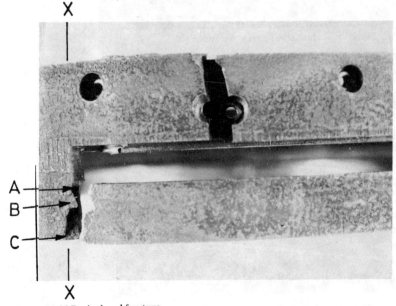

Figure 11.20 Brake band fracture

The wrought-steel brake-band fracture surfaces were examined under a scanning electron microscope. Figures 11.19 and 11.20 show a typical brake-band fracture. Fracture always occurred at section x-x (see also Figure 11.14) in the thinner band section and across one of the rivet holes in the thicker band section.

Striations, which are characteristic of fatigue failure[8] were present on the surface at region A, as shown in Figure 11.21. Dimples, characteristic of slow growth, were present on the fracture surface at region B (Figure 11.22). At region C, the elongated dimples (Figure 11.23) indicated tearing. It was concluded that, due to alternating loads, fatigue cracks were initiated by the high stress concentrations of region A, propagated slowly to B until it could no longer withstand the load, and then the thinner section tore off at C. At this point the thicker section fractured across the rivet hole.

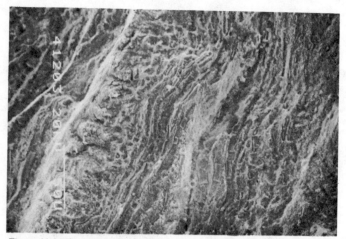

Figure 11.21 Fracture surface at A showing striations

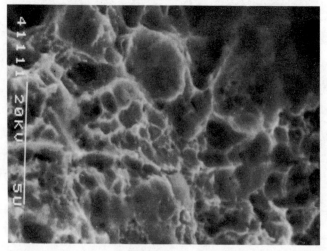

Figure 11.22 Fracture surface at B showing dimples

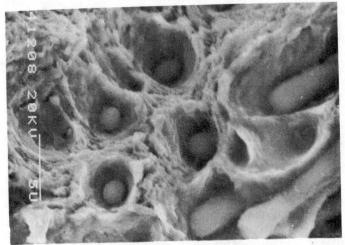

Figure 11.23 Fracture surface at C showing elongated dimples

The low life and random failure of reconditioned gearboxes resulted mainly from the practice of using reconditioned brake bands when reconditioning the gearbox. A brake band fitted into the 2nd gear position (greatest use and stress) in a reconditioned box might have already operated for a considerable amount of its fatigue life. The remaining life obtained from such bands will vary randomly, being dependent quite fortuitously on previous gear position and previous operating life.

The actions recommended for increasing the MTTF were as follows :

(i) Replacement of all five brake bands with new ones, during reconditioning. This would minimise fatigue fracture but would increase the reconditioning cost by about £500. This latter would, however, result in a considerable potential saving in labour and in bus unavailability costs.

(ii) Instrumented crack-detection surveys of all gear trains and shafts before refitting. The previously used visual check was too subjective and would not detect hairline cracks.

(iii) Gearbox manufacturer to be asked to reduce stress concentrations by rounding off all sharp edges on the brake bands.

Discussion

The experience gained from this study showed that in order to control the level of plant failures an organisation needs to adopt a systematic procedure for the recording, storing, analysing and feedback of failure data. A model of such a procedure was shown in Figure 5.16 and involved three main levels of control : the shop floor and first-line supervision, the history record and spares system, the equipment manufacturer.

The advantages to be gained at the first level of control were shown in this study. Considerable data and information were obtained by observing repairs and reconditioning procedures and by discussing the history of failures with tradesmen and supervisors.

The study also showed that unless a data collection system has been properly designed it is extremely difficult to extract the type of information necessary for maintenance decision making. A passenger transport organisation using many identical buses should have a data collection system which will gather information on failures down to the item (e.g. gearbox), level of plant and, where necessary, down to component level. Such information should include the times-to-failure, the symptoms and, above all, the causes of failure (where known). Through the use of computers it is now a straightforward matter to arrange for indication, on a monthly basis (or less) of the main problem areas, in terms of frequency of failures or cost. The spares system can also be designed to be used as an additional source of information. For example, it can indicate high spare-part usage-rate. In each case determination of the cause of failure should be followed by selection of the most appropriate corrective action. Where this has been achieved, the information should be passed to the manufacturer, either directly or via specifications for new equipment. In the same way the manufacturer passes such information through to the equipment user.

References

1. Birnbaum, Z.W. and Saunders, S.C. *A new family of life distributions*. J. Appl.Prob. (1969), 6, 319–327.
2. Whitaker, G.D. *Statistical reliability models for chemical process plant*. Instn.Chem.Engrs, Symposium on Design for reliability, April (1973).
3. Weibull, W. *A statistical distribution function of wide applicability*, Journal of Applied Mechanics, 293, Sept (1951).
4. Johnson, L.G. *Theory and technique of variation research*, Elsevier (1964).
5. Kelly, A., and Harris, M.J., *Management of industrial maintenance*, Butterworths, London (1979).
6. Jardine, A.K.S., *Maintenance, replacement and reliability*, Pitman (1973).
7. Cox, D.A. *Operating experience with power shift epicycle transmission on public service vehicles*, I.Mech.E. Conference on Automatic and Semi-Automatic Gearboxes for Heavy Commercial Vehicles, Solihull, March (1978).
8. *SEM/TEM Fractography Handbook*, Metals and Ceramics Centre, Columbia, Ohio, USA, Dec (1975).

Chapter 12

Motivation

The major part of this book has been devoted to analysing the production-maintenance system, clarifying maintenance objectives and formulating the structure of the organisation which would be needed if these objectives were going to be attained. Emphasis has been placed on creating systems which ensure that tradesmen are provided with all necessary spares, tools and information. However, it is also essential to have a tradeforce that is both diligent and committed, i.e. properly *motivated*. This can only be achieved by giving careful thought to the needs of the individual tradesman and creating a work environment that is conducive to the satisfaction of those needs.

What is motivation?

Maintenance work cannot be closely supervised and controlled in the same way as production work. By the very nature of his tasks, the maintenance tradesman is one of the few shop-floor workers who still has a considerable autonomy over his day-to-day actions and decisions. For example, it is difficult to check on how well a preventive maintenance inspection routine has been carried out. It is also difficult to judge how well a repair has been carried out and, in some cases, whether the method used has been the best (from the company's point of view). It is important that the maintenance objective should be expressed in terms that have meaning for the trades-man so that he has a basis for his own decisions and will be able to utilise his time in the most efficient way. The tradesman will be properly motivated if he knows what is wanted from him and does his best to provide it.

The human relations approach

One of the difficulties of creating an effective organisation is that although the *objectives* of the individual and the company may be compatible, their needs may not be. On the one hand classical organisation theory suggests that work should be divided into simple units, each one only a few motions (thus facilitating specialisation), the worker being motivated monetarily. On the other hand behavioural science suggests that such arrangements are inimical to psychological health. A number of studies have aimed at identifying those factors in the industrial situation which are conducive to the generation of a contented and motivated workforce.

Maslow[1] identifies and ranks what he considers to be the needs of the individual i.e.

Higher needs	5. Self fulfilment
	4. Autonomy
	3. Self-esteem
Basic needs	2. Sociality
	1. Security

Maslow argues that when the first need, security of employment and sufficiency of income, is satisfied, the individual's attention turns to social needs, i.e. group membership and acceptance. When these also have been satisfied attention turns to those attributes, skills, etc., which others are believed to recognise, i.e. to self-esteem. Next comes the desire for autonomy, for a greater opportunity to be one's own boss, and for a corresponding reduction in the constraints upon individual freedom imposed by an immediate supervisor. Finally, and hardly ever achieved, comes self fulfilment—the maximum development, at work, of all the individual's skills, abilities and attributes. Although Maslow's approach is over-simplified, it does provide a useful framework for assessing an industrial situation as it affects the individual.

Herzberg[2] also divides the needs of the individual into basic (biological) and higher (growth) needs; he furthermore identifies and quantifies the factors affecting those needs (see Figure 12.1). He emphasises that it is factors associated with the higher needs that can affect job satisfaction and that, in the industrial setting, these factors are to be found in the job content. Factors which are associated with the basic needs affect job dissatisfaction and these are to be found in the job environment. Herzberg believes that while different factors, under different circumstances, can be used to 'get work done' only the factors associated with job content are truly motivating. He argues that this is because a 'motivated worker is responding to an internal stimulus, a desire to carry out the work'. He points out that if a man works as a result of an external stimulus he will tailor the resultant work in a way that suits him best (he minimises the pain of working), and his preoccupation at work is with the balance of the external stimulus and his effort rather than with the organisational need. The man 'gets work done' but the motivation lies with someone else. This motivation-hygiene theory provides an insight into the conflict of the organisation and the individual. The theory suggests that, rather than rationalising work in order to increase efficiency, the work should be enriched in order to bring about effective motivation.

McGregor[3] looks at the situation from a different viewpoint. He is more concerned with providing managers with an insight into the characteristics of the worker so that they, the managers, can understand their own attitudes and the effects of these attitudes on the worker and the organisation. He points out that the traditional view of the worker (theory

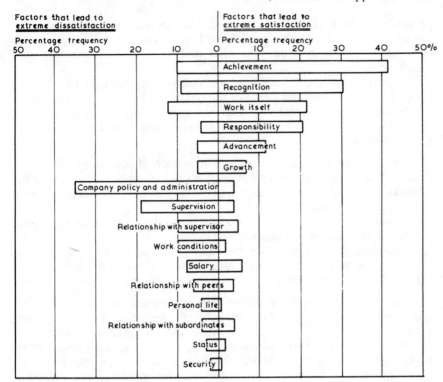

Factors that lead to extreme dissatisfaction	Factors that lead to extreme satisfaction

Figure 12.1 Factors affecting job attitudes

X) asserts that he has an inherent dislike of work and will avoid it if he can. Because of this dislike most workers must be controlled, directed, threatened, or coerced, to make an effort to achieve organisational objectives. Thus, the average worker prefers to be directed, wishes to avoid responsibility, has relatively little ambition and wants security above all. McGregor points out that this view assumes that the worker is motivated by Maslow's lower needs. A manager will, therefore, create an organisation and work situation that reflects these views. This will, in turn, create a worker with these attitudes—the manager is involved in a self-fulfilling prophesy.

McGregor's 'theory Y', on the other hand, more closely reflects Herzberg's view of work and postulates that the majority of workers can be self-directed if they become committed to an objective which they value. They will not only accept responsibility but will often seek it. Furthermore, working is as natural as eating or sleeping. Creativity is widely, not narrowly, distributed among the population. He believes that a manager should not try to decide which theory is 'right', but should examine his own assumptions about his workers in the light of a realistic analysis of the situation he is managing.

Danial[4] is more cautious about the way forward. He suggests that there are different sets of priorities for different contexts, the critical task being to decide not what the worker is really interested in, but which aspects of all the different things that he is interested in are most important in a particular context. He goes on to say that job security, pay and conditions attract a worker to a job but to keep him there he must be given the opportunity to use his ability in a creative way that is interesting and satisfying.

The problem as the behavioural scientists see it, can now be summarised. They argue that the needs of the individual have been sacrificed to the needs of the organisation. This has resulted in work that is over-controlled and unnecessarily boring. If job enrichment is the way forward a manager should:

1. Replace detailed instruction by clarification of objectives.
2. Increase responsibility and provide greater chance of achievement by making the jobs of planning, organising, directing and controlling a joint function with employees.
3. Study the organisation of jobs and try to design them so as to give greater satisfaction of human needs.
4. Replace control activities by those which seek to emphasise the manager as a helper/supporter/tutor, in order to develop abilities.
5. Set out to build effective teams in his workforce.

While the author broadly accepts that insufficient attention has been given to the needs of the individual, he still feels that the behaviourist theories are far too general and insufficiently dynamic to describe the motivational characteristics of the shop-floor. It is the author's observation (in the UK) that in general the industrial worker sees his job as a means of obtaining money, a lower order need, in order to satisfy elsewhere his other, higher order, needs. In other words, his main concern with his job is that it should give him high wages (allowing *financial* flexibility outside work). This view is based on the observation that a person is only truly motivated when he is doing something (work, hobby, sport, home repairs) that he really wants to do. In general, the worker does not find that he is doing what he *wants* to do at work. In addition, the nature of the work is such that it is usually difficult (and sometimes impossible) to institute changes sufficiently to arouse true motivation.

Applying these views to maintenance work is not without difficulty. To a certain extent maintenance work has many of the ingredients necessary to promote Herzberg's idea of worker satisfaction and motivation—a trades-man has autonomy, craftsman status, pride in the quality of his work, varied and interesting job content, etc. In spite of this it is the author's observation that there is no motivation in the Herzberg sense of the word even when management have introduced the ideas of job enrichment. A worker will still attempt to do the work he likes best, in the way he likes best, irrespective of the company's objective. If a tradesman's work programme is to suit the company's requirements then there must be an efficient work planning system coupled with good first-line supervision aware of how far the ideas of job enrichment and participation decision-making can be taken.

Financial incentives

The last section promotes the thesis that if money does not act as a true motivator then at least it can be used to get work done. Consideration of the Maslow hierarchy shows just how complicated financial motivation can be. To some it may mean more bread and circuses, to others a better chance for their children. It can also be linked with security, self-esteem group pressures and autonomy. In other words, it can get entangled with a lot of other motives that have little to do with money. The behavioural scientists would have us believe that once the shop floor worker has had his lower needs satisfied, he will only find satisfaction and therefore motivation in the higher needs. I can only answer this by pointing out that the pressures of the consumer society constantly raise the level of what is regarded as basic need and hence spur on the demand for wage increases to meet these needs.

The last twenty years has seen the introduction of many incentive schemes aimed at the maintenance worker. These have ranged from 'more money for more products out of the factory door' to 'more money for more work'. The most sophisticated and most popular of the work-measurement based incentive schemes uses *comparative estimating* based on Universal Maintenance Standards (see Appendix 4) as the basis of a group incentive scheme. Its first application in the UK was in 1964 at the Leigh Works of BICC Ltd., and it is still used in one form or another, in a wide variety of industries. The standard time for each maintenance job is estimated by comparison with a catalogue of jobs of known standard time. The aggregate of the standard times performed by the whole maintenance team over some agreed period (say a month) is used to assess the team performance on the basis of which an incentive bonus is added to the basic pay. Thus a tradesman is paid to come to work and he is also given an incentive while there. Also, since each job is measured, the information can be used to improve the effectiveness of work planning and work control. Although it is difficult to question its usefulness in this last respect, its effectiveness as a motivator can be questioned on two grounds.

Firstly, does the system motivate at all? In a number of companies studied by the author productivity had risen considerably in the short term. The author felt that this improvement was mainly due to the consequent improvement in organisation rather than to improved work performance. However, in the majority of companies the difficulty was that once the incentive became an established part of the workers payment, its effectiveness as a motivator tailed off and productivity dropped away, the workers wanting the bonus to be consolidated into their basic pay. Management were left with improved control but no motivation. Work-measured maintenance incentive schemes would therefore appear to be successful only in the short-term.

Secondly, do work-measured schemes motivate the tradesman in the right way? It would appear that the tradesman is being paid to do the job quicker rather than in the best way. With close supervision and rigid control (which are de-motivators) this problem can, admittedly, be overcome. Nevertheless, an incentive scheme that concentrates on only one of the maintenance cost-factors—labour—is questionable. What is wanted is a financial incentive that involves, as far as possible, all the costs attached to the maintenance function, one which will motivate the tradesman to take decisions and work at a rate that will benefit the function. The only payment scheme, based on all these costs, with which the author is familiar, is that used by Greater Manchester Transport (see Appendix 5).

In this scheme, if a tradesman is faced with a maintenance repair he is prompted to consider the balance between the quality and effectiveness of the repair (its influence on availability), the speed of the repair (its influence on labour costs) and the usage of spare parts (its influence on material cost). He also has an incentive to re-use or recondition the removed items and components.

The GMT system is limited in many ways (e.g. it lacks the detailed control of a work-measured system) but it is undoubtedly a move in the right direction. It does not take much imagination to realise that a suitably modified work-measured comparative-estimating system could incorporate the GMT ideas.

The influence of organisational structure

The type of organisation, the resource or administrative structure, determines the tasks and responsibilities of the individuals concerned and also determines the grouping of individuals. This can have an influence on the motivation of the tradesman via the nature of his work, the degree of his autonomy and the nature of his 'group'.

It was shown in Chapter 5 that individuals coalesce into a group when they pursue a common objective, communicate between themselves and develop common attitudes, feelings, values and standards. It has been shown in many studies that the group has considerable influence on the motivation and performance of the individual. In addition, the compatibility of its objective with the company objective, and its relationship with other groups has considerable influence on the performance of the company. Thus, when creating or changing an organisation, care has to be taken to form groups which meet the needs both of the organisation and the individual. This is particularly important in the case of maintenance.

Earlier it was stated that two of the main causes of high maintenance costs are maloperation and poor maintenance. The author has observed that maloperation is least evident where the plant operators identify with the plant, i.e. feel it belongs to them. They therefore operate it with care and see that it is maintained properly. A number of companies have attempted to promote this 'operator-plant identity' through arranging, as far as possible, for one operator (or a small group of operators) to use one machine (or area of plant). In addition, the operators carry out simple maintenance and routine inspections and are trained at an elementary level to understand the relationship between symptoms and failure and plant condition and quality.

The same idea holds true for the maintenance tradesman, but is far more difficult to apply because, for high utilisation of his time, a tradesman needs to be responsible for a far wider area of plant. However, in some industries (plastic moulding, machine tools) individual fitters have been allocated total maintenance responsibility for a set number of machines, being responsible directly to the production foreman in that area. This is an example of *production-maintenance integration* at the lowest level. The advantages of this arrangement are obvious in that not only does the fitter identify with the plant but he also identifies with the production operators as a part of the same group.

A contrary arrangement is that of Figure 5.8 where the maintenance resources are centralised and the production-maintenance link is at a much higher level, The advantages of such a structure were discussed earlier but not its disadvantages. The maintenance tradesman acts as a mere service to the production departments and feels no sense of attachment to the equipment or the operations teams. The tradesman has his own responsibilities and belongs to his own trade group with its own code and objectives. Often a communication barrier builds up between the production and maintenance groups (horizontal polarisation)—it is difficult for them to see that their objectives are compatible—and the department operates in spite of these groups rather than because of them.

An investigation[5] into the application of maintenance/production integration in Swedish industry reported that it had achieved excellent results but went on to point out the following limitations—

(i) the demand for specialised maintenance knowledge acts as a barrier to integration,
(ii) the need for expensive maintenance equipment prevents the smaller unit from handling all the maintenance problems,
(iii) the fluctuating nature of the maintenance workload tends to act against a decentralised unit handling all the maintenance work.

The author is not advocating that all companies should attempt to re-integrate maintenance with production but is simply pointing out the advantages of such a move. In any particular case they should be weighed against the advantages of centralised maintenance.

The advantages of trade integration (as discussed in Chapter 5) are easier planning and higher utilisation of the tradeforce. It also simplifies the maintenance structure and provides job enrichment. There is usually also a move towards multi-trade supervision. The net result is the promotion of the 'maintenance group', based on plant rather than on trade. This again promotes identification with the plant.

External social and political environment

It was pointed out earlier in this chapter that one of the most important factors in motivation was identification with the aims of the company. The individual tradesman will then get work done in spite of finding it uninteresting because he feels that it benefits the company and that this must therefore benefit him. He does not see his relationship with the company or with the management as a negative 'them and us' situation where he is motivated to oppose smooth function, e.g. to 'beat the rate' or to 'pull wool over the management's eyes'.

Compatibility between management and worker can be affected not only by the type of internal factors already discussed (job content, money, etc.) but also by the external political and social environment. For example, in the UK it is often the case that Directors and Senior Management come from middle-class professional family backgrounds, having received public school and university educations. Their values and attitudes tend to be very different from those of the manual worker. Such differences can be exacerbated by the political climate and are often exploited by the trade unions, creating a communication barrier between management and shop floor (vertical polarisation). Many UK companies reinforce this polarisation through different conditions of employment for staff and shop floor, e.g. separate dining rooms, different starting times, different holiday entitlement, different job security etc. It is hardly surprising therefore that the worker then develops an inherent distrust of management, making participative management particularly difficult. In other words, the external environment governs, to a large extent, the changes that management can make to the internal environment and also influences the workers reaction to such changes.

The external environment varies considerably between different countries. For example, the social and political environment in Japan is totally different from that of Sweden, yet both countries appear to have engendered worker co-operation and commitment.

Swedish views on job reform

Although this book is concerned with the maintenance function, organisational changes and job re-design in the production function in Sweden merit brief description because of the relationship between the two functions. The aim of Swedish unions and management has been to improve the lot of the shop-floor worker by implementing the ideas of job enrichment and participative management discussed earlier. This has required a complete re-think of methods of work and about the organisation of such work. In summary, job enrichment has been obtained by—

(1) extending the work cycle with additional production tasks,
(2) integrating production and auxiliary tasks such as simple short-cycle maintenance tasks.
(3) decentralising authority and responsibility so that the worker has more control over his own actions.

The Swedes have found that extending the work cycle (say, from 2 minutes to 13 minutes and above) does not, for most people, lead to loss of efficiency. Integration has been favourably received by the production worker and is particularly important in the case of functional groups such as maintenance departments. Decentralisation of authority has probably the most favourable overall impact since, in addition to enriching the work it has also resulted in shop floor workers having a more responsible attitude towards company objectives, management and equipment. This becomes particularly significant from the point of view of maintenance when it is realised that a large proportion of the corrective workload arises from maloperation.

The above techniques are encapsulated in the Norwegian and Swedish concept of autonomous groups. This is based on 'job rotation' and was first used in the production industries where job enlargement by other methods was difficult. The concept has now been adapted to other types of production work. The method differs from the normal methods of job rotation in that job rotation occurs as the work situation demands. The group has considerable autonomy of action and appoints its own team leader; changes within the group and outside it are conducted via informal participation procedures. It has been found that group work is most successful when it is arranged along the production line (with the grain) rather than across the production line (across the grain).

Such fundamental changes in the work situation have compelled changes in the supervisory role and in organisation and planning methods. Although the supervisor is still necessary, his role has changed; he has to learn to discuss, not order. Increasingly, he presents and discusses problems with the groups rather than offering ready-made solutions. One of his main functions is co-ordination between the groups and the back-up services and planning systems. Careful study was also made of the planning system. This concluded that over-planning and control dehumanised the work and was also ineffective. In a number of companies the organisation was re-simplified, the central idea being that the less important administrative tasks were dealt with at appropriate lower levels. Administrative resources were then freed to concentrate on important strategic and economic matters.

Clearly, the general advantages of 're-simplification', of participation and of decentralisation of authority, apply to both the maintenance and production functions. Some of these changes, however, affect maintenance work more directly. Integration of the simpler, routine, maintenance tasks with the production work not only enlarges the production job but also fosters the production worker's commitment to the plant. The maintenance worker's particular skills are utilised more efficiently. For practical reasons, such as the complexity of the plant, there are limits to the process of integration and the need for large maintenance departments still remains.

Integration within maintenance departments has taken two principal forms:

1. Considerable effort has been devoted to reducing inter-trade demarcation, e.g. development of the 'electro-mechanic' who, as well as carrying out the electrician's work, undertakes the simpler fitting tasks.
2. In the more substantial process companies, operating a number of large self-contained plants, efforts were made to form autonomous, multi-trade-supervised, maintenance groups (see Figure 5.13). It was found that while such arrangements facilitated co-ordination of multi-trade maintenance work they led to isolation of specialised tradesmen and poor labour utilisation in the more specialised work. A number of companies have overcome this problem by adopting a so-called 'matrix organisation' (see Figure 5.9). Every individual is attached to a certain maintenance plant-group and also to a certain occupational group. This organisational technique has now been in operation for a number of years and has given good results.

It is also important to point out that while the managers in Sweden have applied, with success, many of the ideas of the behavioural scientists, they have found that these ideas are not without limitations. They argue that the

Payment by results —

behavioural scientists have not sufficiently studied the relationship between motivation and performance and that the latters' views on payment-by-results are questionable. It is their opinion, based on considerable experience, that a properly constructed payment-by-results system (a group system in the case of maintenance) is a powerful motivator.

Although there is much to be learned from the Swedish experience it cannot be emphasised too strongly that Swedish social and political evolution has created a feeling of relative fairness between company, manager and worker. The trade unions are strong but company-based. The problems of trade demarcation do not exist to any great extent. Trade unions and management recognise the necessity to co-operate in the achievement of efficiency and profitability.

Motivation in Japan

The author visited Japan in 1977, has maintained contact with elements of their senior management, and has been able to study the attitudes and values of both workers and management in a wide variety of industries. It is extremely difficult to compare motivation in Japan with that in the western industrialised countries because of the different characteristics of the Japanese worker and the complex structures of Japanese industry.

The individual Japanese worker is extremely well-disciplined, has a considerable work ethic and an exceptional respect for authority. These characteristics have evolved as a result of the social history of the country and are reinforced by the existing political climate (e.g. social welfare is at a very minimal level).

The structure of Japanese industry can be thought of as a pyramid with the elite large companies at the top employing some 40% of the workforce. It is these companies which have created the reputation for high labour motivation, efficiency and high productivity. While this reputation is deserved the effect of the environment in which these companies operate must be borne in mind. For example, the smaller companies (often suppliers to the larger companies) very frequently have poor working conditions, poor conditions of employment and motivation can be considered as deriving from Maslow's lower order needs. Trade unions are almost non-existent at this level. It is, therefore, no surprise that shopfloor positions in the elite companies are highly sought after and that in these companies there is a close relationship between the worker and the management. This relationship is encouraged by educational programmes and excellent conditions of employment. Vertical polarisation is minimised by the realisation that all are in the 'same boat' and although salary goes up with responsibility, holidays and other fringe benefits do not. Trade unions are based on the company (but, unlike Sweden, are relatively weak), there is an understanding between union and management that productivity is good for profitability, and there is an acceptance that profitability means expansion and more opportunity for high wages and jobs. Under these conditions the introduction of the ideas of participative management and of job enrichment schemes is relatively easy, as is illustrated by the following example.

Toyoda Gosei Co. Ltd., is a medium-sized company supplying plastic injection mouldings and rubber mouldings to the automobile industry. In the early 1970's the company was expanding rapidly, had neglected preventive maintenance and was in the classic 'maintain it when it fails' situation which is expensive in downtime and which engenders ineffective use of resources. In order to improve plant availability, product quality and resource utilisation, the management used a Japanese maintenance philosophy called 'Total Productive Maintenance' (TPM). (TPM is based on the assumption that the causes of failure and poor quality are interdisciplinary and that it is necessary to have a plant-oriented management organisation to deal with the problem. Many of the maintenance management ideas used in TPM are non-Japanese but they have been expertly adapted to Japanese traditions and culture.)

In order to incorporate the ideas of TPM into its existing organisation the management used a 'small group circle' approach (see Figure 12.2). It

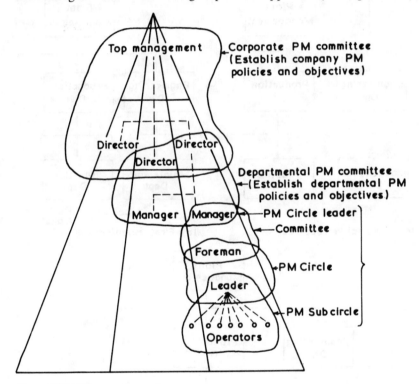

Figure 12.2 TPM promotion system

can be seen that the first step was to form the Corporate PM Committee to decide on PM policies and objectives, and the Departmental PM Committees to interact with the Corporate Committee and the voluntary small group circles of the shop floor. (This type of small group activity is a major theme of Japanese organisation. For example, Toyota Motor Company at one time had over 4000 circles in operation.) Each of the committees and the circles has a membership which cuts across departmental boundaries.

The committee suggests the aims and themes to the circles and also acts in a supporting role. The circle (or sub-circle) appoints its own leader and establishes its aims (within the theme set for them). It is expected to find ways of achieving these aims and is given help and support as necessary. One of the first conclusions of the Senior Committee (TPM Promotion Committee) was that the Maintenance Department should be more closely linked with production. This was carried out in two stages, as shown in Figure 12.3. The Maintenance Department was responsible for procurement of new equipment, setting technical standards and maintenance

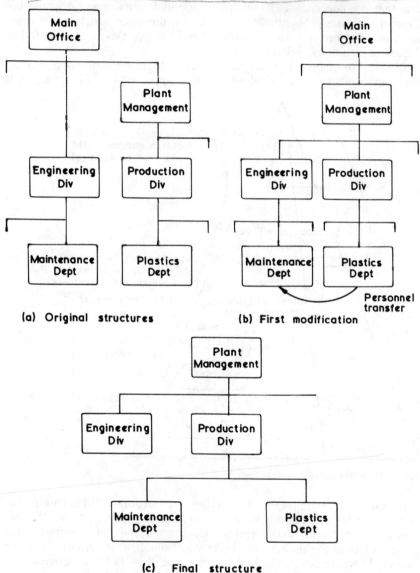

(a) Original structures   (b) First modification

(c)   Final structure

Figure 12.3 Modification of structure to carry out TPM

policy, overall maintenance planning. The Production Manager was given the responsibility for the production and maintenance of his plant and had the Maintenance Foreman reporting directly to him. Within this new plant-oriented maintenance organisation the most important change was the new role of the plant operators who were expected to 'maintain normal operating conditions of machinery'. This meant that they had to operate the machinery, carry out inspection and cleaning routines, perform simple maintenance tasks and assist tradesmen as required. Creation of this new role necessitated expenditure of considerable effort to upgrade the operators' understanding of their machines and of maintenance 'know-how'. The small group circles were successfully used for this training activity and also for the promotion of a closer relationship between maintenance tradesmen and plant operators. The TPM Promotions Committee introduced a new maintenance policy the thrust of which was based on the following points:

(1) Enforced daily and weekly inspections carried out by the plant operators (considerable effort was put into improving the plant for ease of condition monitoring).

(2) Improved corrective maintenance techniques (considerable effort was put into upgrading the tradesman's maintenance 'know-how').

(3) Identification and correction of those plant abnormalities that caused low availability/high maintenance costs/poor quality and feedback of such information to design for plant modification.

The TPM committee also emphasised the most important change of all—'that the new plan was to be carried out through the positive participation of all concerned'. The following example illustrates that such co-operation was achieved. A suggestion from a small circle, for reducing die-replacement time on moulding machines was implemented as a joint project by engineers from the Die Department, Maintenance Department and Production Division. Over a period of two years this joint effort reduced the replacement time from 49 minutes to 40 seconds.

The success of the efforts of the management and workers of Toyota Gosei will be appreciated from the fact that the failure rate fell to 25% of its original level, over a period of two years.

Summary

A maintenance worker will only be motivated effectively if

(i) he finds his work interesting and stimulating,
(ii) his own aims are compatible with those of the management,
(iii) he is given a financial incentive that is compatible with the maintenance objective.

These internal motivations are strongly influenced by the social and political climate (see Figure 12.4). The maintenance manager will, of course, be mainly concerned with the needs of the organisation and will only be concerned with the needs of the individual if this facilitates achievement of the organisational objective. He will be operating in his

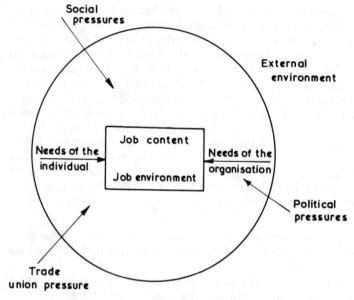

Figure 12.4 Conjunction of individual and organisational needs

own particular set of circumstances and will have to arrive at his own best approach to motivation. The following guidelines might be of some help :

(1) He must study and understand his own shop floor, its history, its present position and its deficiencies (has a work-measured incentive scheme been used? At what level is there maintenance-production integration, etc.)

(2) He must understand the factors that can influence the job content and job environment.

(3) He should be aware of the external environment and its influence since this governs the extent to which internal change is possible.

(4) Above all he must understand that the most important single factor in motivation is getting the tradeforce to identify with the objectives of the management, perhaps this is where we have the most to learn from the Japanese[6].

References

1. Maslow, A.A., *Motivation and Personality*, Harper and Brothers, New York (1954)
2. Herzberg, F., *'One more time : how do you motivate employees?'* Harvard Business Review, Jan/Feb (1968)
3. McGregor, D. *'The human side of enterprise'*, McGraw Hill, New York (1960)
4. Danial, W.W. *'What interests a worker'*, New Society, March, 1972
5. Swedish Employer's Confederation (Technical Departments) *Job Reform in Sweden* (1975)
6. Ouchi, W.G., *'Theory Z'*, Avon paperback (1983)

Functional systems documentation (FSD)

FSD is based on a structural hierarchy of functional block diagrams (see Figure A1.1) showing a system logic in a way that guides the maintainer to that unit or item of a plant which may be faulty.

The top level in the FSD hierarchy (see Figure 4.9(a)) is the general level, covering the whole system. It indicates how and where the equipment fits into the overall system. One of the aims of the top level diagram is to direct the attention of the maintainer as quickly as possible to that area of the system that is most likely to be the cause of any particular trouble. Ideally, a visual test should be used at this level.

The second level consists of a series of diagrams each one of which is a breakdown of one of the individual blocks of the first level (see Figure 4.9(b)). This analysis can be continued down to a level at which the equipment carrying out a function becomes a replaceable item (see Figure 4.9(c)). Thus a hierarchy of diagrams, becoming progressively more detailed, is generated. Each functional block diagram (see Figure 4.10) is accompanied by a test data chart (see Table 4.6). Such test data charts should contain actual operating data relating to the equipment when it is functioning normally.

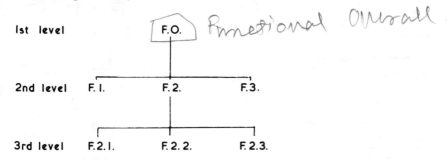

Figure A1.1 Hierarchy of functional diagrams

Rules for the construction of FSD diagrams

(1) The logic flow of the system must always be from left to right.
(2) Inputs to the system's functional blocks are always on the left vertical side.
(3) Outputs from the functional blocks are always from the right vertical side.
(4) Power supplies always enter the bottom horizontal side.
(5) Functional block diagram wording must
    (a) be brief, concise and appropriate to the craftsmen,
    (b) be restricted to explaining *what* the function does and *when* it does it,
    (c) reflect the *maintainers* view of the function, and not the designer's.
(6) Test points
    (a) A forked symbol indicates some sort of test equipment is needed,
    (b) A black spot symbol indicates that the maintainer can use his own senses, or may merely require to operate built-in test equipment.
(7) Several blocks linked by a patterned shading indicates a function that is itself a single piece of hardware. Where two functions are linked together by a common area of shading, it signifies that they are, in fact, the same piece of hardware.
(8) A black triangle at the bottom right hand corner of a block indicates that there is no further analysis of that function. This directs the maintainer to the recommended replacement or repair manual.
(9) A number of functional blocks can be shown twice—to maintain the logic flow from left to right.
(10) The first thing to do when attempting to produce a functional diagram is to understand the logic flow. This may be a signal flow, an electrical signal flow, hydraulic flow, force transmitted or the actual flow of material itself.
(11) Mechanical drives connect the top and bottom horizontal edges.

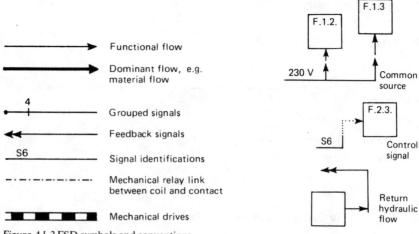

Figure A1.2 FSD symbols and conventions

(12) Every system can be considered in a functional manner. Very often hardware boundaries and functional boundaries are the same, especially at the lower levels.
(13) Symbols and conventions are shown in Figure A1.2. Where recourse, at the lower levels, has to be made to simple circuit diagrams, then the conventional standard circuit symbols are used.
(14) The layout diagrams must assist the maintainer to locate the position of the test points. Group test point numbers in an imaginary inner circle around the diagrams, and functional numbers on an imaginary outer circle.

Work sampling

Work sampling can be used as a means of obtaining information about the proportion of time a maintenance workforce spends on different activities. The technique is based on the same statistical principles as quality control.

Snap observations of man or machine are made at perfectly random times throughout the working period studied. Thus if N random observations are made on a maintenance fitter during a representative study period, and he is found to be inactive on x of these occasions then the proportion of time for which he is estimated to be inactive is simply x/N. The precision of the estimate increases with N. Continuous observation would give a precise analysis of the time spent on different activities, but would normally be prohibitively expensive or inconvenient (and misleading, due to the biassing effect of the ever-present observer!). Conversely, a very few observations would provide information of insufficient precision. Therefore, it is important to know the value of N that will result in the desired precision. This can be obtained from the expression

$$N = \frac{4P(100 - P)}{L^2}$$

where L is the desired percentage precision and P is the estimated percentage of time spent on the particular activity. If P is quite unknown a small pilot study is required to obtain an initial crude estimate. As the main study proceeds the value of P, and hence of N, can be continually updated.

A list obtained by a pilot study of the activities and delays of a maintenance tradeforce is shown in Table A2.1. N was obtained as discussed. Snap observation tours were carried out at random intervals over a representative period of time. The results of this sampling exercise are shown in column 2 and the percentage utilisation in column 3.

The information thus obtained for management control was

(a) total utilisation of the group,
(b) percentage of time spent on different tasks and hence areas where improvement was needed (e.g. areas of excessive relaxation, waiting, and walking time).

TABLE A2.1. Activity sampling exercise

Activity	No. of samples	Per cent utilisation
Working with tools or equipment	205	23.6
Diagnosing/pressure testing/welding	101	11.6
Housekeeping and cleaning		
Lubricating	1	0.9
Service tours and visual inspection	2	0.2
Job consultation time (corrected)	28	3.2
Walking loaded	101	11.6
Walking unloaded	104	11.9
Resolving instructions	24	2.8
Setting up	33	3.7
Checking availability and safety		
Clerical work on job cards	4	0.5
Searching for equipment	13	1.5
Salvaging		
Loading and unloading		
Reading and checking drawings	18	2.1
Official tea break and changing allowance	87	10.0
Authorised work study Rx. allowance	78	9.0
TOTAL % UTILISATION OF GROUP	799	91.8
Excess relaxation allowance taken	57	6.7
Waiting for equipment or materials	3	0.3
Waiting because of adverse weather		
Waiting for prod. clearance		
Waiting for other tradesmen or mates	8	0.9
Other waiting time	3	0.3
TOTALS:	870	100.0

Although not shown in this exercise it is possible to provide information on the proportion of time spent on the different classifications of maintenance work (e.g. preventive routines, lubrication, engineering maintenance etc).

Appendix 3

Queueing theory

It was shown in Section 5.4 that the repair situation can be represented by a queueing model, the simplest form of which was shown in Figure 5.5. It was pointed out that the task of the maintenance manager is to manipulate the factors under his control so as to minimise the sum of the direct and indirect costs of the repair.

Queueing theory is the mathematical analysis of queueing situations and although it has been used to determine, for example, an optimum breakdown gang size it is not sufficiently flexible to reflect the complexities of most maintenance situations. Nevertheless it does illuminate the dynamics of the repair situation and it can sometimes be used to provide an approximate solution to the more straightforward maintenance organisation problems.

Fundamentals

Figures A3.1 and A3.2 model the simplest maintenance queues. The jobs arrive at the maintenance department, perhaps wait in a queue, and are dealt with by a repair gang.

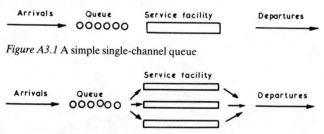

Figure A3.1 A simple single-channel queue

Figure A3.2 A multi-channel queue

A queue forms when the arrival rate exceeds the repair rate and if this is the average condition then the queue is said to be unstable. However, even when the reverse is the case, queues can form if the incidence of arrivals and the variation in service times are probabilistic and, for short periods, the arrival rate exceeds the repair rate. Thus, in this latter situation the queue length is continually changing but always finite and the queue is said to be stable. Prior to mathematical analysis of a queueing system the following, minimum, information must be obtained:

1. The probability distribution, expressed as an analytical function or PDF (see Chapter 11), of the intervals between the arrivals of consecutive jobs. It has been found that the distribution of inter-arrival times for emergency and corrective maintenance jobs is effectively negative exponential since all times of arrival are equally likely and thus the incidence of arrivals per unit time has a Poisson distribution.

2. The probability distribution of repair times, expressed as a PDF.

3. The queueing discipline, i.e. the rules governing the queues.

4. The repair gang structure (e.g. single repair gang, or multiple gangs in parallel).

Simple and multi-channel queueing models

The simple queue (Figure A3.1) assumes that both the arrival and service incidence are Poissonian and that the discipline is 'first-in, first-out' with no restriction on the queue length. Let

Mean arrival rate of jobs	$= \lambda$ per unit time,
Mean service rate of jobs	$= \mu$ per unit time,
Utilization factor ρ	$= \dfrac{\lambda}{\mu}$

It can be shown that—

(a) The probability of n jobs being in the system is

$$P(n) = \rho^n(1 - \rho)$$

(b) The average number of jobs in the queue is

$$L_q = \frac{\lambda^2}{\mu(\mu - \lambda)}$$

(c) The average waiting time for a job in the queue is

$$W_q = \frac{\rho}{(\mu - \lambda)}$$

The effect of the utilization factor, ρ, on queue length is illustrated in Figure A3.3

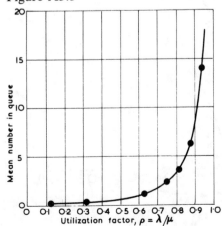

Figure A3.3 Relationship of queue length to the factor ρ

Example A: Simple queue

A factory has many identical pneumatic machines. A study is made of the time between the arrival of machine breakdowns and of the time required for repair. Both distributions are found to be adequately described by the negative exponential PDF. The average time between arrivals is found to be 60 min. and the average time for repair 50 min.
If repairs are carried out by one gang (three men) calculate

(a) the mean number of machines in the queue,
(b) the mean time a machine spends in a queue,
(c) the utilization of the gang.

Mean time between arrivals is 60 min, i.e. $\lambda = 1/h$
Mean time for repair is 50 min, i.e. $\mu = 1.2/h$
Utilization factor $\rho = 0.83$

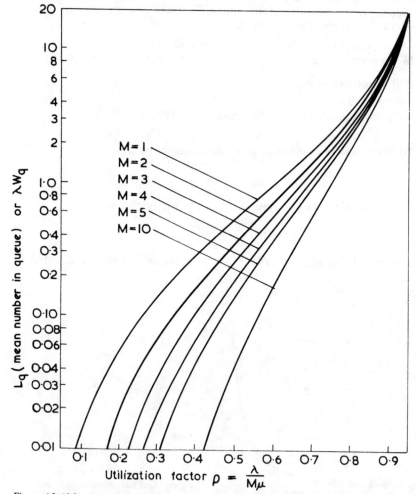

Figure A3.4 Mean number in queue

Mean number of machines $L_q = \dfrac{1}{1.2(1.2-1)} = 4.2$

Mean time a machine spends in a queue $W_q = \dfrac{4.2}{1} = 4.2$ h

Utilization $= 1 - P(0)$
$= 1 - (1 - \rho)$
$= 1 - (1 - 0.83) = 83\%$

One of the most obvious practical ways of reducing queue length is to increase the number of repair gangs. This is illustrated in the multi-channel queueing model, Figure A3.2. The mathematical analysis of such models is complex and the results are better presented as tables or graphs. The graphs shown in Figure A3.4 are derived from a multi-channel model based on the same assumptions as for the simple queue. Each curve assumes a different number M of gangs. Thus, assuming λ and μ remain unchanged, ρ can be calculated for different values of M and the average number of jobs in queue read off the graph.

Example B: Multi-channel queues

For the situation outlined in Example A determine the number of repair gangs which will minimise the queuing costs. A fitter is paid £2 per hour and the unavailability cost of a machine is £40 per hour.

One-gang policy
Labour cost per hour $= 3 \times 2 = £6$
Unavailability cost $= 4.2 \times 40 = £168$
(from Example A)
Total cost $= £174$

Two-gang policy
Labour cost £12
Determine unavailability cost using Figure A3.4 i.e.

$M = 2$ and $\varrho = \dfrac{1}{2 \times 1.2} = 0.415$ giving $L_q \approx 0.18$

Thus unavailability cost $= 0.18 \times 40 = £7.20$
Total cost $= £19.20$.

Three-gang policy
Labour cost £18

$M = 3$ and $\varrho = \dfrac{1}{3 \times 1.2} = 0.28$ giving $L_q \approx 0.02$

Thus unavailability cost $= 0.02 \times 40 = £0.80$
Total cost $= £18.80$
i.e. use a three-gang policy

Appendix 4

Comparative estimating

A number of maintenance work measurement techniques, based on the traditional techniques of work measurement, but also involving some degree of estimation, were developed during the 1950's and 1960's. They are shown in Figure A4.1.

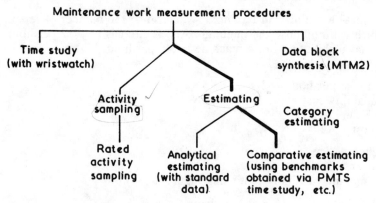

Figure A4.1 Maintenance work measurement procedures

Fundamental concepts and traditional techniques

The 'standard time' for a job (see Figure A4.2) is made up of the time taken (the basic time) to complete a job, when working at the accepted 'standard rate', and time allowances for the ergonomic and environmental conditions under which the job is being carried out. The British Standards Institution definition of standard rate is the rating corresponding to the

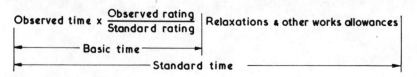

Figure A4.2 Standard time

average rate at which qualified workers will naturally work at a job provided they are motivated to apply themselves.

Work measurement procedures are concerned with using data obtained from past or present observations to make reliable predictions about the times (standard times) that future jobs should take. Generally (see Figure A4.3) the standard times are based on data obtained by direct observations (e.g. time study) and synthetic methods.

Time study: The standard time for a job is obtained by 'timing' and 'rating' the job as it is being carried out. In order to facilitate this the job is divided into easily distinguishable 'job elements'.

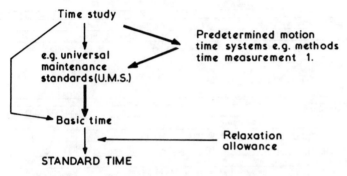

Figure A4.3 Work measurement procedures for obtaining standard time

The basic time for an element is obtained by modifying the observed time to allow for the rate at which the element was judged to be performed (see Figure A4.2). The standard time is then obtained by adding the appropriate allowances to this basic time. The standard time for the complete job is then deduced by summing the standard times of each of its constituent elements.

TABLE A4.1. Part of the MTM1 reach table of time elements

Distance moved in	Time TMU				Hand in motion		Case and description
	A	B	C or D	E	A	B	A. Reach to object in fixed location or to object in other hand or on which other hand rests
3/4 or less	2.0	2.0	2.0	2.0	1.6	1.6	B. Reach to single object in location which may vary
1	2.5	2.5	3.6	2.4	2.3	2.3	slightly from cycle to cycle
2	4.0	4.0	5.9	3.8	3.5	2.7	C. Reach to object jumbled with other objects in a group
3	5.3	5.3	7.3	5.3	4.5	3.6	so that search and select occur
4	6.1	6.4	8.4	6.8	4.9	4.3	
							D. Reach to a very small
5	6.5	7.8	9.4	7.4	5.3	5.0	object or where accurate
etc.							grasp is required
							E. Reach to indefinite
30	17.5	25.8	26.7	22.9	15.3	23.2	location to get hand in position for body balance or next motion or out of way

Element analysis chart — Code 0720.02

Description Left Hand	No.	L.H.	T.M.U.	R.H.	No.	Description Right Hand
A Skin end of wire with knife # IO or smaller						A
Move to area		MIOB	18·7	MI6C		Move knife to work
			16·2	P2SE		Align
			2·9	MIB		
			16.2	API		
			5.4	T9OS		Skin wire
			16.2	API		
			7.5	D2E		
			13·4	MI2B		Move knife away
			96·5			

Operation synthesis — Code 0720.02

Symbol	Ref.	Operation or element description	T.M.U.	Freq.	Total
720.0211		Skin wire # IO,12 and smaller (Levelled hrs.			.0023)
	05.0004	Handle knife			100.5
	04.0001	Handle wire			34.2
	A	Skin end of wire			96.5
					231.2

Universal standard data — Code 0720.02

Skinning

Symbol	Skin electrical conductor # 18 thru MCM			Hours
720.0211	Single	Small	# IO, 12 gauge and smaller	.0023
720.0212	conductor	Medium	# 4, 6, 8 gauge	.0034
720.0213	cable	Large	# 2 thru MCM gauge	.0076

Bench mark analysis sheet — Code 0720.02

Description : Medium size junction box   Date 26.4.61   BM 0790 3

4 holes, 85 wires # 12, crimped   Craft. elect. Gen. install.

connections, mount and connect   Dwgs : None

No. of men: 1   Analyst W.M.   Sht 1 of 1

Line	Men	Operation description	Reference Symbol	Unit time	Freq.	Total time
1		Mount medium size box	750.0207			·3243
2		Select proper wire	13.0002	.0035	85	.2975
3		Move marker on wire	720.0660	.0094	85	.7990
4		Cut off 85 # 12 wires	720.0101	.0021	85	.1785
5		Skin 85 # 12 wires	720.0211	.0023	85	.1955
6		Connect 85 # 12 wires	720.0323	.0110	85	.9350
7						
30						
Notes:			Bench mark time			2.7298
			Standard work group			G

Spread sheet   task area, general insulation — Code .0795   Craft : Electrical

Group E 1·2	Group F 2·0	Group G 3·0
1·5	2·5	
0790-16-Conduit, 15'- 1¼" 2–30° bends, 2 condulets, 2 nipples between junction boxes. prepare conduit and install; 2 men. 0790-2 Medium size junction box. 4 holes, 37 wires.	0790 15 Conduit 35' 2" 2 30° bends, 2 condulets, 2 nipples between junction boxes. prepare conduit and install.	0790-3 Medium size junction box, 4 holes 85 wires # 12 crimped connections, mount and connect.

Figure A4.4 The build-up of a spread sheet from MTM1 and UMS

Synthesis: Many job elements are common to a range of activities and their basic elemental times can be compiled into a library of 'standard data' from which standard complete job times can be synthesised without recourse to actual timing. Standard data can be compiled directly from time study or less directly from predetermined motion time systems (PMTS).

Predetermined motion time systems: Several systems are in use but only methods-time measurement 1 (MTM1), which is relevant to comparative estimating, will be described. This is a system in which the standardised time date for basic human movements are tabulated in time units (TMU) of 0.000 01 h at a BS rating of 83.3. There are ten tables of standardised data covering the following movements: reach, move, turn and apply pressure, grasp, position, release, disengage, eye-travel, body motions, simultaneous motions. The reach table is shown in Table A4.1. In the case of highly repetitive short-cycle productive work such tables can be used to establish the standard time directly. They can also be used to build standard data elements for maintenance work (e.g. Universal Maintenance Standards (UMS) employing much larger time elements than MTM). This is shown in the top three cards of Figure A4.4.

Maintenance work measurement techniques

The most sophisticated of the techniques shown in Figure A4.1 is comparative estimating. Comparative estimating is based on UMS and was developed in the early 1950's by the Methods Engineering Council of Pittsburgh, U.S.A. as a yardstick for use in the introduction of incentives in maintenance. Its first UK application was in 1964 at the Leigh Works of BICC Ltd. and has been used, in one form or another, in a wide variety of UK industries.

The standard time for a job is estimated by comparison with a range of classified jobs, called benchmarks, whose basic times have been derived from UMS or one of the alternative procedures. The bench marks are classified according to trade, task-area and time-range and are arranged on spread sheets as shown in Figure A4.4. Numerous spread sheets are necessary for a maintenance tradeforce. The job being estimated (or slotted) is given the average basic time for that range of work content which it best fits; the times for job travel and personal needs are added. It has been shown that, over a period of time, the positive and negative job-time errors that inevitably occur cancel each other to a level acceptable for use with maintenance group incentive schemes.

Comparative estimating based on UMS is installed by consultants as a package (costing some tens of thousands of pounds) which includes supervision of the installation and training of the system applicators (one of whom is required for approximately every fifteen tradesmen). The objective is the raising of productivity via improved planning and tradeforce performance; a group incentive scheme is usually operated giving 30% bonus for a standard performance.

Outline of Greater Manchester Transport payment scheme

The tradesman's earnings are made up of the following three parts—

Weekly basic pay : based on hours clocked—
Weekly performance payment : an incentive, calculated from an agreed payment curve based on the following formula

$$\text{Weekly performance factor} = \frac{\left(\begin{array}{c}\text{Av. buses provided} \\ \text{at peak hours} \\ \text{Mon. to Friday}\end{array}\right) - \left(\begin{array}{c}\text{Failures on the} \\ \text{road 7 days/week}\end{array}\right)}{\dfrac{\text{clocked hours}}{38}}$$

The weekly performance pay is pro-rata to hours worked.

Overall performance pay : an incentive calculated by monitoring the savings on the following elements of maintenance expenditure—

(i) tradesman's wages,
(ii) cost of spare parts and maintenance material usage,
(iii) cost of spare buses,
(iv) cost of sub-contract labour

This payment is made monthly.

A Maintenance Computer Check List*

General

1 Name of package
2 Supplier name
3 Contact details—name
                      address
                      telephone number
4 Is supplier
      hardware manufacturer?
      maintenance consultant?
      software supplier?
      operating company?
5 Does supplier offer complete package?
6 How long has package been in use?
7 How many in use?
8 List of main users
9 Does supplier's package price include training costs?
10 Lead time to system operation from placing of order?
11 Reliability (M.T.B.F.?)
12 Servicing facilities?

Software facilities

13 What documentation available?
14 What guarantees available on software?
15 What software modules in package?
16 User-definable fields, which?
17 User-definable programs, which?
18 Database querying facilities?
19 Security facilities?

*Compiled by A. Kelly; M. Bamford; R. Hurford.

20 Portability (how much of software is hardware dependent?)
21 Expandability?
22 Does contract include future modification?
23 What language?
24 System menu-driven/command-driven/combination?

Inventory

25 Number of explicit levels in system?
26 Number of digits per level?
27 How determine codes from description?
28 System relationships determinable from unit codes?

Plant data

29 How many technical data fields?
30 Number of characters per field?
31 Drawing numbers/reference/index?
32 Spares details, or reference, or neither?
33 What search facilities?
34 Item-unique numbering system?

Preventive maintenance

35 What job details on computer?
36 Job specification on computer?
37 Scheduling?
   (a) lubrication,
   (b) inspection,
   (c) major overhaul.
38 Corrective maintenance details stored?
39 What condition monitoring?

Work planning

40 (a) Minimum working period?
   (b) Variable working period?
41 (a) Dynamic job backlog list?
   (b) Graphical backlog display?
42 On-line defect entry and feedback?
43 Work orders printed?
44 Permits to work printed?
45 Stores requisitions printed?
46 Statutory inspections printed?
47 Workload projection, tabular or graphical?

48 Resource scheduling?
49 Batch rescheduling?
50 What job feedback?
51 What reports?
52 What search facilities?

History and maintenance control?

53 (a) Chronological plant history?
    (b) What information? What level?
54 'Top ten' reports? Pareto?
55 Condition analyses?
56 Trend monitoring?
57 Cost information? What level?
58 Cost analyses?
59 Availability/output? What level?
60 Search facilities?

Hardware

61 What operating hardware?
62 Examples?
63 RAM?
64 Disk type and storage capacity?
65 Multi-user?
66 Operating system?
67 Data management system?
68 Language?
69 Communication capabilities?

Costs

Buying, renting, leasing?
70 Hardware.
71 Hardware maintenance.
72 Software.
73 Software maintenance.
74 Training costs.
75 Five-year cost (hardware, software, maintenance and training).

Index